BATTARBEE AND NAMATJIRA

BOOKS BY MARTIN EDMOND

THE AUTOBIOGRAPHY OF MY FATHER

THE RESURRECTION OF PHILIP CLAIRMONT

CHRONICLE OF THE UNSUNG

LUCA ANTARA

WAIMARINO COUNTY

THE SUPPLY PARTY

ZONE OF THE MARVELLOUS

DARK NIGHT – WALKING WITH McCAHON

for Matthew

MARTIN EDMOND

Battarbee and Namatjira

Martin Edmond

GIRAMONDO

FIRST PUBLISHED 2014
FROM THE WRITING & SOCIETY RESEARCH CENTRE
AT THE UNIVERSITY OF WESTERN SYDNEY
BY THE GIRAMONDO PUBLISHING COMPANY
PO BOX 752
ARTARMON NSW 1570 AUSTRALIA
WWW.GIRAMONDOPUBLISHING.COM

© MARTIN EDMOND 2014

DESIGNED BY HARRY WILLIAMSON
TYPESET BY ANDREW DAVIES
IN 10/17 PT BASKERVILLE

PRINTED AND BOUND BY LIGARE BOOK PRINTERS
DISTRIBUTED IN AUSTRALIA BY NEWSOUTH BOOKS

NATIONAL LIBRARY OF AUSTRALIA
CATALOGUING-IN-PUBLICATION DATA:

EDMOND, MARTIN, AUTHOR
BATTARBEE AND NAMATJIRA / MARTIN EDMOND

ISBN 978-1-922146-68-7 (PB)

NAMATJIRA, ALBERT, 1902–1959
BATTARBEE, REX, 1893–1973
ARTISTS–AUSTRALIA–20TH CENTURY–BIOGRAPHY
LANDSCAPE PAINTERS–AUSTRALIA–BIOGRAPHY
ART, AUSTRALIAN–ABORIGINAL ARTISTS
759.994

ALL RIGHTS RESERVED.
NO PART OF THIS PUBLICATION MAY BE
REPRODUCED, STORED IN A RETRIEVAL SYSTEM
OR TRANSMITTED IN ANY FORM OR BY ANY MEANS
ELECTRONIC, MECHANICAL, PHOTOCOPYING OR
OTHERWISE WITHOUT THE PRIOR PERMISSION OF
THE PUBLISHER.

CONTENTS

Introduction **1**
1. *The Revenant* **27**
2. *Initiation* **52**
3. *Taos or the Alice?* **84**
4. *Achieving Luminosity* **117**
5. *Blind Man / New Man* **151**
6. *The Offerings of War* **180**
7. *High National Policy* **208**
8. *Tmara Mara* **240**
9. *Painting from Memory* **271**
10. *Papunya and After* **301**
    Note on Sources **330**
    Acknowledgements **338**

The landscape is a social map whose legend you must learn.
The human body and the body of the land share a common language.
Person and place coalesce. Whatever happens to one,
happens to the other.
MICHAEL JACKSON

It would be better for us if all the pictures in the world perished,
than that the birds should cease to build nests.
JOHN RUSKIN

The money belongs to the ancestors.
TIM LEURA TJAPALTJARRI

Introduction

1 The Arrernte

In the beginning the land was a dark level featureless plain: no hills or mountains, rivers or streams. No trees, birds or animals; perhaps no sky. Then, from beneath the crust of the earth, giant beings emerged, convulsing the ground, shaking the dirt from their gargantuan forms. They had the shapes of creatures but the habits of men and women; like the people they became, they were wanderers and in the paths of their wanderings made the landscape what it is today. They established the sacred sites, created the ceremonies that would be performed there and left their essence behind at the places where they came from, or went back into, the earth.

This essence, *tjurunga*, persisted; which word can also mean song as well as ritual, drama or painted design; might refer to an actual object, usually an inscribed stone or piece of wood; and carries a sense of naming along with qualities that might be called trust and belief. The time of the beginning is the *alcheringa* (there are many alternate forms of transliteration), usually translated as the Dreaming; another version is Everywhen.

The ancestors who brought the world into being are as

multitudinous as the things of the world. Among those of the Arrernte are the two Euro brothers who invented the spear and the spear thrower and taught the art of cooking on hot coals; the Lakabara, cannibalistic hawk-men who came from the north and pioneered the rite of circumcision; the Tjilpa or native cat-men who came from the south and introduced the rite of sub-incision. There are kangaroo, wallaby, dingo, opossum, echidna ancestors; emu, eaglehawk, duck, crow and white bat ancestors; carpet snake, goanna, lizard, frog; honey ant, flying ant, green caterpillar, green cicada, witchetty grub; bush onion, hakea flower, rain and wind, fire and water, sun and twin ancestors; an ancestor for every plant or animal or element or attribute that was of significance in the daily life of the people. And for every ancestor there was a story.

Before 1900 the Arrernte were one of the largest Aboriginal groups in central Australia; there were probably several thousand of them, divided later into Northern, Eastern, Central, Western, and Southern groups, with the Southern section possibly distinct and perhaps also to be subdivided into upper and lower moieties. The term Arrernte (Aranda; Arrente; Arunda; Arunta), like these geographical divisions, is a European innovation and refers essentially to a language cluster, of which the divisions are dialect groups. Linguists classify Arandic in the Pama-Nyungan phyla, which includes most if not all of the Indigenous languages spoken outside of the Top End and the north-west of the Australian continent.

The land of the Arrernte stretches from Charlotte Waters in the south to Conners Well in the north; from Haasts Bluff in the west to Loves Creek in the east. It rises from low flats in the south, only about twenty metres above sea level, to the 1500-metre-high peaks of the MacDonnell Ranges to the north. The MacDonnells and associated ranges run west to east but the rivers that flow through them – the Finke, the Hugh, the Todd – tend north-south, cutting great gorges in the mass of the mountains as they make their way south and east towards Lake Eyre. In the ranges and to the south of them the land is relatively well watered; to the west is true desert where the only surface water lies in rock holes in the bare sand hills.

The climate is hot and dry. There are just two seasons: a long parching summer and a short, irregular rainy winter. It is not unusual for no rain at all to fall for two or three years at a time and droughts as long as seven or eight years' duration have been recorded. January and February are the hottest months, during which the temperature can remain in the high thirties or early forties centigrade for weeks. In the cold months, from May to August, it can fall to as low as five degrees or less at night. There are sometimes white frosts.

The people lived by hunting and collecting; but the land over which they foraged was subtly shaped through generations so that it was at once a wilderness and a garden, a park and a farm. This shaping was a matter of intuition as much as of design; it was the sum of innumerable individual acts, each of which was intended to allow the repetition of that act by some other person, at some other time: the taking of a euro as much as the disinterring of a tuber. Water, the most precious resource of all, was conserved with a discipline that is, to us, unimaginable: the best and purest reservoirs, those with the greatest longevity, were left intact and utilised only in times of extreme need.

Trees and shrubs provided wood, gums, herbs and fruits for weapons, tools, medicines and food. A variety of plant bulbs, seeds and tubers, of which yams were a favourite, were collected, along with lizards, frogs, bee's honey and honey ants, grubs, caterpillars, fish, freshwater mussels and land snails. Also eaten were exotica like certain flies and clay from ant nests. Collecting these foods, from which perhaps seventy percent of sustenance came, was primarily women's and children's work. The men tracked, stalked and, using spears and boomerangs, killed the larger animals; some of their methods were elaborate and inventive: waterholes where emus were known to come to drink would be laced with the narcotic juice of the *pituri* plant, after which the drugged birds were easily taken. Dingos accompanied men on the hunt; later they were replaced by European dogs.

Every woman carried a *pitchi*, a scooped implement up to a metre long made from a hollowed-out piece of the wood of the bean tree; a digging stick; and also a string bag woven from fur or vegetable fibre, containing an entire tool-making and repairing kit as well as selected decorative items. They usually wore a fur string around their neck or head; a thread of bright red beads of the bean tree; and an apron of fur covering their genitals. In some areas it was customary to attach to the forehead, using porcupine grass resin, a few kangaroo incisors or small bright red seeds. Women's hair was usually shorter than the men's because it was the duty of every mother-in-law to provide her daughter's husband with some of her own hair with which he would make a waistband; sometimes also, or alternatively, a headband.

Men carried stone knives; stone axes; a shield which was also made out of the wood of the bean tree; one or both of the two types of spear in use; a spear thrower, called a *woomera*, which would usually have a quartz knife blade attached to the handle; a non-returning boomerang; and a wallet made of skin or fur. This might contain, along with the tool-kit, feathers for decoration; a spare piece of quartz; some red ochre; a wooden knout which was used for disciplining refractory women; and a charm made out of a dead man's hair or similar. Older men might also carry a bull-roarer and a sacred inscribed stone, a *tjurunga*: artefacts that could never, on pain of death, be seen by a woman, a child or an uninitiated youth.

Men plucked individual hairs out of their foreheads and tied back their remaining locks, which might be very long, with a band, typically made out of fur, called a *chilara*; both the *chilara* and the hair itself might be painted or decorated with feathers. The waist-belt woven from their mother-in-law's hair would be tightened while travelling or in times of famine; in older men a characteristic flap of skin at the base of the stomach was the result. A pubic tassel was also worn, the design emphasised rather than concealed what lay beneath. Men might insert a bone through the pierced septum of the nose or put on a necklace of beads like those the women wore. Scarification was common to both men and women; some of the marks were associated with mourning or initiation rituals; others were apparently decorative.

Arrernte used just four colours in their pictorial and their body art: white, black, red and yellow, which were derived from white ochre, pipe clay or gypsum; manganese oxide, powdered charcoal, burnt bark; and red and yellow ochre, respectively. Pigment would be ground up on a flat stone then mixed with water, urine or some kind of fixative – bee's wax or honey, egg, emu fat, tree-orchid sap. Brushes were made from chewed twigs, strips of stringybark, palm leaves, feathers. Or the paint might be applied using the fingers or the palm of the hand; or blown from the mouth.

Using these methods and substances – along with their own, or animal's blood – they painted designs on shields and other weapons; on rocks and rock-carvings; decorated the skin of those appearing in ceremonies or in the traditional dances associated with the various totems; and inscribed the symbols on *tjurunga*. It was thus an art associated with both utilitarian and ceremonial objects; though its themes came exclusively from the sacred traditions of the tribe and its forms were typically geometric: circles, half-circles, spirals, zig-zags and straight or curved lines, along with representations of the tracks of animals and birds.

These motifs were combined into balanced patterns of greater or lesser complexity which, however abstract they may look to outsiders, were never seen as abstractions by the Arrernte themselves. It is also the case that, at least in so far as ceremonial art was concerned, spoken word and chanted verse made the representational aspect of the designs apparent. Arrernte art characteristically showed a scene as viewed from above, through the eyes of a people whose existence depended on their tracking ability and who had thereby developed the habit of looking down into a landscape rather than at it from the side. Trees were depicted as circles, animals as lying on their bellies with their legs stretched out on either flank and human beings as recumbent, usually supine, ovals or half ovals.

The Arrernte lived in small local groups or bands, each with its own, ancestrally defined, territory. Marital residence was predominantly virilocal; that is, a woman usually joined her husband's family. Marriages might be contracted, usually between a father and the mother of the girl his son would marry, while both parties were young, or even unborn: typically, older men married younger women or even girls, that is, into the generation below them. Bands were quite small, made up of just two or three families, consisting perhaps of a set of brothers with their wives and children. Towards the turn of the twentieth century a group of exactly forty individuals lived in and around what was then called Stuart and is now Alice Springs, ranging across a territory of about 260 square kilometres; but at various times of the year, and especially in times of plenty, much larger ceremonial gatherings were held, which could go on for weeks or months.

The sparseness of the country meant that the people were nomadic most of the time, although each local band also had rights to a permanent central camp. While travelling, dwellings usually consisted of lean-tos made of brush, each occupied by a man, his wife or wives, their children and, after Europeans arrived, dogs, which were never killed and quickly became numerous. These lean-tos were almost always built against the prevailing south-westerly winds of the region. More permanent houses were made out of small branches set in a circle and leaning together at the top. Both kinds of dwelling were used for shade or for protection against rain or cold; in hotter weather, people slept outside.

A temporary camp would be established near a water supply, the area would be hunted and collected until it became depleted, then the group would move on. More permanent camps had a definite organisation, constructed after the moieties, sections, and subsections of the tribe and also divided according to the marriage affiliations, potential or actual, of the members: a system of great complexity that has fascinated generations of European anthropologists.

Arrernte camps were divided initially in two, with the moieties Panangka and Paltara in one half and the Purula and Kamara moieties in the other; in some areas the four sections were further divided to make eight sub-sections (Bangata and Mbitjana, Ngala and Knguarea). Each of the four main groupings had its own men's section, on the outside edge of the circular camp, and a women's section on the inside. The complexities of social organisation were thus reflected in spatial terms.

Marriage was strictly regulated. All divisions were exogamous; husbands or wives had to be chosen from the proper section or subsection of the opposite moiety. Descent was patrilineal, in that children of a marriage always belonged to the other section of the same moiety as that of the father. The Arrernte, in common with other Aboriginal peoples, used a classificatory kinship system: everyone in a particular generation was called father, mother, brother, sister and so on, irrespective of what Europeans think of as actual blood relationship. The kinship system was a universal; not only did it put every person into some kind of relation with all others, it also served to include strangers who could, on coming into a camp, be categorised and thus the proper behaviour displayed towards them.

The various totems constituted a further subdivision of the Arrernte. Each person, from before birth, belonged to a particular totem group, which traced its descent from a natural being, usually a plant or an animal. Totem groups were independent of the kinship and marriage system and only partially hereditary. Souls of legendary ancestors associated with the founding of totems in the Dreaming persisted in the places where they had gone back into the earth and could enter women passing by; and so were born again in the infant she was carrying. Sometimes a spirit approached a woman in a whirlwind; sometimes she attempted, usually without success, to flee.

The individual into which the totemic spirit was born again thereby also inherited a *tjurunga*, which expressed both the quotidian and the timeless aspects of the reborn soul; but a man's *tjurunga* was never fully explained to him, nor properly understood, until he had gone through the intricate stages of initiation. Some totems had many members, for example the witchetty grub totem centred around Alice Springs; while at the same time, in the same area, a single solitary individual represented the wild plum totem.

There were no hereditary chiefs as such although some kinds of authority were handed down the generations; in general, law was consensual and in the hands of old men. Nevertheless, each initiated man inherited from his totemic affiliation, and those of his mother(s) and his father(s), obligations, as either a manager (*kutungula*) or an owner (*pmaragatuia*), with respect to country. Some were, or became, *ingkata*, whose responsibility it was to care for repositories where *tjurunga* were kept; and to lead ceremonies. Each local group had its own *ingkata* and the office usually passed from father to son; or went to a brother or brother's son if a son was too young, incapable, or of the wrong totem.

Besides the *ingkata* there were medicine men and spirit mediums. Medicine men were curers who removed the causes of illness from a patient and determined who was responsible for the malady; if the sickness turned to death, revenge was usually taken. Spirit mediums were able to communicate with the *iruntarinia*, the spirits. These vocations were neither hereditary nor ubiquitous; but the exercise of their powers and its consequences were a constant preoccupation.

Death was considered unnatural and usually the result of sorcery, which obliged revenge; thus every death meant the killing of at least one other individual. After death, the body of an adult (children and young people were usually buried) was burned along with all the individual possessions of the deceased, whose name itself would be proscribed: total erasure of self, complete re-absorption in the Dreaming.

Wife stealing, taking a wife from the wrong marriage section (a kind of incest), the accusation of causing another's death, were all likely to result in a duel or an execution; organised fighting as such did not go much beyond group skirmishes that ceased once retribution had been effected. Groups could feud with each other for generations and yet lay aside their grievances to join in essential ceremonies. Here, as in all other facets of life, reciprocity ruled. Relations between local groups were generally amicable and people were able to travel widely without fear. The Arrernte were and are extremely adaptable; despite the depredations consequent upon European invasion of their land, while there are records of skirmishing, there are none of sustained hostilities between the two.

2 The Lutherans

A religious dispute on the other side of the world had incalculable effects for these remote and self-sufficient people. In 1798, one year after taking the throne, King Frederick William III of Prussia, who was also Supreme Governor of the Protestant churches, decreed the publication of a new service book to be used by both Lutheran and Reformed (Calvinist) congregations in the kingdom. The two churches had existed side by side since the early seventeenth century, but they differed on points of doctrine that seem arcane now but were crucial then: predestination; whether the blood and body of Christ were actually or only metaphorically present during the communion; how divine grace operated. An essential irritant to Protestant reformers like Frederick William III was the fact that the Lutherans retained aspects of the liturgy and sacraments as practised by the Catholic church.

A commission was formed to write a common liturgical agenda; but the Napoleonic Wars intervened and it wasn't until twenty years later, on 31 October 1817, Reformation Day, that two flocks, Lutheran and Reformed, who worshipped in the same garrison church in Potsdam were united, by Imperial fiat, into one Evangelical Christian congregation: the Prussian Union. Frederick William at that time expressed the hope that Lutheran and Reformed churches throughout Prussia would follow the Potsdam example and also unite. The new liturgy was promulgated in 1821 and the next year all Protestant congregations were directed to use it. Some among the Lutherans dissented and a revised document, re-incorporating aspects of Lutheran practice, was issued in time to be proclaimed for 1830's three-hundredth anniversary of the publication of the Augsburg Confession.

This still did not satisfy the more doctrinaire, henceforth known as Old Lutherans; they liked to assert the age of their ancient church and the incontrovertibility of their doctrine, which was expressed primarily in their Confessions, written by Luther himself or his systematiser, Philipp Melanchthon, and generally recited during divine service. *The doctrine*, Luther said, *is not ours but God's...He cannot, will not, and shall not tolerate a man's altering or abolishing doctrine.* For Old Lutherans, then, to change the liturgy was to change the Word of God and was therefore inconceivable. They also believed in the separation of Church and State and held to the notion that the body and blood of Christ were actually present during communion. Those who saw an absolute contradiction between the will of God and the King's decree felt conscience-bound to disobey the latter. In 1831, in the face of their intransigence, the persecutions began.

Congregations using the traditional liturgy went underground; they met and worshipped secretly in houses or barns; or at night in the fields and in the forest. Paid spies infiltrated these illicit congregations and pastors discovered using the old forms were suspended from their ministry; if they continued to act, they were imprisoned. Naturally, the persecutions had the effect of confirming people in their faith and also encouraged other potential dissenters to join them. Under these circumstances some congregations, and their pastors, decided to seek religious freedom in new lands, and emigrated: principally to the United States of America but also to Australia.

Pastor August Kavel, Berlin-born, university-educated, pastor of the Prussian state church at Klemzig, was among those who dissented; in January 1835 he wrote a letter to the King informing him that he would no longer use the prescribed order of service. He was removed from his ministry and his parishioners, many of whom also dissented, were prohibited from entering their church. Kavel, a man with messianic yearnings, went to Hamburg to inquire as to the possibility of emigrating with his flock – to Russia or perhaps the United States. In Hamburg he came across publicity material circulated among dissenting congregations across Europe by Scots banker George Fife Angas, who was seeking recruits for the new colony of South Australia; he wanted *to provide a place of refuge for Pious Dissenters...who could in their new home discharge their consciences before God in civil and religious duties without any disabilities.*

Kavel went to London and there met Angas; who, as one of the South Australian Colonisation Commissioners, tried to obtain money from the Emigration Fund for Kavel's people to travel to the Antipodes as sponsored migrants. After the funds were granted, then withdrawn, Angas put up £8000 of his own for the charter of four ships. He sent his agent, the confidential clerk Charles Flaxman, to Germany to negotiate with and for the Lutherans.

There were complexities at the German end too; Kavel's flock was given permission to emigrate, sold their land, goods and chattels and travelled by river barge, singing as they went, down the Oder to embark for the New World; only to be told that the permission had been withdrawn. They remained for some time in dire poverty, subsisting on potatoes and milk, on their ships in the port of Hamburg. Many who saw this group of pilgrims remarked upon their frugality, piety, simplicity and their beautiful singing. Kavel's seventy-three year-old mother was among them; as was a woman who had, while living on the land, sometimes drawn her husband's plow while yoked up next to the family cow.

The four ships – the *Prince George*, the *Bengalee*, the *Zebra* and the *Catherina* – left in three stages during 1838; by January 1839 all were in Adelaide, along with the 596 people who survived the journey; and here, on rented land, three separate settlements were established: Klemzig, Hahndorf (named after the Dutch captain of the *Zebra*) and Glen Osmond. In mid-1839 Kavel convened a meeting of the elders of the three villages and a constitution for a new synod was promulgated; at the same time, a letter was dispatched to Germany requesting further migrants and another pastor. Later Kavel led the majority of his followers on a pilgrimage north to the Barossa Valley; but some of those living in Hahndorf refused to uproot themselves and come along; and therein lay the seeds of schism.

The new pastor, Gotthard Fritzsche, with a further 274 Lutherans, again sponsored by Angas, arrived on the *Skold* in 1841: coincidentally, while they were waiting to leave Germany Frederick William III died and religious freedom returned to Prussia; but it was too late for them to turn back. Fritzsche, at Kavel's request, tried to mediate between the fractured communities but ultimately identified himself with the Hahndorf people; when Kavel, who had by now fully embraced millenarianism, attempted to amend the Lutheran Confessions, the infant church split into two opposed groups: the more orthodox South Australian Synod, based at Hahndorf, and Kavel's millennial Immanuel Synod in the Barossa. There would be further schisms over the years until six different varieties of Lutheranism co-existed, uneasily, in the new country.

Nevertheless the German community as a whole flourished. With their ethic of hard work, simple living, frugality and piety they built prosperous and stable communities; and it was perhaps that very prosperity that led them to evangelise further afield. In fact, Lutheran efforts to proselytise among the Aborigines had begun in 1839; but initial results were discouraging and by the mid-1850s most of the early missions had closed. The renewed impetus to evangelise the north came from India, courtesy of two ex-Leipzig missionaries, JF Meischel and E Appelt, who resigned from service on the sub-continent because of differences with their superiors over how to deal with the caste system there. Both advocated abolition over the extant policy of compromise, which prevailed; both subsequently came on to South Australia.

For Pastor Meischel the obligation to proselytise was unequivocal. By 1862 he was actively urging the South Australian Synod to preach the gospel among the heathen: *I share the clear conviction that it is the first vocation of the Lutheran Church in Australia to carry on mission work among those heathen in whose lands she dwells, for they are our neighbours, and if we do not have pity on them and endeavour to help them to life through the Holy Gospel of Jesus Christ, they must without the means of grace be irretrievably lost.*

At Meischel's behest the Synod wrote to Ludwig Harms, director of the Hermannsburg Mission Institute north of Hanover, to ask for assistance and further personnel. Harms was interested but declined to send missionaries to work with refractory and divisive congregations. Under pressure, and with Kavel and Fritzsche now both dead, the two Lutheran factions attempted to reconcile. The South Australian Synod agreed to the teaching of millenarianism so long as it did not degenerate into *enthusiasm*; while the millennial Immanuels retreated from their desire to rewrite the Confessions.

In October 1866 the Barossa Valley German community gathered at their church at Langmeil to farewell the first party of missionaries sent north, under the auspices of the South Australian Synod: five men, two of whom had trained at Hermannsburg in Germany, seven horses, two wagons and two dogs. After many trials the missionaries settled at Lake Killalpaninna on the lower reaches of Coopers Creek near the south-eastern shores of Lake Eyre on what is now the Birdsville Track and began to proselytise among the Dieri people.

Misunderstandings were total and immediate: as the wagons were being unloaded, the Dieri sent women across for the missionaries – a traditional means of securing peace with possible enemies by offering sexual favours. The Germans refused, the women persisted, so the outraged Lutherans drove them away with horsewhips. Local practices of polygamy and polyandry were just as confronting; and when the missionaries witnessed some Dieri eating a dead child *like nasty pigs* it almost made them pack up and return south. Under certain circumstances the Dieri also ritually, and avidly, consumed their adult dead; but by the time this act was witnessed the characteristic Lutheran oscillation between repulsion and fascination had shifted in the direction of the latter.

The Killalpaninna Mission, also known as Bethesda, was active well into the next century, persisting until it was closed and the land sold in 1915. Its early years were characterised by a series of retreats and returns and it is likely that, in May 1867, the entire mission, and that of the Moravians at nearby Kopperamanna, would have been massacred by a force of Aborigines several hundreds strong if it had not been for the fortuitous arrival of a group of armed police from Lake Hope. The police had not come specifically to protect the missionaries but were merely on a routine visit; however, their presence emphasises the fact that, with the pastoralists and the missionaries themselves, the police were the crucial term in a three way nexus of power that sustained European incursions into remote areas; and at the same time radically dispossessed Aborigines.

This was how it generally happened: a stock lease would be granted to a prospective station holder in an area where there was permanent water. This water would invariably sustain a local Aboriginal group, which might number anywhere between twenty and two-hundred people. The stock would first ruin the water, then destroy most of the bush tucker; and thereby estrange the wild life. Those Aboriginals who survived this despoliation of their economic support had two choices: to work for the station owner, which was an option only for a few; or to go elsewhere.

Hence the drift to the missions and towns, where charity,

rations, replaced bush tucker: white flour, tea, sugar. Tobacco. Eventually alcohol. Health declined. Some among the white men took, were given, or solicited women for sex. Venereal disease began to spread. If stock was speared, and it was, a general 'dispersal' of the Aborigines was usually the result. These were massacres. One of the more destructive, longer term aspects of this process was the way in which it undermined the structure of traditional society: young men and women, ordinarily powerless, were suddenly, in white terms, most desirable, the men as workers, the women as sexual companions; while the old, concomitantly, were reckoned useless.

The Lutherans at Killalpaninna saw the stages of this devastation unfolding before their eyes; and, while necessarily blind to their own complicity in it, their concern for the souls of those they had come to evangelise nevertheless became increasingly refocussed upon the protection of their lives. This redirection of pastoral care was accompanied by, and augmented with, the typical Lutheran enterprise of language study and translation of Biblical and other texts into Indigenous tongues; which in turn, and naturally, itself encouraged both the understanding and the recording of local customs.

Nevertheless the rate of conversion was very slow: many among the Dieri were interested in what the Mission could offer materially but did not necessarily see that this involved spiritual commitment as well; or, if they did, found such commitment to be in conflict with their own beliefs. Mission boys continued to undergo the stages of initiation; young women continued to marry older men to whom they were betrothed according to the arcane proscriptions of tribal custom. Traditional life thus continued alongside the new, notionally exclusive way promoted by the missionaries; as it did at the next station further north.

The Lutheran Mission of Hermannsburg at Ntaria on the Larapinta (Finke) River in the MacDonnell Ranges, west of Alice Springs, was established ten years after Bethesda in June 1877; the land, over nine-hundred square miles, was given to the South Australian Synod after the Surveyor General, GW Goyder, took advice from explorers Ernest Giles and William Gosse, both of whom had been through that part of the country in the previous decade when the route for the Overland Telegraph Line to Darwin was being surveyed.

Pastors Hermann Kempe and Wilhelm Schwartz, a blacksmith and a baker, came from Germany to begin the mission; they were commissioned in St Michael's church in Hahnsdorf before setting out for the north. It took them twenty months to travel the thousand miles to the Finke and before they were halfway Kempe, to the dismay of his partner Schwartz, fell almost into despair: *How gladly I would have preferred to relate only good news. Yes often our courage nearly fails us. Often I have been almost tempted to exclaim in the words of the prophet: It is enough now, O Lord, take away my life, for I am sick at heart.*

At the same time a flock of sheep was driven overland from Killalpaninna to be pastured at the new station; although it was soon found that cattle fared better on the harsh land. A year after their arrival Kempe and Schwarz were joined by a third pastor, Louis Schultze, who brought wives for the two men and also three lay workers; by 1883 there were twenty-one Europeans, including seven children, living there. A school and church were built out of stone, date palms and orchard trees were planted, and cultivation began of experimental crops of cereals – wheat, barley and oats – which, however, failed.

The intention was to establish a permanent, self-sustaining community that included the local Aboriginal people, who would learn from the missionaries both practical skills and spiritual truths.

The Mission was subsidised by the South Australian government and, in the early stages, the Arrernte practised *intelligent exploitation...content with the exchange of their labour or artefacts for food and steel.*

In 1880 Pastor Kempe published a small primer in the Arrernte language for use in the Mission school, where children were taught reading, writing, arithmetic, some geography as well as being given religious instruction. They were encouraged to sing and Pastor Kempe followed up his primer with a small book of hymns and devotions. In 1881, he also produced a dictionary of 1750 Arrernte words and in 1891 a *Grammar and Vocabulary of the Language spoken by the Aborigines of the MacDonnell Ranges.*

Visual aids towards the education of the young were minimal and those that were used, strictly representational: naïve pictures illustrating Biblical scenes that would be displayed in the course of classes in religious instruction, which were often held outside. They would be accompanied by a text, recalling the amplification of Arrernte visual motifs in song, dance and story. One which survives shows John the Baptist preaching in the desert to an assembled congregation seated at his feet; the memory verse reads *Be Thou Faithful*.

Lutherans did not usually indulge in the iconoclasm common among the other reformed faiths; indeed, some Lutheran congregations continued to worship in previously Catholic churches, which retained their pre-reformation character and kept their paintings, their screens and altarpieces, and their statuary. Post-reformation Lutheran churches are notable for the balance and restraint in their decoration. Many have stained-glass windows; most have an organ of some kind, since Lutheran services are always musical. The interior of the church at Hermannsburg was unadorned apart from a lurid, anonymous painting of the crucified Christ behind the altar.

In 1887 the first seven baptisms took place. One of the early converts was Tjalkabotta, also known as Blind Moses who, sixty years later, still recalled with wonder his first sight of the church and his curiosity as to how such a thing could have been built. He was living on the cusp of contrasting world views and could also remember his father spearing emu and his mother grinding up seeds to make bread; and *men with boots whose feet cannot be seen* riding upon *horses with round feet*.

Europeans were first thought to be spirits of the dead returning to haunt the places where they had once lived; their clothes were assumed to be exotic skin. There were contradictions, however. Thomas, another of the earliest converts, would later join the notorious Mounted Constable William Willshire's detachment of armed native police and was implicated in the double murder committed at Tempe Downs station that led to Willshire's sensational trial (and acquittal) in Port Augusta in 1891.

The Hermannsburg Mission failed in the late 1880s and early 1890s as, one by one, the pastors left or were withdrawn: the effects of the harsh climate, hard work, loneliness, isolation, ill-health and the constant lack of financial resources were factors. Their inability to get along with each other was profoundly troubling to themselves and their superiors in Adelaide and in Germany: the three missionary families, unchristianly, ate separate meals at separate tables. Their complicity, in method if not in fact, with police, was even more disquieting.

Pastor Schwarz was recalled to Adelaide in September 1889 and, the following January, made shocking allegations about the conduct of Willshire and his six Mounted Native Police. Willshire responded with accusations of his own against the missionaries – he said he had seen Arrernte converts imprisoned, chained and whipped – and while the subsequent inquiry did not confirm that these practices occurred, neither did it deny that they had. They were part of a regime of punishment and learning that the missionaries themselves had grown up with and which they defended in their writings.

Schultze left in November 1891 and Kempe, after the deaths of his wife and their six year-old son, followed some weeks later. He was so weak he had to be lifted onto the wagon that carried him and his surviving children to Alice Springs on the first stage of the journey back to Adelaide. Two lay workers remained at Hermannsburg, literally to keep the flag flying and to carry out essential maintenance; but they too left in 1893 and the Mission went into abeyance: a collection of neglected, more or less derelict buildings haunted sporadically by the few surviving Arrernte converts.

3 The Anthropologists

In 1862 the indomitable Scots explorer, John McDouall Stuart, returned to Adelaide from his latest, and successful attempt, to cross the continent to the north; unlike his immediate predecessor and rival, Robert O'Hara Burke of the Victorian Exploring Expedition, he lived to tell the tale. Stuart reported the existence of vast tracts of land suitable for grazing sheep or cattle, along with an expectation of fabulous mineral wealth to be extracted from the ground; and thereby set off a land rush.

The rush pushed the frontier north towards the allegedly rich pastoral country he said he saw; and planning commenced for the Overland Telegraph Line from Adelaide to Darwin, which was built between 1870 and 1872. The first sheep had already, in 1870, been driven up in expectation of lush new pastures; but, as mentioned, they were soon largely replaced with cattle. Further explorations were made, for example by Ernest Giles, who went looking for land where Indian hemp, useful in those days for making rope, could be cultivated. And in the wake of the explorers and the pastoralists came the anthropologists.

When Robert O'Hara Burke failed to return from the over-supplied and over-hyped Victorian Exploring Expedition, search parties were sent to find out what might have happened to him and his men. One of these was led by Alfred William Howitt, who many in Melbourne thought would have been a better choice than Burke as leader of the Expedition. WEH Stanner wrote that *Howitt's discharge of this assignment was exemplary. Without blunder or loss he twice led large parties on the long journey to Cooper's Creek. He soon found King, the only survivor, and took him to a public welcome in Melbourne but avoided the limelight for himself. Then, at request, he returned to bring the remains of Burke and Wills to the capital for interment.*

Howitt had the scientific curiosity that Stuart lacked, as well as the ability to systematise what he saw and to theorise upon it. He was a geologist and a naturalist who became, by degrees, an anthropologist; he saw Aborigines *as a people doomed to extinction by an extraordinary primitivity, and this quality aroused his scientific interest.* Despite his early espousal of geological metaphors to describe social facts – the imaginary stratigraphy of fossil customs – he was in time able to see that *aboriginal society as it exists in Australia is organized in a comparatively complete manner…in order to understand any part it becomes necessary to study the whole.*

Sometime in the late 1850s, while droving between Melbourne and the Murray River, Howitt met Lorimer Fison, another Englishman who had been sent down from Cambridge, emigrated and was prospecting for gold. Fison came to a point of crisis after his father's death in 1861 and, at an open air evangelical meeting on the Victorian goldfields, underwent an ecstatic conversion to Christianity. He became a Wesleyan, was ordained in Melbourne and in 1863 went to Fiji as a missionary, where he served for seven years at the Viwa, Lakeba and Rewa stations. He was, a contemporary wrote, *one of the best missionaries whom God has ever given to our church*.

In 1869, in Fiji, Fison responded to a request by Lewis Henry Morgan, the American ethnologist, for detail about kinship systems among Indigenous peoples and wrote an account of Tongan and Fijian kin organisation which was published as a supplement to Morgan's 1871 book *Systems of Consanguinity and Affinity of the Human Family*. He also contributed to Morgan's *Ancient Society* (1877) but this work, while written during his second sojourn in Fiji, actually concerned Aboriginal kinship systems. Fison had returned to Australia in 1871; in 1872 he advertised in the Melbourne newspapers for help in pursuing his study of social organisation among Aborigines. Howitt responded, the two men renewed their acquaintance and thereby initiated a friendship and collaboration that lasted the rest of the century.

Howitt and Fison's book, *Kamilaroi and Kurnau*, published in 1880, was prefaced by, and dedicated to, Lewis Morgan. It was a landmark of Australian anthropology. Fison's contributions tend towards the theoretical and the general but Howitt's are full of detailed observations that include names of informants and descriptions of localities where ceremonies were held – information that has outlasted the author's outmoded belief in evolutionist doctrine and remains valuable today, not least to the dispossessed. *Kamilaroi and Kurnau* was also influential internationally. A paper by Howitt on initiation was read subsequently by the anthropologist Edward Tylor to the Royal Anthropological Institute in London in December 1883; and praised by him for its lucidity and detail.

Howitt and Fison, one an adventurer–explorer turned scientist, the other a missionary who became an anthropologist, in their collaboration united two dominant frontier traditions. Howitt in particular is a significant figure because of the emphasis in his work upon information gathered in the field and his inclination to revise theoretical positions in response to actual data. Both men retired to Melbourne, where there was already a flourishing scientific community based in the university and at the museum; one of those scientists was the botanist Ferdinand von Mueller, a sponsor of the Burke and Wills expedition, who arranged the experimental planting of cereals at Hermannsburg.

The construction of a railway north from Adelaide began in 1878 and by 1891 the line had reached Oodnadatta (from Arrernte *utnadata*, mulga blossom); and it was by means of the new railway that the first major scientific expedition into the centre began. The Horn Expedition was funded by wealthy Adelaide pastoralist and mining magnate Alexander Horn and organised under the auspices of the three existing universities at Adelaide, Melbourne and Sydney. Their joint project was to investigate in detail the MacDonnell Ranges and surrounding areas; the expedition's members included a geologist, a botanist, a zoologist, an ethnologist and a meteorologist, as well as two collectors (one an ornithologist), a cook, four cameleers and local Aboriginal guides.

The zoologist, also the expedition's photographer, was Baldwin Spencer, a young academic from Manchester who took up the foundation chair of biology at the University of Melbourne in 1887; he was director of the National Museum of Victoria from 1899; and in 1912, for one year, Chief Protector of Aborigines in the Northern Territory. He also became, through a series of accidents and coincidences, the editor of the Horn Expedition's report; furthermore, what he saw during those few months in the MacDonnells led to a profound re-orientation of his academic interests and, without relinquishing zoology, he became a pioneering anthropologist. It was while on the Horn Expedition, at Alice Springs, that Baldwin Spencer met Frank Gillen, the Superintendent of the Telegraph

Station there; and the two men, like Howitt and Fison, to whom their first book was dedicated, became collaborators in a series of enterprises that outlasted Gillen's death in 1912.

Frank Gillen was Anglo-Irish; with his luxuriant moustaches, his fondness for whiskey, his advocacy of Home Rule, his inveterate gambling, he was to some a stage Irishman. He was insouciant, enthusiastic and disrespectful of proprieties; an efficient administrator and a defender of Aborigines who became a public figure, known locally in the north as The Pontiff. He was proud of the fact that he never carried a pistol; however, like Spencer and many others, he usually referred to Aborigines as *niggers*.

Neither was he immune from the prevailing *philosophical confusion, the dogma of the evolution of the mind and the certainty of white superiority*; but he could show surprising insight. Of his own attempt to uncover gold on Arrernte land east of Alice Springs he wrote: *his dream of riches from beneath the earth dealt a crippling blow to those tribesmen who had exploited its surface since the Dreamtime*. Indeed, he may have been responsible for the invention of the term Dreamtime, as a translation of the Arrernte *Alterrenge* based upon its homophonic resemblance to their word for dream.

Gillen was already a collector when Spencer met him and had in his possession over one hundred *tjurunga* stones. Even if he did not entirely understand what they were and what they meant, he was capable of the beguiling speculation that there was an analogy to be drawn between them and the tablets bearing the commandments that Moses brought down from the mountain. Initially he collected zoological and botanical specimens for Spencer; their ethnological pursuit grew into a shared obsession and Gillen became an indispensable source of information for Spencer, who reciprocated throughout their friendship with gifts of various kinds: apples and oranges; books for Gillen's wife and children.

Spencer was himself an amateur whose initial interest in

ethnology was sparked when he helped Edward Tylor remove the famous Pitt-Rivers collection from London to the Oxford museum. He began to specialise in anthropology partly because Stirling, the ethnographer on the Horn Expedition, was dilatory in the preparation of his report. His description of his and Gillen's methodology, given to Sir James Frazer, author of *The Golden Bough*, is illuminating: *I send him up endless questions and things to find out, and by mutual agreement he reads no-one else's work so as to keep him quite unprejudiced in the way of theories.* Spencer did not understand or speak any Aboriginal languages and Gillen himself was not fluent in any of the Arrernte dialects; much of his information came from men who talked to him in broken English or some kind of patois; but he had fervour, great energy and the trust of his informants.

During the Horn Expedition, Spencer visited the abandoned Hermannsburg Mission; its owners had considered auctioning it on the open market but in the event sold it to their Lutheran rivals, the Immanuel Synod, for £5000; a new pastor had been appointed but had not yet arrived to take up his position. This was a young man called Carl Strehlow who, at Bethesda, had shown himself to be a remarkable linguist. With JG Reuther he translated, in only two years, most of the New Testament into the Dieri language. Now he would turn his attention to the Arrernte and, like Fison in Fiji, move from evangelising to ethnology, from trying to convert his people to trying to understand them.

Baldwin Spencer and Carl Strehlow never met; but they became rivals nevertheless, with their respective merits as ethnologists discussed by eminent scholars in metropolitan centres in Europe. Spencer and Gillen's *The Native Tribes of Central Australia* (1899) was hugely influential. James Frazer facilitated publication, by Macmillan in London, of the book, which led directly to his own *Totemism and Exogamy* (1910); which in turn helped inspire Sigmund Freud's *Totem and Taboo* (1913) and Emile Durkheim's *The*

Elementary Forms of Religious Life (1915). Carl Strehlow's *Die Aranda und Loritja Staemme in Zentral-Australien* (1907–20), which has not yet appeared in an English translation, also entered the tradition as a pioneering work of scholarship: *on the myths, legends, material culture and customs of these archaic tribes.*

Despite differences in interpretation as to the nature of Arrernte culture, they became, for European intellectuals in the early twentieth century, *the icon of the primitive...their culture has become **the** culture of a people lodged in mythological time.* Here, held in suspension as if in a kind of pristine solution, was a living example of the veritable past of the human race; this precious example would inevitably disappear and so must be described before it did. It was *an anthropology devoted to discovering the 'essential Aborigine' locked in a disappearing present.*

While Carl Strehlow's election to Hermannsburg was being promulgated, and Baldwin Spencer was preparing for the expedition to the centre that would define his career, half a continent away, in rural Victoria, in the family home on their farm above the Hopkins River, a child was born whose fate would become irretrievably entwined with that of the actual, as opposed to the anthropologised, Arrernte; and especially with those in the west ministered to by Strehlow. And among those Western Arrernte lived a man who was in the early 1890s undergoing the arcane trials of initiation into adulthood; with his future wife, then an adolescent girl, he would raise a son at Hermannsburg who, briefly, tragically, became *the most famous Aborigine in the world.*

1. The Revenant

Rex Battarbee was born Reginald Ernest Battarbee at Warrnambool, Victoria, on 16 December 1893, the fifth and youngest child of George and Mary Battarbee; his parents married in 1881 at St John's Presbyterian Church in Warrnambool where they worshipped and, it is likely, also met. Their other children were a girl, Florinda, the eldest, and three boys, Malpas, David and Preston. There was an eleven-year gap between Rex and Florinda but she, of all the siblings, was the one who became an enduring influence upon how his life unfolded. He signed a youthful letter to her *your boy, Rex*.

George Edward Battarbee, their father, was born in 1840 at Malpas near the Welsh border in Cheshire; the Battarbee name, found across the north of England, probably originated in Yorkshire where, in the Esk Valley, on the edge of the moors, there is a village called Battersby. The branch of the family George came from, however, traces back across the border to the parish of Hanmer in Flintshire, Wales where, in 1740, a grocer and baker named John Battarbee married Elizabeth Kempster; their descendents, many of whom farmed, lived in the border country at Hanmer, Worthenbury, Threapwood, Tallarn Green and Malpas.

George Battarbee left Gravesend, England, on the *Hampshire* in February 1875 and arrived in Melbourne in May of the same year; he was thirty-four years old and described himself as a miner. He settled at Warrnambool, west of Melbourne where, in 1881, the year of his marriage, he bought some land upon which he established a pig farm; and a flourishing bacon and ham curing business.

His wife Mary Miller Battarbee, née Wilson, Rex's mother, was born in 1856 at Upper Ballytresna, County Antrim, Northern Ireland; that is, north and west of Belfast on the shores of Lough Neagh. Mary's mother was Florinda Church Cust who in 1851 married David Wilson in nearby Randalstown; the Wilson family embarked in 1864 on the *Blue Jacket* out of Liverpool for a difficult passage during which one of their five children, a four year old boy, died of nephritis; Mary herself, along with her father David, was ill for most of the voyage. He was spitting blood when they arrived in Melbourne and took an open boat to Warrnambool; she was a seven year-old girl who soon recovered her health once they were safely ashore.

Her mother, Florinda, Rex's grandmother, was the daughter of a textile manufacturer and brought with her to Australia a small piece of blue and white checked linen made from flax grown and woven by her father. She was *a handsome woman with a bright outgoing personality...would never speak ill of anyone...and never turned away anyone in need.*

Both the Battarbee and the Cust–Wilson families were part of the mid-nineteenth-century movement of free settlers from the British Isles, migrating to seek opportunities not available at home and thereby better themselves; they joined a thriving, mostly Protestant community, many of whom were Northern Irish, in Warrnambool and nearby settlements like Port Fairy (formerly

Belfast) on the south coast of Victoria. The Battarbees were pious, hard-working, plain-living folk with solid values that were strictly adhered to; their recreations included singing, especially the singing of hymns, and an enthusiasm for croquet and lawn bowls. And, latterly, watercolour painting.

The Battarbee property, downstream from Tower Hill and looking seaward from the west bank of the Hopkins River, was called Skiddaw and there are still a Skiddaw Heights and a Skiddaw Crescent in that part of Warrnambool. It was named after the mountain in Cumbria in the Lake District and perhaps represents a homage to some more distant origin of the Welsh and Cheshire branch of the family from which George Battarbee came; or, equally, the name might have arrived with the Custs, who originated in Yorkshire and other places across the north of England.

In the Australian Commonwealth between Federation and the outbreak of World War I a new kind of society began to form, a working class paradise in which, so long as you were not Asian or an indentured labourer from the Pacific Islands – or Aboriginal – daily life became an egalitarian exercise in healthy optimism along the way towards the achievement of Australia Felix. These were the years of Rex Battarbee's childhood, adolescence and early manhood – he was seven at Federation, twenty when war broke out – and, although many details of his growing up are unknown, it is possible to reconstruct, largely from the recall of his cousin Bob Cust, something of the kind of place in which he lived and the mode of living he shared. It is now a lost world in which most people, in spite of whatever personal afflictions as individuals they may have suffered, lived in hope and a naïve simplicity: a dream that the carnage of war destroyed forever.

Warrnambool was a port town, built at the mouth of the

Hopkins River and serving a flourishing rural hinterland – and the goldfields after the strikes in the 1850s. It is subject to earthquakes, because of the volcanic nature of the landscape; the name comes from the Aboriginal word for the extinct cone now called Tower Hill and means *land between two rivers*.

Sailing ships entering the harbour, laden with timber from New Zealand, to be made into boxes at the town's two box factories were a common sight. A big black ball would be raised on the Lady Bay lighthouse flagpole when a ship was approaching. Later steamers berthed outside the breakwater and their cargos were moved by train from the docks to the huge goods shed at the railway station.

Bullock wagons brought bales of wool for the local woollen mill. Cattle, pigs and sheep were driven through the streets by herders on foot to the abattoirs near the showgrounds. House cows would be collected each morning by a cowherd who grazed them on the common during the day and returned them to their owners in the evening. There were four working sandstone quarries; and, later, the Nestlé Milk factory: in one of the photographs of Rex painting in the outback he is sitting on a box that once held condensed milk.

Food and produce was weighed and bagged using jute sacks for bulk items. Milk was delivered scooped straight from the can into a household receptacle. Bakers, butchers and other goods providers also went door to door. Hawkers were ubiquitous, for instance selling rabbits at a shilling a pair. Most people had their own vegetable plots but you could also buy fresh from Chinese market gardeners or from their shops on Lava Street. The night cart called weekly to take the contents of the dunny away to be buried in the sand dunes behind the surf beach at the mouth of the river.

National news came in by Morse telegraph; overseas news via cable. Newspapers could be bought at Reeds newsagency on Timor Street and press reports viewed by passers-by on a bulletin-board outside the offices of the Warrnambool *Standard*. Silent movies, with piano accompaniment, were shown at the Town Hall. Picnics in Jubilee Park, on Shelly Beach or along the banks of the Hopkins River were popular, as was boating: rowboats could be hired from Fleets or Proudfoots and there were river-boats for larger parties. All major religious denominations were represented in Warrnambool; the Battarbees and the Custs attended St John's Presbyterian church.

Balls were held on Saturday nights when up to three hundred people might attend and the dancing would go on until three or four in the morning. On Sunday afternoons the Citizens and the City bands alternated playing music in the rotunda in the gardens on Cannon Hill. People who owned one held sing-songs around the piano at home. Mixed sea-bathing was illegal and swimming costumes were, by law, neck-to-knee. There were separate dressing sheds for men and women on either side of the jetty, which was built out over the ocean so that sea water could be pumped up to the city baths in Gillies Street, where there were hot salt water baths with private cubicles for hire. The fee to get in to the public arena was a penny and classes from the local school used to march to the pool for swimming lessons.

In Albert Park there was a golf course and there too the school kids went to play football. The annual Warrnambool to Melbourne bicycle race, inaugurated in 1895, used to start at 6am, when crowds would gather to urge on local heroes. Warrnambool had a Town Crier, his name was Monkey Bellis, he ran a junk yard in Raglan Parade and was the main seller of race books on race day, ringing on his bell to attract buyers.

Rex went to Warrnambool State School for his primary education and to Warrnambool College Academy for his secondary. He does not seem to have liked either place; much later, in 1938, he remarked, speaking of a Mr Quinn who ran the school at

Hermannsburg: *I am sure I would have enjoyed my schooling if I had had such a teacher.* From the age of eight, he would wag school, with his cousin Claude Freckleton jumping the fence at the back of the Battarbee property and going to Selby Forest to visit an old Aboriginal man, Wilmot Abraham, who sometimes lived back there. Rex loved birds and from a young age looked after the chooks, choosing the best for special care, entering them in competitions, winning prizes.

The Battarbee name turns up in newspaper notices of births, deaths and marriages and in the results of lawn bowling and croquet tournaments; but the records at St John's, presumably a rich store of information, were destroyed when the church burned down. Nevertheless, Rex kept the Roll of Honour from the Skiddaw Sunday School he attended; and the photograph of himself and his fellows on a picnic down by the banks of the Hopkins.

There are more arcane sources: on 5 September 1901 the Melbourne *Argus* noticed that among the Additional Prizes for produce entered in the Royal Agricultural Show of that year GE Battarbee's six sides of bacon (three smoked and three unsmoked) and his six hams (three bagged and three unbagged) had been awarded second and third respectively; in both cases the winner was JC Hutton of Melbourne – who would go on to much bigger things in the ham and smallgoods industry.

It's also possible Rex's sister Florinda was in Melbourne at this time, taking painting lessons; she was, wrote Ted Strehlow, *trained as a painter under Walter Withers.* Withers, from Birmingham, was the grandson of an artist and the son of a roper; he studied at the Royal Academy and Kensington Schools, visited Paris and undertook sketching tours of England. His father, however, opposed his choice of a career as an artist and, in 1883, aged twenty-nine, he came out to Australia to work on the land as a jackaroo.

In Melbourne he resumed art lessons at the Gallery School, worked as a draughtsman for two firms of lithographic printers and became a member of the Buonarotti Society, a group of artists, musicians and writers who met fortnightly in the city. In 1887 he returned to England, married and undertook further study at the Académie Julian in Paris before returning, via Italy, to Melbourne late in 1888.

Withers was a founding member, with Arthur Streeton, of the Heidelberg School; Tom Roberts called him the Orderly Colonel because of his organisational efficiency. By 1890 he was living in one wing of Chartersville, the Heidelberg mansion, painting and teaching while his wife gave music lessons, and sub-letting the cottages ('lodges') to other artists for half a crown a week. The next year he opened a teaching studio in the Provident Building, Collins Street, in the city; and in 1893 at Creswick gave *plein air* painting classes which both Norman and Percy Lindsay attended. He lost most of his freelance graphic work in the depression of the early 1890s and turned to school teaching instead; Frederick McCubbin found him work in three separate secondary schools and he taught on and off for the rest of his life.

Withers' painting *The Storm* won the inaugural Wynn Prize for landscape painting in 1897 and he took the prize again with *Still Autumn* in 1900; his *Tranquil Winter* was exhibited in England. Also in 1897 he revived Tom Roberts' idea of open studio days during which the public might visit and see the painter at work. In 1901 Withers succeeded Portuguese artist Artur Loureiro as Professor of Design – really art master – at Melbourne's Presbyterian Ladies' College after Loureiro decided to return to Oporto, and it was perhaps here, at the PLC, that Florinda Battarbee took lessons in watercolour painting from him.

Withers worked in both oils and watercolours – he had an early interest in the English watercolour artists Peter De Wint and David

Cox – and elaborated a style of his own influenced on the one hand by Constable's sombre, muted landscapes and on the other by experiments with broken colour, light and the ephemeral by those French impressionists whose work he had seen and admired: Bastien LePage, Manet, Monet and Anton Mauve. If there is an artistic genealogy for the mostly self-taught Rex Battarbee, it begins here, with Withers' *distinctive, poetic style, capturing nature in all her moods*.

In 1960 Rex remarked that he had *a sister who was an artist and had a certain amount of art background but in our family it wasn't considered proper for a boy to be an artist...she had an art class of about fifty girls but didn't have any boys or men in her class*. They painted flowers rather than nudes; a modest study of pink geraniums, in oils, survives. Florinda, Strehlow also recorded, *guided the cultural life of the district*. She was nineteen in 1901; a decade later, in 1912, she married the Reverend Hugh Adams, then minister at St John's Presbyterian church in Warrnambool; and subsequently lived out her days with her husband and their four children, at Winkleigh near Launceston in Tasmania.

She must have recognised something in Rex, her youngest brother, that she wanted to encourage and that encouragement took various forms; an early manifestation is a book she gave him in 1906, when he was thirteen. It appears in the inventory of his estate as *Ruskin Treasuries*: one of the very many editions of essays John Ruskin wrote on art and related matters during his long life. This particular volume includes two of the most famous, originally given as lectures in December 1864, at Rusholme Town Hall, Manchester, and published the next year, 1865, under the title *Sesame and Lilies*.

Ruskin believed the practice of art to be an enterprise that involved the whole person in pursuit of facts that might then be reshaped by the imagination: by facts he meant things of the world apprehended by our senses. The purpose, indeed the duty, of art was to impart vital truths, pertaining not simply to vision, but to religion and the conduct of life. *Whether in making or perceiving a work of art, we bring to bear on it feeling, intellect, morals, knowledge, memory, and every other human capacity, all focused in a flash on a single point.*

Art should reveal beauty of form in the same way that an organism – an insect, a flower, a bird, an animal – attains through natural growth an individual perfection: *appearance of felicitous fulfillment of function.* Good art should be done with enjoyment and an artist must feel that he is free, that he is wanted by society, and that the ideas he is asked to express are true and important; great art is the expression of epochs where people are united by a common faith and a common purpose, accept their laws, believe in their leaders and take a serious view of human destiny.

Ruskin himself, in the introduction to a later edition that added the essay 'The Mystery of Life and its Arts' to *Sesame and Lilies*, expressed his fundamental views on the conduct of life thus: *whatever our station in life may be, at this crisis, those of us who mean to fulfil our duty ought first to live on as little as we can; and, secondly, to do all the wholesome work for it we can, and to spend all we can spare in doing all the sure good we can. And sure good is, first in feeding people, then in dressing people, then in lodging people, and lastly in rightly pleasing people, with arts, or sciences, or any other subject of thought.*

This kind of practical idealism, this Christian socialism, seems to have homed so early and so securely into the consciousness of the young Rex Battarbee that its effects reverberate throughout his life. It is rare for a man to live out in a pure form the beliefs to which he subscribes while young but in this Battarbee was exemplary. Just as his Christian faith seems never to have wavered, neither did his belief in the need he felt to fulfil his duty as articulated by Ruskin. Everyone needs food, clothes and shelter; only when these needs are satisfied may we then go about *rightly pleasing people.*

In a biographical sketch of Battarbee published in 1956 Ted Strehlow wrote: *His interest in the Australian aboriginal was first awakened by acquaintance with an old man, the last of his tribe, who lived in a mia mia near the Battarbee farm.* This was Wilmot Abraham and, rather than the last of his tribe, he was perhaps something more like the first: in some accounts he is the half-caste son of a European father and an Aboriginal mother. In this version Wilmot's father, Billy Abraham, came down as a boy from the Riverina to the Warrnambool district in 1839, seeking work; he was shadowing a mob of cattle driven south by a family he knew, who eventually employed him as a boundary rider on their lands east of the town. It was while he was camped out there, making sure the cattle didn't stray past Childers Cove, that he began a liaison with an Aboriginal woman that produced the child, Wilmot.

His mother took Wilmot away and he was raised as a tribal Aboriginal; but he knew who his father was and, when he was grown, returned to the Abraham house one night and dumped his swag on the veranda. One of the children rushed inside and told her father – another son of Billy's, also called Billy – that there was a black man outside. Billy Abraham came out and asked him what he wanted; he replied: *Well, I'm Wilmot, I'm your half-brother and I'm here to stay.* To their credit, the Abrahams took him in and he lived and worked on the family farm for a time. He was, however, a wanderer by nature and didn't stay.

When, in 1865, the Central Board to Watch over the Interests of Aborigines received a request from the Church of England Mission to the Aborigines of Victoria that a reserve be established to ameliorate the appalling conditions in which local people lived, the Aboriginal Station was founded at Framlingham up the Hopkins River from Warrnambool. All Aborigines were supposed by law to go there but Wilmot Abraham refused and continued to lead a nomadic life, moving seasonally from place to place and acknowledged as a local in districts far afield. He was Corwhorong, of the Gunditjmara people, he had his own places and his own stories and he refused to exchange them for a stationary life.

Among those stories is an alternate account of how Corwhorong became Wilmot. It was said that he was one of a mob gathering witchetty grubs that was set upon by a party of white men on horseback – *dispersal* was the euphemism – and as they fled his younger brother, whom he was carrying on his back, was shot and killed. Wilmot fell down as if dead himself and lay there covered in his brother's blood. He was captured by the dispersal party and taken to live with a white family called Murray. In this version, then, he is a stolen child, removed from his people and raised in something like captivity.

Another story concerned a woman, Queen Fanny, perhaps Wilmot's own mother, and one of the few survivors of another massacre, during which she too took her child on her back and swam to safety across a mile-wide lagoon. Wilmot was consulted about Fanny's ancestry when a dispute arose as to whether she was a full blood or not; some believed her to be the half-caste daughter of William Buckley, the escaped convict who lived with the Watha Warrung people west of Port Philip Bay in Victoria for some years in the 1820s and 30s. His reply, which satisfied his interlocutors at the time, now sounds ambivalent. *She was as black as – blacker than me*, said Wilmot.

In the later years of the nineteenth century Wilmot was a common sight in and around Warrnambool, with the dubious distinction of having been arrested more times for drunkenness than anyone else. If convicted he usually got a forty-eight hour sentence but on one occasion when, because she would not serve him, he threw a jug at Miss Tieman, the barmaid in the Victoria Market Hotel, he was given three months in jail. Nevertheless he was a trusted source of local knowledge and in the early 1860s twice guided parties of gold prospectors into the Otway Ranges looking for ore.

His wife, in her red blouse and purple skirt, became as well known as he was and children who did not wash were told they would end up *as black as Diana*. After Diana's death Wilmot took up with a woman called Lily who, he said when upbraided for his backsliding ways, was sure to get him into heaven by importuning St Peter on his behalf; by the time Rex got to know him, in the early years of the twentieth century, he appears to have been alone, an old man in his sixties who sometimes lived up behind the Battarbee farm at Skiddaw.

Wilmot was much photographed and often drawn: indeed, it has been suggested that he was an early subject of Rex's although there is no evidence for this. In the photographs he is invariably dressed in European clothes, sometimes a suit-jacket, waistcoat and trousers, in others checked pants, an overcoat, with a handkerchief knotted at his neck and sturdy boots on his feet. He usually wears a bowler hat as well as a white beard; smokes a short pipe and carries a slender knobbed stick. His expression is calm, in most shots he looks straight down the lens of the camera (but in one poses hatless in profile) and it is impossible not to think that he knows exactly who he is and what is happening to him.

For he was an intelligent man; witty too. He said to the magistrate at one of his court hearings that he was only drunk because it was the Queen's birthday and he felt obliged to toast her good health. On another occasion he told a white man shooting possums to desist, otherwise there would be none left for him, Wilmot, and his fellows to eat. The local belief that he was the last of his tribe was clearly a convenience for those who would have found the truth of his mixed origins too confronting; but what about Rex? Did he believe he was hearing ancient stories from a pure unsullied source or did he know, as Wilmot certainly did, that they were in fact tales from a new dispensation that had utterly replaced the old? It seems inconceivable that he did not realise, in some part of his being, that Wilmot was a man who lived simultaneously in two worlds; as Rex himself, along with many of those whom he knew and worked with in later life, would also do.

A not unrelated enthusiasm Rex had was for the collection of what in his diaries he usually called *Abo stones*. In this he was by no means alone: it was a late nineteenth- and early twentieth-century pursuit shared by many, most of them men whose occupations took them regularly into the bush. They were professionals who were also amateurs – doctors, engineers, farmers, geologists, metallurgists, teachers – and among them were some, like AS Kenyon and RH (Bob) Croll, who became eminent in their fields.

Kenyon, a public engineer whose task it was to find out how to make marginal lands such as the Mallee arable, was later Keeper of Antiquities at the National Museum of Victoria, where he initiated the exchange of Aboriginal artefacts for Egyptian antiquities; Croll, who became a mentor for Battarbee, was a well-known educationalist, journalist, broadcaster and writer with a particular interest in literary and artistic matters: *he nowhere ran very deep, perhaps,* as Geoffrey Serle noted, *yet few in his time made a more diverse contribution to cultural and intellectual life.*

The enthusiasm for picking up stones, which seem to have lain scattered in vast numbers across the landscapes of de-populated tribal Victoria, was usually associated with other pursuits; Croll, for example, was a passionate bushwalker, a field naturalist and, by the 1920s, an enthusiastic traveller in central Australia, often on camel back. He was also, in 1934, one of the founder members of the Anthropological Society of Victoria as well as a stalwart of the Victorian Amateur Athletics Association; athletics was an interest

Rex Battarbee shared, one that he took with him when he too began to travel in central Australia.

Tom Griffith has analysed the complex of qualities and peculiarities of the typical fossicker after stones. Such men were, he suggests, akin to prospectors after gold or precious stones, with an avid desire for possession. A good collector left nothing behind for his rivals, whom he was always besting in his mind if not in fact; boasting of a certain kind was endemic to the pursuit. The number and volume of stones collected was always important, as was the range of found objects, their rarity and what was assumed to be their primacy. Once collected the imperative was to order, to display and to compare the various examples.

Curiously, the stones were thought of more as natural than as cultural objects, for the fossickers were not particularly interested in who had made and used the tools nor indeed in what their uses might have been. It was who collected them that was important and where they had been collected – and these constitute the two main recoverable facts from the vast stores of stone tools still extant in Victorian museum collections. This lack of interest in the past of the stones was a function of a belief that such a past was brief, almost negligible. Most collectors did not believe in any great antiquity for the Aboriginal people, they thought of their period of occupation of the land as a shallow horizon only a few hundred years deep. Many of them came to ethnology from a similarly truncated geology and went back there afterwards.

They were surface collectors, then, not diggers: there was no physical depth to their explorations either. Their status as field workers was however important to their sense of their own seriousness. Ideologically they were usually nationalists and sometimes isolationists too. They were, unlike the young Rex Battarbee, uninterested in living Aboriginal informants, who they thought could have nothing to tell them; and, anyway, the puzzle the stones represented was part of their allure. Bob Croll put it this way: *but – and it is an amazing thing – we have to guess at the meaning of much we pick up.* In this sense the fossickers were like amateur detectives assembling a vast jigsaw from disparate pieces and in love as much with the enormity of the task as with any possible solution they might have been able to come up with.

Yet they were often sympathetic to remnant Aboriginal populations, believing they should be allowed to live on at least a portion of their traditional lands and opposing the more violent and ruthless attempts at expulsion; while remaining blind to the implications of the history and geography of possession they were themselves enacting. *Typology was confusing, antiquity was elusive, cultural change was impossible, theory was evil*, writes Griffith. And: *In the tens of thousands of stone tools stored at the museum, the Victorian Stone Circle had built a monument to a timeless, extinct culture. The only history they had recognised – this they helped generate with a pioneering fervour – was the history of a European pastoral ascendency.*

Rex was himself a tiny part of that pastoral ascendency, his days keyed to the rhythm of life on the farm. When he left school towards the end of the first decade of the new century, he joined

his father in the bacon and ham curing business and, later, took over full responsibility for running the family business. *I went on the land,* he said, *and became a very enthusiastic farmer but when the first war broke out I volunteered and went overseas.* A photograph of him survives from this period: four young men, elegant in suits, turned up collars, striped ties and shiny boots lounge side by side together on a park bench. Rex is third from left, looking rather less nonchalant than his fellows; with his large head and forward-looking stance, he seems both older and wiser than they: as if already anticipating a different fate.

Australians stepped up to go to the Great War in numbers far exceeding their government's pre-August 1914 promise to Britain of 20,000 troops. The initiation in 1908 of compulsory military training for all males between the ages of twelve and twenty might have had something to do with this; many were however simply looking for adventure. After the Gallipoli landing in April 1915, the average 8000 enlistments a month with the Australian Imperial Force peaked, in July and August, at 36,575 and 25,714 respectively.

Because of press censorship most people at home did not know the full story of what was happening in the Dardanelles; the newspapers made it sound like a lark. By the time of the battle at Pozières in mid-1916, however, word about the true nature of the conflict had spread and only about 6000 a month were joining up; the bloody encounters on the Western Front never initiated the surge in enlistments that Gallipoli did. Nevertheless, in the words of the poet John Shaw Neilson, *the war fever was very strong in Victoria in 1916.* On the war memorial at Warrnambool are the names of more than 1,200 men of the district who served; one in five of these men died.

Rex was twenty-two years old when he joined up in Melbourne

on 20 January 1916. The farmer from the parish of Wangoom became Private 2616 in the 6th Reinforcement of the 58th Battalion of the 15th Brigade in the 5th Division. He was passed fit at a medical examination then weighed and measured before being given a series of lectures on health, hygiene and the symptoms of various diseases soldiers might encounter overseas. Training in Australia concentrated upon marching and drilling, in the first instance, shooting in the second. Recruits were required to hit a bobbing target – a figure on a chain – at hundred yard intervals up to 900 yards. Presumably, like most farm boys, Rex could already shoot accurately with a rifle.

The 58th Battalion was present at the first action the AIF saw in France, the debacle at Fromelles in July 1916, as a support or 'carrying' battalion; the action, an attempt to take a German salient known as the Sugarloaf, was a diversion to attract the enemy's attention away from the main theatre on the Somme. After the decimation of the 59th and the 60th, mostly by machine-gun fire on the uncut German wire, half of the 58th were sent up in support of a British attack that had already been cancelled by HQ. A survivor wrote: *the air was thick with bullets, swishing in a flat, crisscrossed lattice of death. Hundreds were mown down in the flicker of an eyelid, like great rows of teeth knocked from a comb.* At Fromelles there were 5,500 Australian casualties – dead, wounded, missing or taken prisoner – in just twenty-four hours.

Rex was at this time still in training in Melbourne; he went overseas on 2 October 1916 on His Majesty's Australian Transport ship A71, the *Nestor*; in his wallet was a letter from *Your Old Dad* dated 28 September: *The parting coming very near and none of us can know whether we will ever meet again in this world. My time is short, and the chances are that if you return in a few years, my place will be empty... Dear Rex, have faith in God, do your duty faithfully, keep out of Bad Company...and if sent to the front, you will be as brave as the Australians gone before*. Rex did see his father again, albeit briefly; George died at Warrnambool in 1918.

He also had with him a book of *Daily Prayers & Promises*, with an inscription – *May God guide you, wishing you a safe return* – from his grandmother, Florinda Church Wilson, who died that year; a watch engraved with his name; family photographs, including the one of his mother that he kept all his life; and a New Testament published in 1915.

His detachment arrived by ship in England on 16 November and was sent into the country, in sight of Stonehenge on Salisbury Plain, for further training, this time in the exigencies of trench warfare: how to dig a trench with pick and shovel, how to use grenades, what to do if captured; more lectures on diseases. They were also set to marching wearing full battle-rig, which could weigh as much as a hundred pounds: not just rations and water, not only guns and ammunition, bombs and flares, picks and shovels, but sandbags too and even rolls of expanding wire to throw over the barbed variety. Australian soldiers were kitted out in boots, knee britches, puttees, a khaki tunic; those embarking for France exchanged their slouch hats for the round steel helmet worn by Tommies.

The 6th Reinforcement, after six weeks in England, during which Rex, on leave, visited London, embarked for Calais on 30 December 1916. By early March they were in the trenches near the town of Bapaume, undergoing more training in that peculiar kind of warfare. Rex probably first saw a combat zone on 17 March when the Australians finally entered Bapaume, which had been a primary objective in the Battle of the Somme the previous year; it had taken the Allied forces eight and a half months to cover the nineteen kilometres from Albert and when they reached Bapaume they found its old grass- and tree-covered ramparts undefended and the town buildings largely, and deliberately, destroyed. Fruit trees had been cut down, wells poisoned, even children's toys had been smashed.

The German forces were retreating behind the Hindenburg Line, arduously constructed over the previous winter months using the labour of Russian prisoners of war. With its concrete bunkers, its machine-gun nests, its intricate zig-zag of salients and re-entrants, it was believed by its builders to be impregnable. Naturally the British command did not agree and one of its Generals, Hubert Gough, who commanded the Reserve Army which included the AIF Divisions, was convinced that he knew how and where and when to break it. Gough was *rash, headstrong and prickly. The cavalry charge was forever playing in his head; he didn't want to be held up by detail or doubters.* He was the chief architect of the two battles of Bullecourt, during the second of which the Hindenburg Line was indeed breached; but at what cost?

Rex and his companions in the 58th Battalion were not present at First Bullecourt, they were behind the lines at Albert and environs. Rex himself was at Mametz where the 38th (Welsh) Division had, during the Battle of the Somme the previous year, taken Mametz Wood for the loss of over 4,000 men. Siegfried Sassoon was at Mametz; so too was David Jones, who wrote of the battle in his novel *In Parenthesis*. Rex may have wondered if there were any distant cousins from Flintshire among the Welsh dead. Included in the fragments he brought back is a drawing of a part of the camp at Mametz. The sketch, on a piece of lined paper torn from a note or exercise book, logs the buildings either side of a road, which is divided, to scale, in segments that are measured in yards.

The early part of 1917 saw epochal events on the world stage. In March, in Russia, the army decided it would not suppress revolution among the Petrograd workers, the Tsar abdicated and the Provisional Government took over and attempted to continue the faltering Russian war effort, which had already incurred five million casualties. Then, on 6 April, following the loss to submarine attacks of a number of American merchant ships, and the Zimmerman Telegram suggesting to the Mexicans that they attack their northern neighbours, the US Congress declared war on Germany.

In Australia, in early May, the war-mongering socialist-turned-nationalist, the ersatz Welshman Billy Hughes, was re-elected Prime Minister with a huge majority, even though half the men of the AIF who were eligible to vote had not bothered to do so. His second attempt to introduce conscription by referendum (the first was in October 1916) would fail later in the year; once again a majority of those in the trenches voted 'no', apparently because they didn't want the hell they lived and died in to be compulsorily inflicted upon anyone else.

On the Western Front, the three weeks of moving war initiated by the German retreat behind the Hindenburg Line had been succeeded by the familiar stalemate, the war of attrition. The first Battle of Bullecourt, in early April, was a mad attempt to break the line using tanks, which at that stage of the war were a new and largely unknown quantity. Two junior officers had come up with a plan, which General Gough accepted, to send a dozen British tanks ahead of the infantry against the fortifications around the small town and its satellite villages. The plan, hasty in conception and execution, was spectacularly botched when the tanks failed to arrive on time, broke down or were destroyed by German fire. Those Australians who did manage to breach the line were not given the artillery support they needed to hold their position and fell back with many casualties. Nevertheless, Gough was determined to try again.

Second Bullecourt, from 3–17 May 1917, was part of the Battle of Arras, itself a feint to help prosecute a massive French offensive further south at Aisne. French Commander-in-Chief Robert Nivelle was confident that a million men and 7,000 guns could end the war in forty-eight hours. The offensive, an unmitigated disaster, dragged on through April until early May and by the time of Second Bullecourt the British rationale had changed: the action was not so much to divert attention from the French attack as it was to draw some German forces away from the disaster at Aisne. Nivelle lost his job (he was succeeded by Marshal Pétain) and over subsequent months the French army almost disintegrated in mutinies and rebellions.

In early May 1917, men of the 5th Australian Division were resting in and around Albert. It was spring; they held a horse show, shining up the buckles and oiling the leather on the bridles and harnesses, plaiting manes and combing tails. There were donkey races; a contest for the best travelling kitchen; a wood-chopping competition too. A day or two later they were on a train heading for Bapaume. In his notes Rex says he left Mametz on 8 May and was at Bullecourt on the 9th, by which time the battle had already been raging for six days. The Australians of the 1st Division had broken the Hindenburg Line, taken German trenches to the east of the village and dug in; while the British, who had a fragile hold on a part of the town itself (the Red Patch), were attempting to consolidate their gains and thereby protect the Australian left flank.

On the night of 9 May the 1st Division retired and were relieved by the 5th, many of whom were men, like Rex, from western Victoria. Sergeant Jimmy Downing, the fellow who at Fromelles recalled men falling like *rows of teeth knocked from a comb*, also described the advance to Bullecourt. Body parts protruded from earth that was bare of all but tree stumps, broken railway lines, the odd brick chimney or crumbling wall. The men they were replacing came out *dull-eyed, shambling, half-crazed*. A British soldier with a head wound, a shattered hand and both legs broken said over and over again: *Keep to the left, they want you there, boys, keep to the left*. At the front he saw a man *with both eyeballs hanging like poached eggs on his cheeks*. When the Germans attacked, the Australians beat them off.

Two days later, on 12 May, the British 7th Division was ordered to try to capture the rest of the village of Bullecourt. The 58th Battalion was to assist by attacking westward along two lines of German trenches and then to join up with the British at the crossroads above the north-east corner of the village. Their objectives were clearly stated: one party was to storm a concrete machine gun post; a second would push the Germans back to the crossroads and capture a large dugout there; a third would take other German dugouts beyond the crossroads.

Miraculously, all three of these objectives were met, although the leaders of groups two and three, Norman Pelton and Jimmy Topp, were both killed. The leader of group one, Rupert 'Mick' Moon, a twenty-four year-old bank clerk from Melbourne, who was instrumental in capturing all three German positions, was wounded four times and was later awarded a Victoria Cross. It isn't known which of these parties Rex was with but he did preserve a newspaper clipping about Mick Moon's exploits among his things.

Soldiers in the AIF, as mentioned, went into battle carrying up to a hundred pounds of gear. They had to go over the top thus burdened and run towards the enemy lines before they could engage. Ideally, the German wire would have already been cut by artillery fire, their machine gunners taken out the same way, but this frequently did not happen. Casualties were always heavy, often amounting to half or two-thirds of all soldiers. Those who died did so weighted down with paraphernalia meant to be used to construct a future that would never eventuate.

Rex was one of 7,482 Australian casualties at 2nd Bullecourt; *mown down in the flicker of an eyelid*. He was hit by machine-gun fire and so badly wounded that he was, like Robert Graves the year before, left for dead. Two days after the events of 12 May, a burial detail sent to dispose of a pile of bodies found among them one who, while unconscious, was still breathing. He was pulled out of the heap of corpses and two men began to carry him back towards a casualty-clearing station behind the lines. Shrapnel from a shell-burst killed both stretcher-bearers and yet somehow left Rex alive. He had to be rescued a second time.

His left hand was smashed; his right elbow and shoulder too; he took bullets in the chest as well. One of these pieces of shot, a round ball of lead, emerged years later from his armpit on the opposite side of the body upon which it entered; another token was a 1914 Australian penny with a dent in it where a bullet had glanced off. His injuries were so bad that it took years of treatment before he recovered – four months in an English hospital, a ship home, which arrived on 5 November, Guy Fawkes Day, 1917, then three more years in the Number Five Australian General Hospital in Melbourne. This was partly because of complications that ensued when he contracted tuberculosis in his bullet- and gas-scarred lungs.

Rex's daughter wrote that her father's pain was *never spoken about, but he had* **That Look** *as he marched in the Anzac Parade. His eyes were fixed on the flag in front.* A lot of men, Mick Moon among them, didn't want to talk about what happened to them though it is unlikely that they did not remember. Rex was unconscious for the two days and nights that he lay among the dead so perhaps there wasn't a lot to recall; but he didn't write about the actual moment when he was shot either, nor of what amounts to a re-birth afterwards.

He was of course maimed for life. His left hand was paralysed, just a claw, that he used to put a sock over when he was out painting;

he couldn't properly hold a knife and fork, nor tie his shoelaces. The skin on the back of that hand never healed completely, was susceptible to cancers and there were, over the years, numerous grafts taken from his buttocks or thighs. His right shoulder and elbow remained stiff; and you can see in the photographs that his chest had the pigeon pout of the tubercular or the asthmatic.

Nevertheless, Rex did begin to document his life after this near-death experience. His first surviving writings log his progress from Melbourne to Bullecourt and included with these brief notations are two drawings. One is the map referred to above, a top-down view of road and buildings; the other is a scale drawing of a piece of the battleground. North is indicated off to the left so we are looking from west to east. Across the central portion of the drawing runs a line of trenches, conventionally drawn like the squared-off zig-zag of battlements. Before and behind this line of trenches are asterisks which probably represent artillery batteries. Several of these asterisks are enclosed and most of them are on the far, that is the eastern, side of the trenches; likely behind German lines. Beyond, the land rises to a series of low ridges and the one towards the south-east has standing upon it a black cross.

The drawing is signed and Rex has given his number as well as that of his battalion: 2616 RE Battarbee, 58 B. There are other annotations with arrows pointing east, north and west and if they could be deciphered would tell us exactly where this battle-ground was. But perhaps that is not necessary; for what is remarkable about this simple sketch is, firstly, that it mixes a top-down with a conventional perspective so that you seem at once to be within the landscape and above it looking down; and secondly the austere emotion conveyed by the presence of that single black cross on the stark ridge above the battle ground.

If something of what Rex would attempt and achieve as a painter is prefigured in the awkwardness and poignancy of this drawing, there is also a clue to his later writing in the notations that accompany it. He would fill dozens of diaries with accounts of things he did and places he went but in amongst all of that detail there is scarcely any reflection upon the past. They are the work of someone who does not introspect nor turn events over in search of their meaning. Neither does he examine his conscience or arraign the actions or motives of others. The diaries are written in the present as a record of the immediate past; their focus is always upon the future.

Perhaps this determination to record without reflection, to live without a backward glance, to keep a record of yesterday while remaining determinedly focussed upon tomorrow, was born when Rex came back to life again in the aftermath of the battle of Bullecourt. He was probably too modest, too unassuming to have thought that he had been spared for some task; but once this method of don't-look-back living had been adopted, he brought to it the clarity, the certitude and the generosity of those who survive near-death experiences; as well as that quality of visionary perception frequently possessed by revenants.

2. Initiation

Albert Namatjira's birth was registered at the Lutheran Finke River Mission at Ntaria–Hermannsburg on 28 July 1902 and his name given as Elea or Ilea; his parents were identified as Namatjira and Ljukuta. 'Namatjira', his father's name and ultimately his own as well, appears to have been an error of hearing or of transcription; the Arrernte word meaning *flying ant* is more properly written and sounded as 'Namatjirritja'. Albert's father came from north and west of Ntaria and was conceived as a member of the flying ant totem at a place called Ntalua in his own father's country. This man, Nguaperaka, Albert's grandfather, was an *achilpa* or native cat; his father Wotta was a honey ant; and Albert's unnamed father's father's father was a duck.

Although Albert's immediate paternal ancestors were members of different totems they all belonged to the same patrilineal clan estate in the north-western part of Western Arrernte territory. This estate included the green caterpillar dreaming place Ulaterka (Mt Zeil), Lukaria, a honey-ant dreaming site west and north of Japalpa (Glen Helen) and Rutjubma (Mt Sonder), which is a place of fire dreaming. Mythological knowledge of these sites was passed down the male line and Albert received some of this teaching. In 1957 he remarked of the country around Glen Helen: *It is my father's country. It is my country too...he was a flying ant, he came flying all the way down from the MacDonnell Ranges, way over from Mt Sonder, way down the Finke River, way down the Ormiston. The old men tell us these things and I tell my sons. They, too, must know about my father's country.*

The man called Namatjirritja was living at Ntaria–Hermannsburg in 1901 and it was there that he met Albert's mother, Ljukuta; they eloped together that year and went east to live at Owen Springs. It was a union unsanctioned by either set of parents and in implicit conflict with the traditional method of marriage by arrangement made between tribal elders. Ljukuta was a Western Arrernte woman with affiliations among the Southern Arrernte; her father's country was Nguamina (Palm Valley) just south and west of Hermannsburg and she was conceived and born there, to a woman called Kaputatjalka, into the twin totem. Her father Erankeraka's totem was a snake while Nguamina itself is a place of the yelka or bush onion dreaming. Albert's relationship to Palm Valley was as strong as his attachment to Glen Helen but expressed differently: he was *kutungula* or caretaker of Palm Valley; *pmaragatuia* or manager of Glen Helen.

The marriage of Namatjirritja and Ljukuta was not just unsanctioned; it was wrong. Or, at least, only half right. Although husband and wife belonged to different among the eight sub-sections, they were on the same side, as it were, of the usual four–four division and thus did not come from moieties which traditionally married each other. She was a *mbitjana* woman and he was a *paltara* man; *mbitjana* women are not *noa* (potential wives) for *paltara* men; so they had to go away for a time and were only allowed back to Ntaria–Hermannsburg as long as Namatjirritja agreed to be speared. He did and he was, in the leg, and the parental couple returned to the mission not long before Elea was born. His conception site was at a place of the carpet-snake dreaming along the east-west track to the north of Ntaria and that became his personal totem.

A consequence of this wrong marriage was that some of the secret knowledge of his clan area that Namatjirritja might otherwise have been entitled to, was withheld from him; and withheld, in turn, from his son. A further consequence was that Albert–Elea was the inheritor of two potential skin classifications: he could have been either *knguarea*, after his father; or *panangka*, after his mother. In such circumstances a male child might ultimately identify with his father's line and this is what Albert did; he is generally remembered as a *knguarea* man.

Elea was the eldest son of his parents – both in their early twenties when he was born – but he was not his mother's first child; she had, from a previous liaison, given birth to a daughter, Clara, in 1898; and later had two more children with her husband: a daughter, Meta, born 1906 who died six years later in 1912; and a second son, Hermann, who was born in 1909 but also died young, succumbing during the prolonged drought and famine that afflicted Hermannsburg in the mid- to late-1920s. And then there was the larger network of extended family and classificatory kin, far too complex to summarise here.

Elea's upbringing on the Finke River Mission of Hermannsburg added more layers of complexity to these tribal intricacies. Although his natural parents remained close by him all their lives, two other men, one German, one English, each played a significant role in his religious upbringing and his childhood education, respectively. Carl Strehlow, the *pater familias* of the Mission as a whole, oversaw, sometimes in a very direct way, Elea's induction into the Lutheran church. Harry Hillier, an artist and a teacher, was the first to teach him his letters and probably also introduced him to the techniques of artistic production.

Carl Strehlow had, by the time of Elea's birth, been Superintendent at Hermannsburg for twelve years. He arrived on 12 October 1894 and remained at the Mission, with just four breaks, for the rest of his life. He was a driven man, on *a relentless schedule which included pastoral, teaching, accounting and administrative duties, tending the sick and management of the mission farm* that ultimately ruined his health and led to an early death, aged fifty years, in 1922.

Born in Fredersdorf, Uckermark, Germany, 1871, Carl was the seventh child of a teacher and attended his own father's Free Lutheran Church school; he early on expressed a desire to become a preacher and, since the family was poor, the local pastor, Superintendent Seidel, gave him religious instruction gratis. Strehlow trained for three years (1888–91) at the Bavarian seminary at Neuendettelsau. Upon his graduation, he was about to go to North America when the summons came to travel instead to South Australia.

He was ordained at Light Pass on 3 July 1892 and sent straight to the Bethesda Mission at Killalpaninna where he began collaborating with Reuther on his translation of the New Testament into the Dieri language; which was incomplete when, after just two years at Bethesda, Strehlow was appointed to Hermannsburg. The next year, 1895, his assistant, Pastor JM Bogner, with wife and child, arrived from Queensland; in July Strehlow travelled south to Adelaide to meet his fiancé, Frieda Keysser, off the ship from Germany; they married, were naturalised and returned together to Hermannsburg in November. The first of their six children, five of them boys, was born soon afterwards.

Carl Strehlow was handsome, stocky and robust, with a full, square beard and blazing amber eyes; *an exceptionally able and determined man.* He was also *strong-willed, with a high opinion of his own ability; his rigid self-discipline made him a stern pedagogue and a strict parent.* When early in his tenure torrential rain destroyed or badly damaged many of the old pug and stone buildings at the Mission, he saw it as an opportunity rather than a disaster. With the help of an experienced bush builder called Dave Hart, he began to restore old buildings and to construct new ones using lime mortar to hold the stone together; and corrugated iron instead of reed-thatch for roofing. Some of these buildings, including the church dedicated on Christmas Day 1897, still stand today.

During his first decade Strehlow also oversaw the building of separate houses for the white missionaries; a kitchen–dining room for Aboriginal workers and dependents; a school; dormitories for boys and girls respectively; workshops and sheds. Most of the tribal people attached to the mission lived in wurlies a short way away from the European dwellings and these too were reconstructed on a more permanent basis than traditional design allowed. By 1899, and perhaps earlier, Strehlow had gangs of Arrernte men down in the bed of the Finke River breaking rocks to bring up as stone suitable for the construction of walls that could be as much as sixty centimetres thick.

The Mission received subsidies at different times from both Church and State (and the Strehlows were personally supported by contributions from their families in Germany) but it was primarily a ranch, raising cattle and horses for sale down south; there was a flock of sheep but this was largely disposed of early in the new century in exchange for bulls and stallions. The outdoor work was managed by a European stockman with a shifting group of Aboriginal helpers who were especially useful for mustering; they could always find lost animals no matter how far they had strayed.

It was the Mission's intent to inculcate practical, saleable skills amongst its people, with the ultimate aim of achieving complete economic self-sufficiency. Men worked the land and with the stock; women were taught to sew and mend and to help in the preparation and dispensation of food. Even the giving of welfare was tied to the notion of work: apart from the young, the old and the sick, those who did not contribute were not supposed to receive rations. Wednesdays were given over to hunting and the gathering of bush tucker and then Carl and Frieda would join their flock in foraging upon the land.

Strehlow was as thorough and committed in his methods of religious instruction. He implemented the intensive Lutheran instruction towards adult baptism and confirmation and admitted Aboriginals into church membership only when he felt sure they were ready. He also insisted upon the separation of proto-Christian children, such as the young Elea, from their parents, so that they could be raised and educated without the intrusion of traditional child-rearing ways. In his early years he attempted to suppress ceremonial life altogether; later he realised this was not only impossible but counter-productive: it was necessary to understand the way of life of those he intended to convert.

Nevertheless, during his twenty-eight years at Hermannsburg, he refused ever to attend any Arrernte ceremony because in his mind that would constitute an endorsement of paganism and a denial of God. At the same time, he became an indefatigable researcher into Aboriginal customs and traditions. As well as writing his monumental seven-volume work, *Die Aranda und Loritja Staemme in Zentral-Australien,* published in stages in Hamburg, he revised the Arrernte dictionary and grammar produced originally by Kempe, wrote a school primer and other workshop materials, translated more than a hundred hymns and made his own version of the New Testament, as well as selected passages from the Old, in the Arrernte language.

Carl Strehlow showed early intimations of an ecological consciousness; he refused to allow donkeys to be kept at Hermannsburg because they destroyed native vegetation with their omnivorous eating habits. He was a good manager and a good rancher; according to his son Ted, competent if not expert at most things but somehow reserved and lacking in warmth and, as a result, a solitary and almost friendless man; one who was respected and trusted but not easily loved. He could inspire fear in those who crossed him and never lacked authority in his dealings with white or black. He was puritanical, had a strong sense of sin and was especially harsh on sexual offenders; but did not hold grudges and, once punishment was given, that was usually the end of the matter. In private, a different man appeared. He would weep as he read Walter Scott novels aloud to his wife in the evenings.

Frieda, who outlived him by many years, remembered him thus: *My husband always tried to exemplify the Christian life to his people. For their sake he denied himself many ordinary privileges. When the people were sent bush every Wednesday to hunt and look for their own food, we likewise went on foot, taking our kitchen staff with us and eating the simplest of food. When at times the people had to be short-rationed, my husband deliberately abstained from the luxury of afternoon coffee or from smoking a favourite cigar. He drank a glass of wine only when we had important guests. And he suffered a lot from insomnia.*

Life at Hermannsburg was unremittingly harsh; alternating drought and flood, month by month and year by year, meant there was never a stable set of circumstances for any length of time; each day was, much as it had been for the pre-European Arrernte, an improvisation in the face of incipient chaos. Drought dried out the gardens and killed the animals; the prevailing south-westerly winds blew great mounds of dust and sand into the Mission compound. Floods swept away buildings and dams and, on occasion, the cattle yards.

It was a frontier and violence was ever-present. Strehlow attempted to protect his people from the depredations of the squatters and the police but his fiat only extended so far and he couldn't always prevent the murders and the other killings that occurred regularly on or about Mission land. The infant mortality rate among both missionaries and Aborigines was high and epidemics common: measles in 1899, whooping cough in 1900. In 1899 camel trains started to bring supplies twice annually up from the south but the loadings, as they were called, didn't always arrive on time and then the people faced deprivation if not starvation.

On the first day of Christmas 1905, with Carl Strehlow officiating, eleven adults and three children were baptised into the church. Among these fourteen people were Namatjirritja, henceforth known as Jonathon; and his son Elea, who received the name Albert. Jonathon's wife, Ljukuta, who was not baptised but only blessed, was called Emilie. The precise facts are not known but it is likely that the child Elea spent  his first years living a traditional life with his parents in a wurly on the encampment near the Mission and accompanying them on any trips they may have taken into the bush; and that his induction into Lutheran ways did not begin until after his baptism towards the end of 1905.

Child-rearing among the Arrernte followed a pattern discernible across the continent; one which astonished nineteenth-century observers. From the moment of birth, those babies who had been elected for survival (infanticide was common) were lavished with care and attention, given unconditional love and allowed a remarkable degree of latitude. Discipline of any kind was rare and corporal punishment almost unknown; disobedient children would be spoken to and, if still unresponsive, might be given a slap. From a young age, children were otherwise, within the highly disciplined but leisure-rich confines of the hunting and gathering way of life, free to do whatever they wanted. In the nature of things this usually involved playing various games with the other members of the cohort or mimicking those activities pursued by elder siblings and the adults.

Children's playthings included round or cylindrical toys that were rolled along; target discs sent racing so that missiles could be aimed at them; wooden tops, to be spun, and balls of fibre or wood to be thrown and caught; marbles made from round pebbles; and ball-in-a-bowl toys. There was a near infinite variety of sticks and therefore of stick games: story-telling sticks; clapping sticks; music sticks; *kukuru* or play sticks. Many of the stick games were preparatory to adult hunting with spears and boomerangs; or, with shields, to mimic male combat; while the girls, in pretence or in fact, gathered and prepared bush tucker for meals. Sand painting, especially after rain, was a universal enthusiasm. Apart from these activities, there was the untrammelled freedom to run and jump and swim and talk and laugh all day long.

Most early European observers also commented upon the delightful nature of Aboriginal children, their evident happiness, their unselfconscious curiosity, their robust appetite for new experiences. Some became censorious, especially when recounting behaviours occasionally indulged in by older boys, who would gang up on the women of the camp and harass them, perhaps going beyond verbal abuse to the actual throwing of stones. But this seems to have been a kind of ritual play that anticipated the coming period of sequestration of adolescents in an all-male society and was tolerated in part because childhood was seen as a privileged, paradisial state that would inevitably come to an end, especially for boys, in the fierce and bloody rite of passage known as initiation.

However, the picture was certainly more complex than this.

Ted Strehlow, who grew up at Ntaria–Hermannsburg, described the terrifying stories that were told to dissuade the young from trespassing upon sacred sites or otherwise transgressing against tribal mores. He wrote, speaking of the hill that constituted the eastern border of the sacred site at nearby Manangananga Cave, that *before white missionaries had come to Ntarea, the warning given to the Aranda children had been of the grimmest nature; they had been told never to play near Alkumbadora, lest their dead bodies should be found there.* Stories of demonic beings, of malign otherworldly sorcerers, of natural or supernatural horrors, were also used to keep children within the bounds of what was considered proper and safe.

Further complexities emerge from data gathered by the Hungarian Freudian anthropologist and psychologist, Géza Róheim, during fieldwork at Hermannsburg in the late 1920s. He undertook a particular study of children and discerned two, and only two, social games: what he calls men-men and women-women games; and the oracle game. The first was an imitation of hunting, gathering and food preparation and essentially rehearsed adult roles. The oracle game (called *altjira* which he glosses as *ancestor*) was played with eucalypt leaves that were representative of people and places, and animated in various ways: *the way the leaves fall is interpreted as a prediction of the future life of the player.*

Róheim also discovered that those he spoke to, both adults and children, possessed a large vocabulary of sexual insults that were meticulous, descriptive and inventive; that children's mimicking of adult behaviour did not confine itself to daylight activities like the hunting of animals and the gathering of food. They became adept at the power games adults indulged in, and boys learned early how and when to practice violence against girls; while the girls in turn knew when to submit and when to retaliate. Their sexual obsessions, as children's usually are, were bound up with prohibitions against activities that were imperfectly understood and both feared and desired; they suggest that sexual education, largely through imitative behaviour, also began at a very young age.

Nevertheless, given the late period of Róheim's researches, it may be the complexes he described were not those of traditional culture but characteristic of mission-educated children. On this matter an observer in the 1920s noted that *in the ordinary bush native camps the children speak freely and thoroughly enjoy, as do their mothers, any notice you take of them. I was astonished to find that, on the mission station, the women and children tried to slink away. It was evident that they had been imbued with a false sense of modesty.*

For the Lutherans, Arrernte child-rearing practices, with their excessive toleration, their lack of discipline and their general air of acceptance of almost any behavioural extreme, were anathema. Carl Strehlow, as mentioned, early on initiated the practice of adopting the children of any adults who converted and of raising them away from their parents as young Christians. Such boys and girls slept in segregated dormitories and entered into the rigours of an education system that attempted to account productively for all the hours of the day; and to enforce learning through punishment. They would be taught to read and write in both Arrernte and English; to count, add, subtract, divide and multiply; to pray; to study the Bible; to sing hymns. And then in the afternoons they would make themselves useful doing simple jobs in and around the Mission.

The Reverend Wettengel, Albert's first instructor, left Hermannsburg in 1906 under a cloud, and returned to Germany. His replacement was HJ (Harry) Hillier, a young Englishman who had been living on the Bethesda Mission at Killalpaninna. Hillier was a doctor's son who at eighteen came out to South Australia for his health; he suffered from some kind of respiratory complaint. He was pious and while in Adelaide met some of the Lutheran missionaries from Bethesda, and was invited to come to live there. He moved up in 1893, while Strehlow was in residence, and remained for twelve years. It was not at first a formal appointment but Hillier was young and keen and was soon helping out with the station and stock work; in 1900 he was offered, and accepted, the position of teacher.

At Bethesda lessons began with a prayer and were conducted from a blackboard on an easel. There was dictation and the spelling out-loud of words in the classroom. Hillier expanded upon this rudimentary outline when he described the routine he followed at Hermannsburg: *The first class reads portions of the New Testament every day and then have English and Aranda translation. Every day new English words are learned (with their Aranda equivalents) and all mistakes in spelling written out and re-learned and heard. In sums, the children are set addition, subtraction and multiplication. The second class learn new English words on three days in the week and write in their copy books the other two days. Multiplication tables are learned. The third class, consisting of children from seven to ten years old, are all beginners. They learn syllables and notations.* The young Albert turned seven in 1909, while Hillier was teaching at Hermannsburg; he joined the third class in that year and began to learn his letters.

Harry Hillier was more than a teacher; he was an accomplished draughtsman and watercolourist and a large body of work he made at Bethesda survives. It is not consciously artistic production but belongs in the tradition of scientific and ethnological documentation. Hillier was a collector, primarily of zoological and botanical subjects, and he drew those things he collected; his pictures of insects are particularly fine. In his capacity as a documentary artist he also made himself useful to Pastor Reuther – drawing up a detailed map of the Lake Eyre region, containing about 2,500 place names; assisting in making a visual record of Reuther's collection of

Dieri artefacts; and painting in exquisite miniatures the 404 small wooden sculptures known as *toa* that were made on and around Bethesda Station over the decade he was there.

Toa are enigmatic, perplexing, resonant; they have great presence. Hillier described them thus: *a Thdoa…was usually a piece of wood (mulga acacia aneura) and on this painted a design, or fastened a few leaves or twigs at the top or moulded a shape of clay or gypsum etc etc on the wood & sticking the pointed end into the ground usually inside one of their huts left it there for any relations or friends who came there after they had left their camps.* All *toa* are representational in the sense that each is tied to a particular locality and encodes a myth or dreaming story belonging to that place; about 300 of these were recorded by Reuther. Most use a string or fibre binding about the typically two-pronged wooden head and this binding anchors the gypsum which, once hard, is painted in black, yellow, red and white. Some of the wooden supports show evidence of metal tool manufacture and these tools probably came from the Killalpaninna workshop of the resident blacksmith, the evocatively named Hermann Vogelsang.

Contemporary with the 404 *toa* are seven small sculptures, moulded in spinifex resin, of dogs; each represents an individual animal that belonged, in Lake Eyre mythology, to an ancestral hero. The Dieri loved their dogs; these images seem to confirm the notion that the closely related *toa* are pieces of art; and yet, paradoxically, they also reinforce the idea that *toa*, like *tjurunga*, represent *title deeds of particular social groups to specific sites and areas of land, and they were owned and lawfully controlled only by people who could claim correct relationships to them.* However, *toa* were not sacred objects and there do not seem to have been restrictions upon who could see, touch or otherwise handle them.

It is probable that the Lutheran missionaries at Bethesda were complicit in the manufacture of *toa*, which they then collected and in some cases sold. A further speculation is that Harry Hillier was himself partly responsible for the production of *toa*; may have given technical advice on their construction; and contributed to the forms which they took. And, more generally, that he was a teacher whose provocations to his pupils included the possibility that they make art: like the unknown child who around 1900 painted in watercolour a view of the Killapaninna Mission, with a group of Aboriginals in European dress picnicking among trees in the foreground; the lake with people boating and water-birds upon it on the middle ground; and along the other shore the Mission buildings outlined in profile along a shallow horizon.

Hillier brought some *toa* up to Hermannsburg from Bethesda and these he gave or sold to Oskar Liebler, Carl Strehlow's stand-in when in 1910 the Strehlow family departed for a long sojourn in Germany. Hillier at this point said he would resign as teacher if a replacement was not appointed before Strehlow left because he did not want to become a de facto missionary: *I certainly cannot do so as I maintain a man must have some theological training before he is able to address and teach others from the Scriptures.* No appointment was made and Hillier did resign, in September 1909, though he did not actually leave Hermannsburg until May 1910, when Albert was in his eighth year.

He returned to Adelaide and went to live with Reuther, now retired, for a time. Subsequently he worked as a station hand on various South Australian properties; and was assistant to the Anglican Bishop of Willochra, a diocese that included vast areas of northern South Australia. In the 1930s he moved to Western Australia and ran a farm near Kojonup. He married late, in 1934, aged fifty-nine, to Lillian Trego-Williams of Adelaide, to which city he returned not long before his death at the age of eighty-three.

Hillier knew the anthropological work of Spencer and Gillen

and was sophisticated enough in his grasp of the matter to compare it unfavourably with that of Strehlow; the German missionary, he said, knew the language intimately whereas neither Spencer nor Gillen did; and this was the cause of many misunderstandings. He was particularly harsh on Gillen's rudimentary pidgin and his inept transliterations. Hillier could have become a primary contributor to these debates but, when asked to write for the publication *Man*, said no. Perhaps he declined out of respect for his seniors Reuther and Strehlow. Or maybe he did not wish to improvise as a scholar in the same way that he refused to become a de facto missionary.

One other thing about this enigmatic, reticent man: he was the godfather of the Strehlow's youngest son Ted, born on the Mission at Hermannsburg in 1908; and present in the church during the baptism, when extraordinary events occurred. The child was sickly and not expected to survive; those present assert that some kind of divine intervention took place and he was saved. Harry Hillier and Ted Strehlow remained in correspondence with each other for the rest of Hillier's life. He had, along with Albert, taught the other Strehlow children as they came of age. With Ted it was different: Hillier was, it seems, both a mentor and a confidante for the younger man until his death in 1958.

The year before Ted Strehlow's birth, in 1907, there was a crisis at the Mission. Carl Strehlow reported: *In April many of the natives participated in an entertainment of a heathenish nature; others fell into sin against the sixth commandment. Hence the Christians who had taken part were excommunicated.* The sixth here means a general lack of chastity rather than adultery per se. It had already been decreed that Christian women should be modestly covered at all times. They wore full-length dresses, with long sleeves and long skirts beneath gathered tops of plain, hand-sewn fabrics. All females, including girls as young as two, also wore head scarves. Yet many must still have remembered their naked days and some were tempted to throw off all that heavy Edwardian clothing and dance as they used to do – as it seems on this occasion they did.

Strehlow the elder's attitude to what he called *ceremonies* was always ambivalent. They were rites that he would have loved to observe but felt, because of his obligations as a Christian and a missionary, he could not. He was an otherwise hospitable man and in many respects broad-minded too. So-called non-mission blacks, for whom he did not have spiritual responsibility, were always welcome; the halal killing of bullocks by Muslim cameleers who visited Hermannsburg was permitted; and he extended de facto protection to the Arrernte's nearby sacred places. Meanwhile he was compulsively recording every detail he could find of the ceremonies that he would not attend and wanted ultimately to suppress.

These contradictions led in time to a falling out with one of his main informants at Hermannsburg, the ceremonial chief Loatjira – over the precise question as to whether traditional ceremonies should be allowed to continue. When Strehlow refused Loatjira's request for latitude, Loatjira left the Mission and afterwards lived mostly at Glen Helen, where ceremonies were permitted so long as they took place away from the cattle yards there. On his infrequent returns to Hermannsburg, Ted Strehlow writes, Loatjira was greeted as a loved ruler, much missed by his people. Subsequent relations between him and Carl Strehlow were polite but not warm; there would be exchanges of rations for *tjurunga*. Loatjira did not farewell Strehlow when he left the Mission for good in 1922.

It was a complex situation. On the one hand the missionaries had to practise some form of tolerance if they were not to alienate their putative flock; on the other, they could hardly endorse behaviour that cut at the roots of the faith they were trying to inculcate. Temptation was rife and abductions, so called, common;

they might better be described as elopements. In 1908 three girls ran off with their 'abductors' to Ellery Creek; on the positive side, on the second day of Christmas, three adults were baptised and two marriages celebrated. There is nothing further in the chronicle about the fate of the Christians excommunicated after those heathenish entertainments but it is likely that some, if not all, returned eventually to the fold.

The missionaries' own entertainments were meagre and consisted of brief excursions to nearby watering holes like Palm Valley for picnics; regular holiday breaks, usually in spring, to places like Gilbert or Owen Springs; and occasional longer furloughs: in 1910, as mentioned, the entire Strehlow family of eight took a year off and went to Germany. Before he left Carl gave his replacement, Oskar Liebler, lessons in Arrernte and also left him four sermons in the native language to preach. Harry Hillier, who was departing too, gave similar lessons to Pastor Kaibal, who came up for the winter as support for the inexperienced Liebler. There was rain in March and, when skies cleared in April, Halley's Comet appeared; in May, the earth passed through the tail of the comet.

The interregnum over which Liebler presided was a near disaster for Hermannsburg; and Liebler himself throws Strehlow's more positive attributes into stark relief. He inherited a mission and a station that were in a healthy state. There were 192 Aborigines in residence: *Each family had a freshly built grass hut. No more wurlies belonging to creek blacks exist.* The vegetable gardens were flourishing and everyone got fresh greens twice a week to go with their meat. Twenty of the seventy newly planted date palms were bearing fruit; and an extraordinary 800 horses, 2,000 cattle, 250 sheep and goats went south to market. Liebler ordered a harmonium and a new organ for the church; but he does not seem to have possessed either inter-personal skills or the natural authority of his predecessor: *work is also a remedy against sin,* he wrote. *I have kept them under stern discipline, whereby I didn't exactly win the favour of the lazy ones.*

The next year, 1911, the Northern Territory ceased to be administered by the South Australian government and passed to the Commonwealth. The Barclay-MacPherson Commonwealth Exploring Expedition, a party of surveyors and scientists, came through in March and stayed a week at Hermannsburg. They were in the newly constituted Territory looking for stock routes, trade routes, a path for the planned railway north to take; indeed anything that might be turned to commercial advantage. Liebler, very disenchanted, afterwards wrote that *Captain Henry Vere Barclay, who reported adversely about the station…drank our small supply of date wine until it was all gone.* He also remarks that, apart from building a sundial, Barclay did little else over the time he was there.

Barclay was a trained observer but he was also getting on in years (he was sixty-six) and had some strange notions: one, which he actively promoted during the 1911–12 Expedition, was that all Aboriginals in the north should be rounded up and sent for their own good to a reservation on Melville Island. Though it isn't clear if he visited Hermannsburg during any of his earlier trips, Barclay had written critically about the Mission before, in an article published in 1905.

The 1911 report on the state of the Mission, plus covering letter, that Barclay sent from Newcastle Waters to his superiors was both inaccurate and unfavourable. Conditions in the eating house were unhygienic, he said, and the school room poorly ventilated; the clothing that was handed out was *rubbish*. People were forced to purchase food and other goods and the money so made, along with that derived from sale of stock, went to the church in the south. The Lutherans, Barclay wrote, had the best land in

Centralia and were misusing it; they should have been growing cereals. As for Oskar Liebler, he was simply unfit for the job he was attempting to do.

These allegations were taken seriously and the Alice Springs policeman, Sergeant Stott, with another officer sent up especially from Melbourne, visited Hermannsburg to investigate, among other things, Barclay's most sensational claim: that children were locked in their dormitories at night. The police said they found the people well-clothed, the mission buildings freshly whitewashed, the gardens well stocked; there was no shop and money came up from the south rather than the other way round. They did not, however, deny the allegation that buildings used by them were poorly ventilated and sometimes unhygienic. As for the dormitories, they were locked at night or, at least, the girls' dorm was: because if it had not been, 'abduction' would have been even more common than it already was.

That there was a double standard at work on the Mission seems undeniable; the boys' dormitory, for example, which is still there, is tiny and must have been fiercely over-crowded when as many as twenty-four children, including the young Albert, slept within. Others apart from Barclay had criticised the Mission: GA Johannsen, for instance, the Danish stone-mason who came up to help build some stock yards and stayed on for two years as station manager and then deputised as teacher after Hillier left. And the then Protector, Baldwin Spencer, who in 1913, on the basis of Barclay's report, agitated for Hermannsburg's closure; although Spencer's animus may have been connected to his professional rivalry with Carl Strehlow. Incidentally, Spencer also wrote critically of Barclay, characterising him as a fool and a pretender.

What seems to have happened is that Liebler mishandled his relationship with Barclay and the adverse report was at least partly the result of that. He mismanaged other things; Carl Strehlow had been collecting and selling Arrernte artefacts without controversy for years; Hillier had done the same among both the Arrernte and the Dieri; Liebler got into trouble for doing exactly what they did, albeit on a grander scale and over a much shorter period of time. When challenged he responded, primly, and speaking of himself in the third person: *Upon request, the missionary privately purchased from the Aranda (men) some of the ethnological items to send to Germany, at high freight costs.* As if he was somehow the unwilling agent of nameless powers, not an active participant in a trade that nearly all white people at the time, missionary or not, indulged in.

In late February 1912 Mission Aboriginals Jakobus, Nathaniel and Thomas set out in the buggy for Oodnadatta to bring the Strehlows back. Just three of the eight family members returned: the five elder children remained to be educated in Germany and only Ted, the youngest and henceforth a de facto only child, accompanied his parents home. He was in his fifth year. The Mission flag, white with a black cross upon it, was flying in the centre of the compound as the people welcomed their returning missionary home, singing *Abide, O dearest Jesus, among us with your grace*.

Later that year the Administrator of the Northern Territory, Dr Gilruth, along with Secretary O'Loughlin and Sergeant Stott, arrived for yet another inspection. Strehlow had recommenced activities with his usual enthusiasm, embarking on a new building programme and carrying out essential maintenance on the old structures. The wells and yards, which had fallen into disrepair, were being renovated, a water tank was under construction and melons, tomatoes, cucumbers and beans were growing in the garden. Along with three confirmations, there were forty catechumens, mostly old people. The inspection report was overwhelmingly positive; the crisis Liebler provoked had passed.

Liebler himself left soon afterwards, his camels loaded up with gear that included the *toa* he got from Hillier as well as artefacts gathered over the past few years. In the photograph taken as he and his wife were about to depart he looks to be an aggrieved, petulant man, always primed to leap to his own defence against any accusation of untoward behaviour; his wife, standing next to him with her right hand on his shoulder, seems long-suffering and full of doubt. She had cancer and not long to live; there were no children. This was December 1913 and they were going back to a Germany that would soon be at war with Australia.

In May 1914, before the major conflict broke out in Europe, there was an event at Hermannsburg which had reverberations that lasted for years and probably intensified the negative reactions to Albert's marriage. It involved a dispute between the Arrernte and their western neighbours, the Loritjas, which word means foreigner; their own name for themselves is Kukatja. A Kukatja man called Ilbalakura speared an Arrernte, Daputa, who pursued Ilbalakura and speared him in turn; whereupon Ilbalakura assembled his Kukatja friends and fell upon the Mission station Aborigines in the night, severely wounding a deaf and dumb man, Rejura, who later died. The terror and resultant anxiety caused among the Mission Aborigines by the raid was extreme and lasting and seems to have exacerbated their unease at their differential status: both native and acculturated, neither one thing or the other.

The war in Europe had consequences for the mission. Anti-German feeling increased and one man in particular, John Verran MP, began to agitate for the closure of Lutheran schools. Verran attacked Hermannsburg for Germanising the natives; for intercepting messages on the Overland Telegraph and passing them to the Kaiser; for teaching in German on the Mission; all of which allegations were false. Strehlow countered accusations of lack of patriotism by playing popular songs on the outdoor gramophone; the assembled Arrernte would sing along to the National Anthem or to tunes like *It's a Long Way to Tipperary*.

Times were hard; there was a huge debt on the Mission, while its sister enterprise, Bethesda, was abandoned and sold for £5000 – the same amount the Immanuels had paid for Hermannsburg more than twenty years before. There was no teacher between 1914–1917 so Strehlow took the classes himself, just as he sometimes doled out food in the eating house. In 1917, too, the annual £300 government subsidy was discontinued and not restored until 1923.

A long argument over water rights commenced and dragged on throughout the war years. It involved dissension with a group of wild horse catchers over the use of Long Water Hole in Ellery Creek on the southern and eastern boundaries of the Mission land. Chief Supervisor Day of Darwin came down to try to determine the southern boundary of the north Ellery Creek block but couldn't find where the historical marker, Gosse's Camp, had been so the matter remained unresolved.

The missionaries were building galvanised iron water tanks next to their houses and, as always in winter, digging for water in the bed of the salty Finke River. The Arrernte dwellings were not neglected; a later observer noted *some 50–60 small thatched roofed huts for the natives...every house had a rain water well beside it and was fenced off from the sandy waste in front of it by a wooden fence bound together with raw-hide and kangaroo hide straps*. Nevertheless the drought brought dust storms that blew great piles of sand into the compound. The horses were too weak to work, at parched waterholes cows and calves collapsed and died, the survivors were savaged by wild dogs.

At about this time we have only the third glimpse on the record, after his birth and baptism, of Albert. It comes courtesy of Ted Strehlow who, many years later, wrote: *my first recollection of him is as a boy in his teens, rather older than myself, waiting for the approach of his tribal initiation rites. When the time finally arrived, he vanished from the Hermannsburg school 'into the bush' for some months. We all knew that, when he returned, he would be regarded officially as a young man, who would be precluded from taking further part in any boyish activities.*

Initiation, then, was a ceremony that had not been suppressed. For those living at the Finke River Mission it typically took place on a ceremonial ground towards Gilbert Springs in the west and this is most likely where Albert was initiated. The first stage in the process, when the subject was between ten and twelve years old, is called by Spencer and Gillen *Throwing the Boy up in the Air*. Men and women assembled and the boys were *taken one by one and tossed in the air several times by the men, who catch them as they fall, while the women dance...shouting loudly.* Afterwards they were painted on their chests and backs, using red and yellow ochre, with designs *emblematic of the totems*; some of these would have been repeated from old rock paintings.

Elaborate protocols surrounded this act of painting, which had to be performed on the boy by a man who was a brother of a woman from the moiety from which the boy's future wife should come. It was this man who chose the design to be painted upon the boy's body and it usually had some relation to his own, not to the boy's, totem. While they were being painted boys were told that the ceremony they had just passed through would aid their growth to manhood and also that, from now on, they were no longer to play with the women and girls, nor camp with them, nor go out gathering food with them; but stay with the men, hunt with them, and so begin the process of learning the sacred knowledge of the tribe.

The second and third procedures of the initiation ceremony were much more elaborate and time-consuming and it is to these two components that Ted Strehlow was referring when he said that Albert was absent from the Mission for some months. They took place only after the boy in question had reached puberty and began with the gathering of a large supply of food and the preparation of the ceremonial ground for the initiation of one, or perhaps two, subjects. The initiation that Spencer and Gillen observed and described in detail occurred at Undiara (Inteyerre) near Henbury Station on the Finke River south of Hermannsburg at a place of the kangaroo dreaming; and hence was directed by kangaroo men and disseminated sacred knowledge associated with that totem; but, they say, it was *typical of the rite of circumcision as carried out by natives living along the Finke River, who are often spoken of as Larapinta blacks.*

The ground consisted of a wide path cleared between heaped banks of earth stretching in an east-west direction with two brakes made of branches and leaves of trees at either end; before the brake at the eastern end men would gather while behind it the women danced; in front of that at the western end was the place where the actual circumcision would occur and behind it, concealed, the novice waited, out of sight but not out of sound of the activities on the ground. Which was extensive; each brake was forty to fifty feet distant from the terminus of the five-foot-wide path that ran at least that distance again from end to end.

On the evening of the first day the boy, who had no exact notion of what was in store for him, was seized at the men's camp by three fellows who dragged him shouting onto the initiation ground and, while the women danced, sat him down among the men; then he was taken away, painted and brought back again, this time to be led through dancing women to the brake at the western end where his body was greased, covered with pinkish-white clay then decorated with bird's down. He would continue to be painted, at intervals and in different styles, throughout the ceremony.

So began a protracted series of events that lasted nine days and included the giving to the boy by his mother of a firestick that was never allowed to go out; an interlude where the boy hunted with the men; ritual incursions onto the ground by the women followed by their retreat; episodes during which men, singly, in pairs or in groups as large as ten, laid their bodies upon the body of the boy; the construction of elaborate props, like *tnatantja* poles, that were used in highly theatrical ceremonials; and, throughout the festivities, the transmission of secret-sacred knowledge in the form of songs, chants and associated dances.

Events were directed by a council of old men and, though guided by tradition, they had an improvisatory aspect, for instance in the selection of the man who would perform the actual circumcision and of his designated assistant. Nevertheless the provision of roles was at all times subordinate to the complex and arcane rules of kinship relations. The boy was expected to remain obedient, was forbidden to speak unless spoken to, sometimes blindfolded and, unless summoned onto the ground, mostly left alone behind his brake under dire admonitions of silence and secrecy.

The culmination was an act, at night, before a blazing fire, to the sound of bull-roarers and the massed chanting of the men, during which the assistant *grasped the foreskin, pulled it out as far as possible and the operator cut it off...the boy, in a more or less dazed condition was led back to where the old brake had stood and...the blood from the wound allowed to flow onto a shield.* It was while he was in this state that the bull-roarers were shown to him and their function explained; then all the men who had acted in the ritual came up, were introduced and embraced the boy; finally, a bundle of wooden *tjurunga* was presented to him, along with the advice that they would help him heal.

The foreskin itself was usually given to a younger boy to swallow while the blood caught in the shield went to the women's camp where those who were elder sisters to the boy or to the boy's mother rubbed it on their breasts and foreheads; but among some sections of the Western Arrernte the circular piece of skin was given instead to one of the boy's (classificatory) sisters, who wore it, dried and painted with red ochre, on a string around her neck.

One curiosity: at the ceremony Spencer and Gillen observed, before the circumcision the boy was painted *on his back* [with] *a design of the Okranina or carpet snake totem from a place called Tharlinga…in the locality of the man who did the painting…the design…was done in white pipe clay* [and] *consisted of a few concentric circles…with corkscrew lines around…the circles represented the snake's hole in the ground, and the other lines…snakes playing round on the hole.* Three men took an hour to finish the painting, which covered most of the boy's back; while they were working an old man *sang in a low monotonous voice about the snakes of Tharlinga.* In the photograph the painting, white on black, is vivid, intricate, maze-like, heart-shaped – an infinite vortex into which you could fall forever. Albert Namatjira's totem was the carpet snake.

The period between circumcision and subincision might last six weeks or longer and was determined by the progress of the healing of the initiate's wound. During this time he lived in the bush and learned the *tjurunga* he had been given; his tasks included hunting for meat and giving it to the older men: initiates were not supposed to eat until they had satisfied their elders. Sometimes the boys went hungry, which did not help them in the hunt; sometimes they died. The initiate would also undergo a painful rite called head biting, performed intermittently by selected groups of from two to five men who sought him out for this arcane purpose: *Their duty is to bite the scalp as hard as they can, until the blood flows freely.* This was thought to promote luxuriant hair growth.

When the boy was brought in for the next stage of his initiation he found no women present on the ceremonial ground. He lay flat on the ground, face down, with his head covered and was joined by older, already initiated members of his cohort while a night of song, dance and story proceeded. A ceremonial pole, *tnatantja*, decorated with bird's down was made and the boy embraced it in order to lessen the pain of the approaching operation. This took place upon a bed made by two men, volunteers lying face down one upon the other. Upon their two prone bodies the initiate stretched out supine looking up at the sky while a third man straddled his body and *grasped the penis and put the urethra on a stretch*. Then a fourth, the operator, *quickly, with a stone knife, laid open the urethra from below*.

Afterwards the boy squatted over a shield in which, as before, the blood was caught. He might also urinate on the fire and stand in the steam to help with the healing; until that was complete he had to sleep on his back so that his penis did not become warped. There were dietary prohibitions – no meat of the opossum, snake, echidna or any kind of lizard, along with a more general restriction against eating the *achilpa* or wild cat, with whom the rite of sub-incision was associated. In the women's camp some of the initiate's relatives, alerted by sounds coming from the ceremonial ground, made cuts upon their own bodies that healed as cicatrices; on the ground itself some men would, out of bravado, excitement or for some other reason have their penises further sub-incised: *down to the root!*

As before, the initiate kept *tjurunga* with him until his wounds had healed, after which the ceremony concluded with a ritual during which all decorations were scrubbed from his skin and he confronted the assembled, dancing women of the tribe as a naked man. Then dressed, ornamented, decorated, given a shield and spear-thrower, he was again shown to the women. The next morning he was presented a third time and on this occasion might throw a boomerang, ritually, in the direction of his mother's country. Prohibitions continued to surround him and he could not speak to any of the actors in the drama of his subincision until he had gone out into the bush and caught food for them.

Spencer and Gillen's account of these events is exhaustively detailed but un-illuminating, as if they were observing something so outlandish that its significance would never become clear. Their own presence as invited guests may have affected what they saw; the purpose of the ceremony, which was to begin the transmission of secret-sacred knowledge to the initiate, remained as dark to them as the lore itself. For the initiate the procedure, in its awe-full solemnity, its theatricality, its esoteric nature and its violence, both implied and actual, was an induction into a reality that would henceforth become the substratum of life itself: the eternal as the ground upon which the everyday is merely an evanescent figure.

WEH Stanner put it thus: *At initiation new psychic paths are made by isolation, terror, fatigue, pain, mystery, drama, grave instruction – means implicitly prescient and in overt use a memorable spectacle. One inward path is ruptured, another substituted, and life thereafter is one continuous re-integration. There are quite probably neural as well as psychic and social reasons why, after initiation, an Aboriginal youth responds but poorly to other possible worlds open to him. Neural, since there has been a cortical integration of intense quality; psychic, since his responses have been deeply conditioned to limited stimuli; social, since a limited range of objects of action have positive valence for him.*

Albert's initiation took place in 1915, the year he turned thirteen. Afterwards he returned to a Mission still afflicted by drought. Even Palm Creek dried out, which had never happened before; there were twenty-seven dead horses in the riverbed and animal corpses had to be cleared continually from all the water holes. In February 1916, the rains came and the rivers ran again. That year surveyors made another attempt to fix the boundaries of the pastoral lease so that water rights could be determined. An employee on the station attempted to sell 400 cattle to an eastern neighbour for £5 a head but was thwarted by quick action from Carl Strehlow, who over the course of a single night had all the cattle branded. There was still no teacher for the school; but at least the government hadn't given in to those who wanted the Mission closed.

In 1917 the men laboured for weeks to remove the sand hills that dust storms had formed within the compound. Rains in February broke the dam on the Finke, destroying the irrigation scheme that watered the gardens. Adolf Heinrich, the new teacher, arrived. By the end of the year, they were in drought again. Over the summer the dam was repaired, extended and deepened and a yard built to hold wild horses. Heavy rain came again in autumn, interrupting the work but, despite a flood in the Finke, the dam held. On 7 April 1918, four Aborigines – Albert, Berthe, Heinrich and Susanna – were confirmed into the church and for the first time took Holy Communion. *May the newly confirmed lead a life in accordance with their vows*, wrote Carl Strehlow. In the case of Albert, at least, he was immediately disappointed.

Among Strehlow's informants were the aforementioned Loatjira; Albert's own father, Jonathon; and a Kukatja man called Wapiti. Wapiti, a ceremonial chief from Mereeni, out west towards Haasts Bluff, was an inveterate cattle thief and eventually paid a price for it. *After police bullets had smashed one of his thigh bones and severely gashed a part of his abdomen...Strehlow...dressed his seemingly fatal wounds and patiently nursed him back to health...he repaid his white benefactor with a wealth of important and secret information.* Wapiti had a daughter, whose name was Ilkalita; and the young Albert, not long after his confirmation, fell in love with her.

Here is how, many years later, he described subsequent events: *Rubina (Ilkalita) was such a nice looking girl and I really fancied her. I sent a message through an old man to her father Wapiti...the fathers talked about it and first the old men said that I was too young and would not give their permission so for a while I felt beaten but then I decided that if I wanted Rubina I must fight for her. There were many who wanted Rubina so it was no use waiting until I was old enough, someone else may have decided before me, or she could have been given away by her father to someone else to whom she had been promised for a long time. I went out to Haasts Bluff and made a little trouble, there was a big fight and I had a spear thrown through my leg and then afterwards when I was well enough to travel we ran away. I was seventeen at the time.*

It was, like his father's, a wrong marriage. It was also a proscribed union so far as the missionaries were concerned: Ilkalita was not a Christian. She was however, one assumes, in love with Albert – otherwise why would they have eloped together? What was courtship like in those days anyway? Once again Géza Róheim is among the few who have ventured an account of how men and women among the Arrernte conducted their intimate affairs. He is writing ten years after Albert went out to Haasts Bluff and claimed Ilkalita; it is a narrative *of a seduction…given…by Renana and some other Aranda men*:

The man and the woman first looked into each other's eyes. Then the man left the group of people and slyly went off into the bush. There they found each other. The woman stood close to the man and they rubbed their breasts together. The man asked the woman if she had come into the bush for his sake and the woman answered that she had come because she loved him. The man then took her into the dense scrub. She opened her legs to him and he put his penis into her vagina. Then the man, who was kneeling, raised the woman, who was lying on the ground, and held her in his arms. The woman held the man with her legs and embraced him with her arms. When they had finished cohabiting they talked. The man asked the woman if she would come to him again. Then they cohabited once more. They remained with each other. When the man went to another place, the woman went with him. They stayed married to each other. When they returned to their home camp, the people all became very excited. They wanted the couple to separate, but the two loved each other. They were married, and remained so.

The child named Elea had become, on baptism, the boy, Albert; as an initiated man he was given a third, a tribal name, Tonanga; there may have been others. A boy passing through the stages of initiation into manhood also inhabited a series of status names, six in all. Of these six stages, it is likely that Albert passed through five; the sixth and last ceremony, called the *Engwura*, which was as elaborate as the foregoing stages and generally undertaken quite some time after the subincision, he did not experience; this is the basis of the repeated claim that he was not a fully initiated man.

According to Spencer and Gillen the Engwura, or Fire Ceremony, was a series of procedures that could last as long as four months and fire played an important role throughout: *at night initiates hurled hundreds of firesticks over the camp, sending them flying through the darkness like rockets to the accompanying screams of women and children and the howling of dogs.* On the last day a large fire was built then covered with green boughs; initiates had to lie for about five minutes on the smoking leaves and endure, while older men fanned the embers, the heat of the burning coals beneath them.

Albert's parents' wrong marriage might have been a cause of his missing this ceremony and maybe also the fact that he was a Christian; but times were changing. One of Ted Strehlow's informants remarked, after a gruesome description of the superseded practise: *Nowadays we make a great concession to the young men in our group. We no longer tear off their finger-nails. The price is too high; we give the tjurunga to them at a much lower cost. Besides, the young men of the present generation are no longer hardy enough to endure such pain.*

Nevertheless the educative function of the ceremonies remained and Albert would have attended other events on other grounds and there learned the songs and dances that belonged to the different totems. Initiation per se was not an end but a beginning: the first stage in what would become, over a lifetime, an increasingly intricate grasp of a cosmogony, a world view, that was both age-old and made-new. It is the same with the names, both given and descriptive: the transition from one to another does not extinguish the previous name, which is instead incorporated as part of the burgeoning identity.

Elea sounds like it could have been either a Mission or an Arrernte name, although it is undoubtedly the latter; Albert, the public name he would carry through his life, was Mission given; the third, Tonanga, not revealed in print until the early 1950s, remains to the uninitiated of unknown provenance. And, as mentioned, there may have been others, making up a complex identity that would itself act upon the complexities of the world, especially once a further component, the surname Namatjira, was added to it. Albert was thus at the time of his marriage already a man of multiple identities folded seamlessly into one: less a wanderer between worlds than a progressive sojourner in a sophisticated, manifold reality.

3. Taos or the Alice?

The story that Rex, in hospital in Melbourne, was given a box of watercolour paints by his sister Florinda, while affecting, is uncorroborated, although he did mention her example when he described how he found his vocation: *After spending several years in hospitals getting treatment I was discharged, although not physically fit enough to go back on the land again. I was rather worried for a long time what to take on, I didn't want to be a lift attendant or something like that which it was suggested at the hospital I could do, but seeing that I had a sister who was an artist, I thought I might take an art course. Eventually I studied commercial art in Melbourne.*

The ambition to become an artist was certainly confirmed during that long period of hospitalisation. Among the memorabilia Rex kept in a cardboard suitcase is a small notebook dated 17.7.19; it contains pen and ink sketches of family members, pets, farm animals and the like, painfully executed and awkward in the way of a child's drawings. They suggest a determination to regain fine motor skills lost in the aftermath of his injuries; and, a more inchoate desire to discover some alternate purchase on the things of the world now that farming was no longer an option for him.

Some of these drawings would have been made while Rex, on leave from the military hospital in Melbourne, was visiting his family in Warrnambool; they are contemporary with two photographs of him, outside, his left arm in a sling, in what seems like the same location – perhaps the hospital garden, perhaps at Skiddaw. In one he wears his army uniform, complete with slouch hat; in the other, civilian clothes. Programs in which he is listed as a singer survive from the same period: on HMT 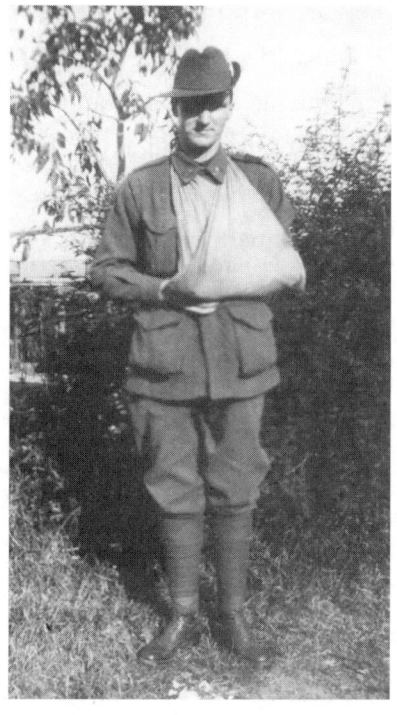 *Themistocles* on 14 December 1917; with Mr Henry Thomas and his students at Melba Hall on 3 December 1921, at which he sang *The Curfew* by Monk Gould; at the St Kilda Dinghy club where his brother Malpas was a member.

Just as, in England, he had been looked after by relatives – the Lees of Malpas, Cheshire, the Thistlethwaites of Ashton on Ribble, cousins in Windermere – back in Australia he was nurtured in the bosom of his immediate family. For many years his eldest brother, Malpas Richard, a chemist and a druggist, provided him with a room in his house from which he could come and go as he pleased; his sister Florinda in Tasmania was a constant correspondent and frequent hostess as well as a mentor; there was a cousin at Lake Bolac with whom he often stayed; he continued to spend time with his mother Mary at the parental home in Warrnambool until her death in 1930.

The art institution he attended was The Commercial Art School in Rickard's Building at 226 Little Collins Street, just behind the Melbourne Town Hall and backing on to the Athenaeum where, later, Rex and Albert both exhibited; the principal was Cyril Leyshon White. He was the same age as Rex and, like him, a returned man; he served as a private with the 6th Field Ambulance and first saw action at Gallipoli in the Dardanelles, where he was awarded the Military Medal. The citation reads: *These two men* [the other was a William James Benfell] *during the Lone Pine Bombardment were doing duty as dressers out at Brown's Dip Advanced Dressing Station. They continued to dress and evacuate patients during the bombardment. These men were especially conspicuous being under shell fire the whole time.*

This was in early August and not long afterwards White became one of the workers on *The Anzac Book*, a miscellany edited at Anzac Cove by journalist, later official war historian, Charles Bean and published in 1915. White's work was described by Bean as *comic stuff…a sharp sense of humour.* His drawings are not all caricature however; some are documentary. When the 6th Ambulance followed the 2nd Division to the Western Front the following year, White continued to work as an unofficial war artist (there were no official artists as yet), producing a set of four humorous, illustrated cards for sale over Christmas 1916. He seems to have remained at the Western Front for the duration; when the war ended he was at Rouen where, under the general editorship of Corporal JRW Taylor, he became the art editor of a publication similar to *The Anzac Book*, called *The Dernière Heure*.

The Dernière Heure was finished in London and published there by the AIF in 1919; it was probably during this period that White went to study art in Paris. However, he was soon back in Melbourne, contributing watercolour illustrations to a book of short stories, *The Ivory Gate* (1919) by Marjorie Barnard, who would, as one half of the portmanteau author M Barnard Eldershaw (the other was

Flora Eldershaw) become a significant contributor to Australian literary culture between the wars.

Leyshon White was an energetic promoter of his school; an advertisement in the *Argus* in 1928 begins: *Ladies, why not take up this lucrative profession?* Another, from 1930, *guarantees thorough training. Each student receives personal attention. Ample assistance provided; thorough instruction given by artists of 21 years' experience.* White wrote a booklet called *Art that Pays* which he gave away for free and also devised a home study plan for those who could not physically attend *the school with a reputation.* Students learned to draw for catalogues, to prepare newspaper advertisements, to paint posters, to make up show cards and write tickets; to do lettering, take photographs, screen prints and etch lithographs.

Rex, who was a commercial artist for most of his life, seems to have acquired his skills quickly. There are two early examples of his work extant, both from 1924. One, a poster for Rosella High Class Preserves, features a brightly coloured parrot, in profile, perched on the twiggy branch of a gum tree above a pile of fruit and a jar of preserves; the background is jet black, the lettering bright yellow, the table upon which the fruit rests a pale green oblong. The rosella has something awkward about it, perhaps there's too pronounced a hump in the back, but it makes up for any lack of verisimilitude with a display of the cheerful insouciance that parrots seem to us to possess. The other work is black and white, gouache on board, advertising Trufood Separated Milk; a cow's head in three quarter view above a selection of milk products which, in the expressive accuracy of the image of the animal, shows a farm boy's observational powers.

Rex is usually said to have been without formal art training but this is not strictly true. In a 1960 interview he acknowledged his teacher and credited him with supplying the motivation to become the kind of artist he was: *while I was studying commercial art my teacher,*

Leyshon White, suggested I should go out and do some landscape paintings for the backgrounds. Once I had gone out to do a bit of sketching, I realised I wanted to be out of doors, I didn't want to be tied up in the city and be just a commercial artist all my life. Many returned men did end up immured in the city, as lift attendants or behind the wheel of a taxi or in some other quasi-sedentary occupation easily pursued by the partially disabled. Rex was not going to be one of those.

It was at The Commercial Art School that Battarbee met John Gardner, a student from the same west Victorian background as himself: *He was a country boy too*, Rex remarked. Gardner (1906–1987) was the son of a dairy farmer from the Stoney Rises between Colac and Camperdown; and later Terang, north and east of Warrnambool. He was twelve years younger and a foot shorter than the lanky Battarbee; garrulous where the other was laconic; a drinker whose carousals sometimes alarmed his largely teetotal mate; they must have made an odd couple. As well as a love of art and of the outdoors, the two shared a passion for music. Gardner played the violin and sometimes while he fiddled, Rex sang. Gardner was, like Leyshon White, a caricaturist. He drew compulsively from a young age and was still a teenager when he came to Melbourne in 1923 to study at the National Gallery Art School.

Gardner's teachers at the NGAS were Charles Nuttal and George Bell; he also took lessons from Harold Herbert, a watercolourist who had himself twice gone to Hans Heysen for instruction. In 1922–23 Herbert spent eighteen months travelling in England, France, Spain and Morocco and upon his return to Melbourne in 1924 staged a major exhibition of the paintings he had done while on safari: it was a sell-out and caused a sensation. He was a naturalist, a *plein air* painter who thought an artist should draw inspiration from the picturesque as it manifested before his eyes; one of those who, in Bernard Smith's words, wanted to resist *the primitivistic assumptions that lay at the heart of modernism and to champion the pastoral tradition of nationalist painting against imported European fashion.*

Herbert's example – to travel and paint, return and sell – was congruent with the practice of the Taos School of Painters, who were already known in Melbourne art circles; Gardner heard about them through Fred Leist, another war artist, who visited Taos in the mid-1920s and showed some of his American paintings at the Fine Art Gallery in Melbourne in 1927. The Taos School dated from the turn of the century, when two New York artists on their way to Mexico for a painting trip were stranded after their covered wagon broke a wheel near the small pueblo town; and ended up staying there.

The artists' colony they founded was formalised in 1915 as the Taos Society of Artists – essentially a sales co-operative, it aimed to promote the work of its members through travelling exhibitions. In this it was wildly successful, not least because of an appetite amongst people in the cities of the eastern seaboard of the United States for the romantic exotica they used as subject matter: Native American life and the wide vistas of the wild western lands. Both forms of exotica existed, albeit in different forms, almost unexploited in Australia and Herbert's and Leist's examples showed that it was possible to travel, paint and bring the results back home to sell.

The commercial imperative was no doubt part of the motivation but it was also in a spirit of pure adventure that Battarbee and Gardner in 1926 tossed a silver shilling: heads they would go to New Mexico; tails into the Outback. It came up tails and they began saving money for the trip. Both men were then employed as salaried artists by advertising agencies. Gardner was getting three guineas a week from Samson Clarkes and when, at the end of 1927, they offered him a rise to seven guineas he knocked it back and went on the road instead.

For £110 he and Battarbee bought a second-hand, black, hand-painted 1924 Model T Ford van which they described as a *caravan* – perhaps a converted ambulance or even a hearse; it had kerosene lamps on either side of the exterior of the windscreen. Neither of them could drive and Rex's crippled hand and stiffened arm and shoulder meant that he never would; he became their cook. Gardner took driving lessons and in time, through necessity, developed into an expert bush mechanic. They gathered supplies – canvas, paper, paints and brushes; a rifle, ammunition, cameras; split peas and barley – named their vehicle Henrietta and, after each spending the summer holidays at home with their respective families, in February 1928 set out on a fifteen-month, 7000-mile painting trip through eastern Australia.

We went west of Rockhampton and back of Bourke, one or other or both of them wrote in a short-lived magazine called *The Art Student* published by Leyshon White in the early 1930s, *and never bought a meal or slept in a house. And while we were sometimes two hundred miles from a town we were never short of food. We carried a good supply of flour for damper, and the gun and the rod got us entrées…the big cost was petrol and repairs. Our work greatly interested the aborigines. They would sit and watch us for hours. They were puzzled at the rough daubs at the start, but when the pictures were completed, they thought we were marvels. Strange meetings? Yes. At a solitary cattle station in Queensland, we discovered that the manager had studied at the National Art School, Melbourne. He gave us a royal welcome.*

2

It's curious the way Rex's hospital years coincide with Albert's time in the wilderness: as if the lock-step between their thus far wholly dissimilar lives began a full decade and a half before they actually met; as if the survivors of two very different wars were already entered upon intersecting paths. Albert and Ilkalita disappeared from Hermannsburg in 1919 and did not return until after the departure for Adelaide of Carl and Frieda Strehlow with their fourteen-year-old son Ted in October 1922. Only Frieda and Ted arrived in the southern capital; twelve days into the overland journey Carl died of dropsy at Horseshoe Bend and was buried there, leaving half a dozen full bottles of whisky as memorial – and equivocal – gifts for Aboriginal men who had helped him in his work.

Nobody knows exactly where Albert and Ilkalita were in these years but it's likely that they spent them moving from station to station where Albert could get work; interspersed with episodes of living a traditional life on the land, most likely among Ilkalita's people around Mereeni and Haasts Bluff in the west. Two children, Enos and Oscar, were born during the exile and when they came in to Hermannsburg Ilkalita was pregnant with their third child, Maisie. A fourth, Hazel, was conceived and born on the Mission soon after.

It's usually been assumed this period of wandering was required by tribal law but that may not have been the case. After all, Albert had already been speared; and his father's exile for a similar, albeit less serious, offence lasted just a single year. One of the sources mentions the family returned only after somebody told them it was safe to go back; perhaps it was actually the departure of Carl Strehlow, who opposed the marriage, that made it so? Other sources suggest that Strehlow protected the marriage of Albert and Ilkalita against those who were outraged that he should have married a Kukatja woman; the bloody raid of 1914 was still vivid in many people's minds and had left bitter and lasting memories behind. Nevertheless, marriages between Arrernte and Kukatja were not unknown and there were certainly ways and means of repairing the social fabric so torn.

The relationship between Albert and the Strehlows is not easily elucidated. To Carl he was perhaps just another young man, of no particular distinction, and so treated accordingly; but every word that Ted Strehlow wrote about him is charged with implications that remain mostly unspoken – as if there was secret-sacred business of an unprecedented kind involved; which is no doubt the case. Ted, had he been Arrernte, at age fourteen would have been initiated; instead he accompanied his dying father south to Horseshoe Bend. It may be that in later life he envied those among his near contemporaries, like Albert, who *were* initiated; that he could neither forgive nor quite forget that the inside knowledge so gained, the intrinsic understanding, would never be his.

Albert built a house, a grass hut, for himself and his family at Hermannsburg then resumed the peripatetic labouring life he began in 1919, ranging widely over the country, travelling to where the opportunities were and working at a variety of occupations – blacksmithing, carpentry, cattle-work, saddle-making, well-digging, yard-building. To these multifarious occupations he added another, that of camel man, going along with the teams and their mostly Afghan drivers as far as Oodnadatta, 300 miles away, to collect or deliver loadings and also doing the runs into Alice Springs and back for Mission supplies. Later in the 1920s he would, as camel man, guide parties of tourists to Palm Valley and other exotic locations. Later still he would offer a curious homage to his Muslim friends, inscribing *Salaam* on the trunk of one of his gum trees; or else painting a tree into which that word had previously been carved.

No immediate replacement for Strehlow the Elder could be found so in his absence superintendent's duties were split between Heinrich, the teacher, who became the congregation's spiritual adviser and Johannsen, the Dane, who was re-appointed station manager even though he lived some distance away at Deep Well Station, where he had been farming since his first tour of duty at Hermannsburg ended before the war. The Mission Board apparently hoped that a lay person might prove more efficient at generating income and developing Aboriginal employment opportunities; unfortunately Heinrich and Johannsen did not get on with each other. Worse, dual responsibility exacerbated matters already made difficult by the onset of a seven-year drought.

Baldwin Spencer, like a baleful spirit, returned to Hermannsburg in May of 1923 in order to make yet another report to the Commonwealth. He stayed ten days and, Heinrich said, *reported on everything*; there is a list that encompasses buildings, the spiritual side of the mission's work, its training policy, history, language, statistics and generalities but the main issue was *the half-caste question*: what to do about those children born of black mothers from white fathers? This amounted to an obsession amongst government officials throughout the 1920s and 1930s and continued to have an impact after the Second World War; the children of the Stolen Generations were often taken away precisely because they were thought to have so-called white blood in their veins.

Spencer reported unfavourably upon conditions at Hermannsburg and, as he had after Barclay's report a decade earlier, recommended the Mission be closed, taken over by the government or given to the Salvation Army; he was critical of the failure to develop a viable pastoral programme while ignoring the fact that living conditions, food and medical supplies for Aborigines were far better than on most cattle stations. Canberra had already, the previous year, granted a seven-year extension of the Mission's lease, which until then had been reviewed annually. The Mission Board felt sufficiently encouraged by this to begin making longer-term plans: they decided to develop tanning and leather industries; and to begin proselytising among the western tribes, those *living within a reachable distance, about two or three days journey*.

Heinrich went on leave towards the end of 1923, going south for an operation, to get married and to have a rest. When he returned some months later with his new wife, they were met at the railhead at Oodnadatta by Albert, driving the Mission's buggy and horses. Mrs Heinrich, who was at first intimidated by a man usually described as *a full-blooded Aboriginal*, soon became not just unafraid but actively fond of Albert. *Each night*, she recalled, *he made sure the camping site was protected from the chill desert winds, lit a big fire, prepared the evening meal and unpacked the sleeping gear before retiring to another campfire that he made for himself at a little distance.*

Heinrich was relieved by Pastor Reidel who, in November, baptised thirteen men, fifteen women and sixteen children; and blessed fourteen marriages. *The men and women*, he wrote, *– besides one who was already confirmed – had been instructed by Mr Strehlow, teacher Heinrich and Moses.* The exception, the man already confirmed, was Albert; and among those who were baptised was Ilkalita, who was given the name Rubina, and their three children Enos, Oscar and Maisie. Also baptised was the ceremonial chief Loatjira, who had for so long resisted Carl Strehlow's attempts to convert him. It was Reidel who in late 1923 sent the first Aboriginal evangelists – Nathaniel and Maria, Jakobus and Alma – into the west to try to convert the Loritjas. They were followed early the next year by Moses and August.

Reidel was less tolerant than Strehlow had become over twenty-eight year's service; it troubled him that the Hermannsburg flock was a mixture of Christians and heathens. *Is it a proper Christian act,* he wondered, *when a Christian man marries a heathen woman or vice versa? In contrast to past practice I have answered the question 'No'.* He also resisted those forms of clan avoidance still practised by the people, considering it a relic of heathenism as well as a denial of Christian fellowship. When some Arrernte men saw a vision of the fiery cross flaming above the altar in the church during the

Lord's Supper, Reidel took it as a sign that his sterner advocacy was reaping just rewards. In this he was, albeit unwittingly, preparing the way for Strehlow's eventual replacement, Pastor Friedrich Albrecht.

Albrecht, with his wife Minna, arrived at the Mission on 16 April 1926, after a rail trip from Adelaide followed by a three-day journey from the railhead at Oodnadatta to Alice Springs, and thence overland to Hermannsburg. He was a Polish German from Kroczyn in the east, one of thirty-seven small, rural, largely Lutheran villages made up of German settlers who had been given the land by the Russian administration after the confiscation and subdivision of large estates following the suppression of the Polish nationalist uprising in 1863.

Born 1894, the eldest of eight, Friedrich was a sociable child who walked with a limp because injuries after a fall down the steps into the cellar of the family home when just twelve months old had left him with one leg shorter than the other. His physical disability was compounded by indifferent performances at school and he was seen as a boy of limited usefulness. The young Albrecht became a reader and a believer and, at the age of ten, decided he wanted to be a missionary.

With the support of his mother, and against the wishes of his father, in Easter 1913 he began studying at the Lutheran missionary institute in the small German town of Hermannsburg, some thirty miles north of Hanover. When, the next year, war broke out, Albrecht refused to enlist as a soldier and chose instead to begin medical training, joining the Red Cross and serving on the eastern front as part of a field hospital. His unit followed the rapid advance of the German armies and was typically in a state of crisis, mainly because of the need to care for large numbers of wounded Russians left behind by the retreating Imperial army. Albrecht, who spoke

Russian as well as Polish and German, often found himself crawling among the wounded, triaging in no man's land; for bravery under fire he was awarded the highest grade of the Iron Cross.

Disease was rife. Albrecht caught cholera and was left for dead, with others so afflicted, in a Russian farmhouse. When, against expectations, he recovered, he rejoined his unit, then stationed near Kroczyn; visited home; and there, in June 1915, learned that, just ten days earlier, the Russians had sent his entire family east by train to Siberia. He was not re-united with the survivors – five of his siblings died of cholera at Kustany – until after he was discharged and returned home again on New Year's Day 1919. Then, after helping his parents re-establish themselves on their farm, he set out to resume his interrupted studies at Hermannsburg.

Poland was occupied, in chaos and the border with Germany closed. It took Albrecht, who had no identity papers, three attempts to find a train that would take him west. He crossed the Polish-German border at Rypin, illegally, on foot, with only a birth certificate as identification, then reported to the German military authorities on the other side. The two men interrogated ahead of him were taken out and shot but when his turn came the lieutenant in charge remarked: *He's only a cripple. He's not worth a bullet* and allowed him to phone Hanover to confirm his identity.

At the Institute in Hermannsburg Albrecht met Minna Gevers (b. 1899), a young woman from the village of Wesseloh to the north-west who had contracted tuberculosis while at *Haushaltungsschule* or finishing school and, during her convalescence, decided she wanted to become a nursing sister in a mission overseas. She was working in the household of one of the lecturers at the seminary when she and Albrecht met; coincidentally, after he arrived at Hermannsburg in 1919 with not much more than the clothes he stood up in, Minna's father, who was devout, had a set of bookshelves constructed for him in such a way that it could be easily dismantled when he went overseas; he did not realise he was also going to give his daughter to the improvident young man.

It was November 1923, when Albrecht received, by letter, the invitation to go as Superintendent to the Finke River Mission in Central Australia; seven other men had previously refused the lonely and difficult posting. He was twenty-nine years old and still getting over the death of his mother the previous year; he asked Minna if she would marry and go with him and she said she would. Albrecht then spent some time alone at Wartburg Seminary, Iowa, in the United States, in order to improve his English. In June 1925, having overcome her parents' objections, Minna left from Hamburg by ship for Quebec then travelled by train across Canada to Winnipeg, where Albrecht met her and they were married. They travelled on together to Vancouver and sailed thence for Adelaide.

Albrecht was short and broad and lame; he was known as *ingkata inurra*, the limping pastor, and widely respected. Like Strehlow before him, he believed in bilingualism and actively promoted the use of Arrernte and English in school and in church. Within a year of his arrival at Hermannsburg he had learned the language well enough to preach a sermon in Arrernte. When 150 copies of Carl Strehlow's translations of the four Gospels from the New Testament, printed by the British and Foreign Bible Society, arrived, there was no money to pay for them so Albrecht and his Arrernte elders asked for donations: a wealth of spears, boomerangs, shields, stone axes, stone knives, strings of human hair, red bean necklaces and *tjurunga* were brought in, crated up and sent by camel to Oodnadatta and ultimately by rail to the Bible Society in Adelaide.

The railway line was gradually progressing north towards Alice Springs (it arrived there in 1929) and there were other indications that the isolation that had pertained since the earliest days of the Mission was breaking down. Just a few months after the Albrechts' arrival the Reverend John Flynn of the Inland Mission, the pioneer of the Flying Doctor service, came out to visit from his new hospital in Alice Springs; he returned in November with an assistant, Alf Traeger, who set up wireless telegraphy for the station. This allowed telegrams to be sent by Morse code to Alice Springs; the replies could be heard live, *louder and better than a telephone on a good night*; but the lack of anyone permanently manning the Alice Springs station meant this service remained at best intermittent. Full radio contact, via Cloncurry in Western Queensland, would not be achieved until 1931.

The first motorcar had come through in 1920 and by the later years of the decade, although there was still no proper road, there were regular visits by car. Often these were dignitaries of some kind or another, usually politicians or vice-regal personnel, but not always; some were simply tourists, attracted by the exotic landscape of the Western MacDonnells and especially the growing reputation of Palm Valley with its exotic, perhaps unique, palms, *Livistonia mariae*. Then, in 1928, the first aeroplane landed: *Some of the Aborigines screamed with fright when the planes appeared over the hills east of the bend in the Finke and approached the station*, Albrecht wrote. He welcomed the growing tourist traffic, seeing it as the economic opportunity it was, but at the same time warned that *for the life of the congregation…there exist numerous dangers.*

Among these early visitors to the Centre was the artist, Jessie Constance Alicia Traill, who came through in April and May of 1928. Her mentor, Tom Roberts, whom she had known since she was ten years old, saw and admired her Centralian work. *I'd love to go and work there myself*, he said. *I had a glimpse once from a high pass of the West streaming away, but things in that day didn't let me go. It's for the later generation and they will love it.* Traill herself wrote that *the country was suffering under the throes of a dreadful drought but the people were wonderfully cheerful and charming. The colour of the landscape…is extraordinarily delicate – pinks, yellows, opals, greys and blue-greens…Oh, the cloudless days of shimmering light, the pale pink dawns, and golden sunsets!…The mornings are fresh, the nights strangely luminous.*

Traill is the first European artist known to have painted the Centre and also the first to have exhibited there. Her show took place in the schoolhouse in Alice Springs, with the works pinned to grey blankets hung from the walls. The entire population of the town is said to have attended and one work was sold – to a man whose house happened to appear in the picture. Among the works Traill completed on that trip is a watercolour of Mt Hermannsburg, dated 1928, and eerily prefiguring the many versions Albert Namatjira would do of the same subject. It is usually called, after an inscription on the left of the picture, *Natives Carry Faggots of Wood* but also has the words *Camel Carts Gathering Sand* written on the right. Traill held another exhibition at Wilpena Pound in the Flinders Range and on her return to Melbourne showed, in November 1928, her Central Australian landscapes, along with those painted in the Flinders Range, at the Little Gallery.

Albrecht already believed that the only way for Hermannsburg to survive as a mission was by becoming self-sufficient; a 1928 increase of the government subsidy from £300–400 annually was never going to suffice: that was approximately the amount spent in any given year on flour alone. But the provision of a twenty-one year lease on the Mission's land was conducive to long-term planning and over the next few years Albrecht would initiate a number of schemes whereby Arrernte could earn money: for instance, he tried to establish a brush-making industry using horsetail hair, which however failed because of the lack of a sales outlet in the south.

Women's fancy work became another source of income. Doilies, tray and tablecloths of Irish linen, with scrolls and flowers printed on them, were ordered from department stores down south and given to the women to complete in lazy daisy, stem and satin stitch. The articles, which were usually worked on in the grass huts where the women lived, often came back black with dirt but were washed in the Mission laundry to a brilliant white, starched and ironed before being sent away to Adelaide.

Albrecht made a virtue out of necessity despatching south, along with the fancy work and the snake and goanna skins, cattle hides with the camel loadings. The hides were all that could be salvaged of their precious stock. *Our cattle are dying in great numbers,* he wrote. *One can still see only miserable skeletons walking about. We try…to retrieve the hides of the dead animals, and, after salting them down, to send them to Adelaide, where they command a good price. The drought continues unbroken. Often severe dust storms rage.* The only way they could get water onto the Mission was by camel from Koporilya Springs, five miles away; and by 1929 there was only one camel fit enough for the task.

The seven year drought in Central Australia in the 1920s was not a period entirely without rain; but the rain that did fall was never enough and hence the effects over time were cumulative and increasingly severe. *Waterholes which had not failed in living memory disappeared, underground water became brackish and unusable before it dried up completely. It was not uncommon to see the carcases of rabbits caught in the lower branches of trees where they had leapt trying to reach the last remnants of vegetation.* Out on the range kangaroos and euros were dying too, bush tucker had virtually disappeared and those called myalls, who followed a traditional way of life, were coming in from the west in numbers, naked and starving, looking for rations. The 1928 winter camel loading was fifteen days late because the camels were so emaciated they could barely walk and, the evening before it finally came in, the Mission was effectively without food.

Prices in Alice Springs sky-rocketed and Albrecht canvassed, then rejected, the option of buying supplies there: they couldn't afford to pay what the merchants were asking, let alone spend the money needed to hire a truck to bring the food back. There was no motorised vehicle on the Mission because Albrecht wasn't prepared to buy one and then have to spend money that could be used for food on fuel. Instead, he allowed his people permission to go out hunting with guns, and gave the meat to the sick.

Disease followed drought with biblical inevitability. Epidemics of influenza on the Mission were succeeded by measles, whooping cough and dysentery; ultimately tuberculosis. The worst affliction of all was one which made the limbs swell, the body ache, the gums ulcerate, the teeth fall out. The very old and the very young suffered most: in some estimates eighty-five per cent of Arrernte children died, including one of Albert and Rubina's children, their third daughter Nelda, who was born with symptoms of malnutrition and lived just seventeen months. Also among the dead was Albert's twenty-one year-old brother Hermann, about whom nothing else is known. Albert took his family, left the Mission and went into the west to mourn.

Nobody knew what the affliction was though there were theories as to its origin. *Jakkai, Kristarinja inkaraka iluma* one old woman told Albrecht. *All the Christians die.* However, because of the dearth of bush tucker, the exact same thing was happening to the myalls in the west so it couldn't only be a disease of the faithful. An old man from Alice Springs had another perspective on the calamity; he gave Heinrich the sardonic advice that they *should pray in English and not in Aranda so that God would understand.*

It seems incredible that neither Albrecht, with his medical training, nor anyone else realised that people were suffering from scurvy. It wasn't until an anthropological expedition came up from the University of Adelaide in August 1929 that vitamin C deficiency was diagnosed and an appeal for help launched: over 200 cases of oranges and lemons arrived during the next few months and most people recovered relatively quickly.

Yet the load on the Mission's resources continued to increase. At the end of 1928 the government decided to move a hundred or so displaced Aborigines who had been camping along the railway line then under construction, out to Hermannsburg. This strategy, held to be for their own good, was also a means of clearing fringe dwellers, many of whom were sick, alcoholic, venereal or otherwise degraded, out of the path of the railway that was nearing Alice Springs and expected to increase tourist traffic substantially. The so-called *government blacks* were meant to be fed with rations bought with money provided by the Commonwealth but, typically, the group was never properly assessed or even counted and included many more people than were officially catered for.

Somehow the Mission coped with the extra demands and then, at the last gasp of 1929, the drought finally broke. *Things were extremely bad during the Christmas days but then there followed lovely rains on the 27th and 28th December, so that the Finke ran in high flood* Albrecht wrote. There was more rain in the new year and, in the first two months of 1930, eight inches fell. *Choruses of crickets and frogs sounded...along the river and...sand and stone became waving vistas of lush green grass.* Wild flowers that the Albrechts had never seen before appeared and fish spawned in the Finke as the floodwaters receded. The dead land recovered so rapidly it seemed, at least to the Christians, a miracle of God.

Albrecht was compassionate, energetic, forthright, dedicated, the *Schweitzer of the Northern Territory*; but he was also, like Strehlow, prepared to use corporal punishment when he felt it was necessary. He told Géza Róheim how he once locked a child of eight, Rufus, in the boys' house and, when he roared and screamed for an hour, took him out again and gave him a beating. When some of the people protested, even going so far as to threaten him with death, Albrecht told them, in typical Lutheran fashion, that it was the only way to make refractory children learn. He was also, in matters of religion, intolerant, especially when it came to the stone-age beliefs of his flock. He did not share Carl Strehlow's interest in ethnology and did not see why he should put up with relics of ancient religion or custom among the Aborigines on the Mission.

A subtle and consummate politician, he decided early on that, rather than lay down the law himself, he would govern – it is not too strong a word – through the agency of a group of Arrernte elders, all of whom had their positions confirmed by election of the congregation. These men – Jakobus and Titus, Nathaniel and Abel, August and Petrus, Albert's own father Jonathon – commanded respect due to their longevity as Christians and, in traditional fashion, also exercised authority because of their age and life experience.

The chief amongst them was Blind Moses, born Tjalkabotta around the time of the arrival of the first Lutherans and baptised aged twelve; he had, subsequently, like Albert, undergone initiation and, not long after that, become partially blind due to heatstroke. This blindness became total following a severe illness in the early 1900s and his activities were as a consequence restricted. He became a baptismal instructor on the Mission and one of Carl Strehlow's chief aids in his translation and anthropological work; it was Blind Moses who helped Albrecht learn the Arrernte language. He often preached in the church and sometimes evangelised, going by donkey amongst the unconverted Aborigines living up and down the Finke River.

Moses and the other elders sometimes proved holier than their pastor. When one of the members of the 1929 Anthropological Expedition, Dr Harold Davies, the Director of the Elder

Conservatorium of Music in Adelaide, returned to Hermannsburg with a request to record traditional Aboriginal music, especially their singing, Albrecht agreed. Men and women from the Mission and beyond were invited to come and perform and were offered a shilling for each song. Sessions lasted for two weeks but, even though they clearly needed the money, none of the Christian Arrernte performed.

Later, after Davies had left, the Arrernte elders came to Albrecht and complained that corroboree dancing had been revived near the Mission. For this they blamed Albrecht himself, because he had encouraged the pagan performances that Davies recorded. Albrecht apologised. Barbara Henson, his biographer, who recounts this episode, remarks that group pride might have been as much a factor in the elders' outrage as simple piety. They, the Western Arrernte, were Christians; the heathen Loritjas were not.

The assertion of their Christian identity was made in far more dramatic fashion on Pentecost Sunday, 9 June 1930, when one of the principal secret-sacred sites of the Western Arrernte, the cave of Manangananga, just a few kilometres from Ntaria at the head of a dry gorge running up into Mt Hermannsburg, was ritually de-sacralised. The immediate provocation for this act was a series of fights on the Mission which, whatever their origin, always resulted in the people opposing each other along the lines of traditional tribal relationships and often led to the suffering of innocents while the guilty escaped.

When one Saturday night a man had his thigh gashed to the bone with a butcher's knife, Albrecht had had enough. That Sunday, instead of a church service, he called a meeting outside at which he told the people that he would not again give communion until the congregation demonstrated that they put God's word before tribal law. The plan to de-sacralise Manangananga was apparently the elders' response to this ultimatum – though it is possible that the suggestion might in the first instance have come from Albrecht himself. He certainly did not oppose it.

The women baked cakes, the men loaded a copper onto a donkey cart and the entire community walked out to the cave, where the copper was filled with water from the sacred rock-hole then boiled to make tea; they picnicked on bread and meat as well as the cake. Before the church service, at which Albrecht, Blind Moses and others preached, the *tjurunga*, the sacred stones, were brought out of the cave, unwrapped and laid down in the open for all to see; even the women and children were invited to handle them, an act which had once meant certain death.

Albrecht took as his text the story of Moses, Aaron and the Golden Calf; Blind Moses delivered an address he gave many times over the years called *Churinga or Christ?*; and after the sermons were over, everybody sang hymns. The scene was photographed and in the picture men, women and children, all in European dress, stand or sit on a rocky hillside in a rough circle about the cave mouth; near the centre of the image, before the dark aperture, white-haired and white-bearded Blind Moses sits with a child in his arms. One of those in the picture is Albert, sitting hatless on the far left in the mid-ground.

Albrecht followed up this epochal act by initiating a series of missions proselytising among the heathen tribes in the west. He led the first attempt himself, with a Warlpiri man called Meranano as his guide and translator; Meranano had taken refuge at Hermannsburg after the Coniston massacres in 1928 and was trying to find his parents, whom he had not seen or heard from for two years. The small party went west by camel past Glen Helen, Haasts Bluff and Mereeni as far as Pikilli Springs in Pintupi lands, meeting people who had never seen whites before. Meranano found his parents alive but traumatised: Albrecht was asked why so many had been killed when the two men who provoked the massacres by murdering the dingo-hunter Brooks were still alive and living in the hills not so far from where they were? All he could say was that he would do his best to make sure such a thing never happened again.

From Pikilli they went south-west to Illbila in the Ehrenburg Ranges, where a man showed them one of the depots Harold Bell Lasseter left behind during his attempt to re-locate his legendary reef of gold in the Petermann Ranges further south. Lasseter was at that moment somewhere to the south-west, with a rogue German named Paul Johns as his cameleer; Johns had worked for a time at Hermannsburg before being fired. The two would soon fall out, Johns would abandon Lasseter and Lasseter would die in a cave sometime during the coming summer; the quest to learn his fate, the search for his body, was co-ordinated in part via Hermannsburg Mission.

From Illbila the party looped south and then east, visiting station Aborigines at Boatswains Hole, Tempe Downs, Middleton Ponds and Henbury on their way back to Hermannsburg; they covered over 500 miles in five weeks and Albrecht returned with the strong conviction that an extension of the Lutheran mission into the west was an absolute necessity if the people were to survive. There was already talk of pastoral leases being granted over their land and he knew that meant certain eviction for the several hundreds whose range it was. As soon as he was back at the Mission he began preparations for another expedition, this time with Aboriginal evangelists who would remain behind as sojourning missionaries.

The party set out the next winter, in May 1931, but Albrecht was taken ill at Glen Helen and could not proceed; the others, with Ernest Kramer, a lay missionary from Alice Springs, in charge, went on without him. There were two pairs of Aboriginal evangelists: Abel and Albert going to Pikilli in the Davenport Ranges; Titus and Rolf heading for Illbila in the Ehrenburgs. They carried with them supplies of food for four or five weeks and were expected subsequently to live on the land and so stay out there for an indeterminate period making friends and co-existing with the local people; the results were however disappointing.

Albrecht wrote with some asperity: *Abel proved, even in this situation, what he had always been, – unreliable, returning to the station with Albert as early as one week after Mr Kramer's return, and only after they had whittled away their supplies of food to the wild men. Titus and Rolf held out longer.* He means that they had given away the food they were meant to subsist upon to those they were trying to convert. Albrecht concluded that the only way properly to evangelise in the west was if the Mission took over the ordering and supply of provisions.

The image of Albert as an Aboriginal evangelist emphasises his position at Hermannsburg at this time as one of the younger men expected to join the cohort of elders who were Albrecht's apostles, advisers and executors. Titus, the man who held out longer, was his uncle; his father Jonathon remained one of the prominent group of old Christians on the Mission; he had other close relatives among the Christian Arrernte. The truth was that Albert had not thrived at Pikilli, had lost two stone in weight and learned, moreover, that his Mission background left him unfit for a long period of living a traditional life off the land.

Coincidentally, an unanticipated consequence of the expedition led to a major turning point in Albert's life. After he fell ill with severe back pains at Glen Helen, Albrecht declined the use of the Flying Doctor service out of Cloncurry because of the money it would cost and returned overland to Alice Springs; from there he went by train to Adelaide, where he was diagnosed with kidney stones. While recuperating after treatment there, he saw boomerangs, woomeras and other carved wooden artefacts for sale; they were not items of traditional manufacture but had been made specifically as souvenirs and Albrecht at once saw the opportunity for a craft industry at Hermannsburg.

Further, he remembered the devotional plaques, made of birch wood and inscribed with Biblical texts or other homilies, that were common in peasant households in northern Germany and in Poland, and thought they might also be adapted for sale on the Mission. A complementary innovation may have come from the Arrernte: in the old days men around a fire in the evening sometimes decorated utilitarian objects using hot coals to burn designs into the wood and this technique was adapted, via the agency of red-hot wire, to make marks on oval sections of mulga cut from the trunk of a tree. Or maybe the idea came from the practice of using hot wire to brand hides, stockwhips, saddles and cattle. Later the marks would be made by a purpose-built machine with a platinum needle that was heated in a methylated-spirits flame. The mulga, with its fine grain, reddish brown heartwood and pale amber halo of sapwood, was an ideal support. It could be polished to a lustrous finish then varnished.

In his Annual Report of 1934 Albrecht wrote: *We noticed how some of the Natives had decidedly artistic inclinations, and as there is a fair growth of mulga on the Reserve, we thought of commercialising this for pokerwork…The first pieces, where we used old engravings of tjurungas as a design, did not sell. But then one of the Natives started making freehand drawings of local animals, palms, etc., which appealed and sold well.*

Albert had already exchanged his putative calling as a preacher for his vocation as an artist: in 1932 he received his first pokerwork commission – a dozen mulga plaques, worth five shillings each, showing the camel train of Constable William McKinnon of the

South West Patrol riding through a landscape of sparse trees and spinifex. The constable rides at the head of the train, a spare mount follows him, then two pack camels, then a black tracker on the fifth beast. Albert, who often remarked that all he ever earned for taking a camel train to Oodnadatta and back was sixpence, executed this commission with skill and alacrity and received payment in full.

As well as a harbinger of things to come, the £3 he earned must have been of considerable immediate help to a man with six children to support: Rubina had given birth to a girl, Martha, in 1929 and a boy, Ewald, in 1930. Albert was for the next few years usually described either as the camel man or as the one who does pokerwork. His work was burned into boomerangs as well as mulga-wood plaques; it included naturalistic scenes and religious messages: *Other Refuge Have I None*, for example. Some were signed *Albert*; others bear his monogram, the four-petalled red desert rose. They were sold directly to the Mission shop, which then resold them. In a manner serendipitous and almost unwitting, then, he had begun his career as an artist.

3

John Gardner estimated that when he and Rex Battarbee returned to Melbourne in May 1929, they had completed 600 paintings between them. Ninety-six of these were exhibited at the Athenaeum Art Gallery in August, 1929; the show was opened by CJ Dennis, the author of *The Songs of a Sentimental Bloke* and there were enough sales to finance their next overland odyssey, which began early in the new year, 1930, in a Henrietta that had been re-painted yellow with a scarlet trim. Gardner was still wearing the red beret he had assumed for their first trip and he would continue to wear it, or one like it, for the rest of his life.

They drove north to New South Wales and west to South Australia and on into the Flinders Range. After eight months on the road, in early November, they were at Hawker, from which they went to Wilpena Pound, where Jessie Traill had been two years before, and spent until just before Christmas in the area painting. Gardner's diary of this section of the trip is full of oddball details of their sojourn: as if they were two young fellows on a lark, which perhaps they were. Gardner spent a lot of time working on the station owner's 1918 Dodge, which he ended up giving a complete overhaul. Then there was the similarly antiquated Ford, a *Lizzie*, that he also repaired.

Meanwhile Rex made jam out of dried apricots or nectarines or, once, disastrously, paddy melons; and went hunting with the rifle they called the *game-getter*. It fired three types of cartridge through its two 13-inch barrels and with it he shot pigeons, goats, kangaroos, turkeys and wallabies. They trapped rabbits and supplemented their diet of meat and home-baked bread or damper with wild greens; there was porridge every morning for breakfast. The truck had separate apartments where they slept, or perhaps one was in the body of the vehicle and the other in the shelter of the attached tarpaulin. It was a home. They kept pets, a galah at Wilpena, cockatiels and budgies in cages, even, for a while, a young euro. Rex grew cycads in pots and lamented when they were destroyed by rabbits.

Their painting regime was always dependent upon the weather and Gardner's diary is full of meteorological observations, including the image of Rex in a violent storm sitting under cover in the truck with his watch in his hand, timing the decreasing intervals between stupendous cracks of thunder as lightning flashed across the land. Reconnaissance was an integral part of their method and they would, separately or together, hike across the landscape looking for prospects they could come back to with their gear to paint.

In this they were, consciously or not, following eighteenth- and nineteenth-century traditions of the picturesque as the appropriate subject for art.

When Gardner, who was primarily an oil painter, ran out of canvas, he painted on sugar bags instead. Sometimes Rex, who used only watercolour because turpentine and oil paint irritated the skin of his maimed hand, painted mirages. They spent a lot of time socialising with their hosts and other locals; and after a forty-two day stay, left the Pound and began to trek back east to Melbourne where, as before, they would exhibit and sell their work at the Athenaeum and use the proceeds to finance their next trip. On Christmas Day they were at Cape Grant, west of Warrnambool, where Rex gave Jack a Christmas gift of a cake of chocolate. There's no mention in his diary of his mother Mary's death, aged seventy-four, in July 1930, while they were outback; but he kept the letter from Florinda advising him of it.

This was of course during the Great Depression; they liked to joke they were so remote from things they did not hear about it until after their first trip into Queensland was over. The roads were full of itinerant men looking for work or food or shelter and many of them went about in pairs. Rex and Jack were, like so many others, mates. And, as so often, the precise nature of their relationship remains occluded: in their writings it does not seem ever to decay into impatience or irritation, on the one hand, nor to go much further in the other direction than genial good-fellowship and a kind of humorous disregard of the other's incorrigible eccentricities.

Rex recorded their 1932 trip in a Sands & McDougall Invicta Rough Diary #4A, with three days to a page. It cost him 4/6 and in it he notes, unfailingly, every day, the weather, including the temperature, the mileage if they are travelling, their numerous breakdowns and blow-outs and anything else of casual or occasional interest; he is always alert to bird life: *I saw a beautiful sight this evening. There was a mob of galahs on the ground with the evening light on them, they looked like beautiful flowers then they rose like fog clearing as we got near them.* Food, the getting, the preparing and the eating, is as constant a concern as the weather but, whatever the subject, he rarely attempts explanation or even comment, seemingly content simply to record.

By contrast, Gardner in his writing, which is mostly retrospective, represents the Centre as mythical land which is difficult of egress, a kind of Shangri-la to which the way can only be found, by good luck or good judgement or perhaps even virtuous conduct, after long searching and much trial and error. On the 1932 trip, their third attempt to find the way to paradise, which like the others began in late summer or early autumn, they came up through Coober Pedy where, on 19 May, Rex paid five shillings for a Miner's Right; a certificate that bought him an entitlement to a year's worth of legal opal prospecting. With it he procured an opal that, twenty years later, he used to make his wife's wedding ring.

They were shocked, upon entering Alice Springs for the first time, to see a chain gang of Aboriginal prisoners, wearing collars of iron, passing. In order to go to Hermannsburg, a reserved area, they had obtain passes from the police station. On the way out they met a fellow called Long Harry who was going into Alice for rations and gave him some tea, sugar and bread. Macarinyah, as Gardner called him, became a friend and they encountered him again later on their journey: *He was a bright chap*, Rex wrote, *and looked as though he has been a wild black...he noticed our parrots and called them Budgies...Harry has also been along to see the sketches, he asked to see them all, he says they will bring a lot of money in Adelaide.*

At Bitter Springs, fifty miles east of Alice, Rex had a breakthrough in his painting. It is a work called *Ghost Gum at Bitter Springs Gorge* and shows the doubled, white and shadow-striped trunk of the tree before the muscular, glowing, ochre and purple rocks and declivities of the gorge. It was during the application of colour that the epiphany came. By layering more pigment over paint that had not yet properly dried, he found a way of reproducing on paper the blazing luminosity the landscape possessed.

Another innovation was his framing of the view: like an extra close close-up of one of Hans Heysen's gums. The trunk, resembling the letter Y, is an enormity, a prodigy; there is no foliage shown, just roots knotting into the stark land like sinews; while the striation of light and shadow on the bark is echoed in the riven hills behind, as if one were an outgrowth of the other: which of course it is. Battarbee often found compositions, as he did here, through the view-finder of the camera; the 1932 diary has a unique photographic companion that runs in parallel to the written word, recording many more views than were actually painted. The camera, then, was part of the travelling studio, an indispensible accompaniment to the pigment, brushes and paper.

Battarbee and Gardner arrived at Hermannsburg on 24 August, drove the Ford into the river bed and found a camping spot down by the Finke. Children buzzed around the vehicle *like a hive of bees* and trade commenced almost immediately – rations for artefacts. Gardner bought a corroboree stone, *tjurunga*, for three shillings. Another, *made out of Blackfellow hair, rabbit hair and cockatoo feathers*, was exchanged only on condition that it never be shown to women or boys. *We felt rather honoured that they would take the risk. When we said we would pack it away and take it out of the country they thanked us very graciously.* Battarbee several times mentions a cameleer who was interested in their paintings but does not name him: *We left the Mission for Palm Valley at about 11…the man with the camels is a real good sort and a very willing worker. He was the chap who was over last night to see the painting of Mangaranka.*

The two artists established cordial relations with Mission staff, attending a church service and hearing Blind Moses preach. The singing was extraordinary and Gardner remarks that it was the first church service he ever attended at which no collection plate went around. A few days later *Mr Albrecht rode over on horseback. He gave us a nice piece of fresh goat, also a tin of cream and a tin of biscuits. It was a beautiful surprise.* Rex encountered a large grey and green snake, allegedly poisonous, and killed it with a stick. Another day he visited the corroboree cave, that is, Manangananga; it reminded him of a similar shelter at Mutawintji, north-east of Broken Hill in western NSW, which they had visited on an earlier expedition; Ludwig Becker had also painted there. Rex was doing watercolour landscapes, taking photographs of naked men fishing in the river and sketching some of the local boys, in particular two called Ukalbi and Urbula, whom he paid with lollies.

It is the lollies that are the main attraction but the ones that have been drawn and painted are very proud to bring their friends over to see the camp…some of the boys are very affectionate at times, poor boys, they can't get many home comforts. It is a wonderful experience to meet these boys in such a natural way. After tea we could hear them singing, it was really beautiful…this is a great place to get models and it is marvellous how they seem to turn up whenever we need something to do. He would leave behind crayons for the children to draw with.

After about six weeks, on 11 October, they decided to move on; but before they did *Jack showed them the pictures of Hermannsburg and did some good business, he got orders for three pictures from Mrs Albrecht and one from Mr Petering. There will be two of the Mission, one of Mt Hermannsburg and one of Palm Valley.* This is the origin of the repeated claim that Battarbee and Gardner held an exhibition the night before they left Hermannsburg – one that Albert, allegedly away at Henbury Station building stockyards, did not see. In fact, the two artists showed their pictures on many occasions to whomever showed an interest in them and often made sales or received commissions as a result.

Battarbee and Gardner went by way of Koporilya Springs and Jay Creek the eighty miles back to Alice Springs, where they camped on the outskirts of town for a few weeks waiting for some mail that had gone astray. There was a rush on to the Granites, to the north, where gold had been discovered. They caught up with the cricket on the radio: the Bodyline series was gearing up to begin. Rex shopped in town or at the market gardener's – *I got a wonderful parsnip* – yarned with the locals, swapped books with other readers, developed photographs in the evenings. He was reading crime writer Edgar Wallace, author of *King Kong*; and, after a visit to Emily's Gap in the east to view the totemic art stencilled on the rock there, remarked *there is a lot about this gap in Sir Baldwin Spencer's book.*

He struck up an acquaintance with an Afghan camel driver, a devout Muslim who told him biblical stories from the Islamic point of view: *The story of Joseph was very good, also Noah. He made them more real than I have ever heard before.* He and Jack acquired some dingo scalps but couldn't sell them at the store. Later they exchanged them for *Abo stones* and other artefacts, including a shield. But Rex didn't really like being in town, even as small a town as Alice was then: *I don't feel at home here, towns are no good to camp at and the people seem different.*

So they packed up and went back onto the land to find places where they could stay in the wild and, weather permitting, do their painting. On 24 November, a Thursday, Rex wrote: *This has been a beautiful day…I worked on three sketches, finishing two. Jack shot another turkey this afternoon. A hen. While we were having tea a couple of blacks came along on camels. They came over. They were from Hermannsburg.*

One was the camel man that comes into Alice Springs. He continues next day: *While I was sketching the camel man from Hermannsburg came up and stayed a while…He became very interested in the painting. He is a very nice chap.*

This meeting late in 1932 at Temple Bar Creek near Simpsons Gap between the thirty-seven year-old itinerant watercolour painter from Bakers Road, Blackburn, Victoria and the camel man from Hermannsburg, like the earlier encounters on the banks of the Finke, was not certainly one between Rex Battarbee and Albert Namatjira. Albert is at this stage still indistinct, anonymous, a man generally described by means of his occupation not his name. Nevertheless, those meetings can stand as a beginning of the story of their collaboration, which would prove lifelong for both men. And, like many events that, in retrospect, are highly significant, they must at the time have seemed commonplace: a casual encounter like hundreds of others that happen every day among people on the road.

4. Achieving Luminosity

In 1932 the artist Jessie Traill made her second visit to Hermannsburg, this time in the company of her friend, Una Teague. They were, according to Betty Churcher, *part of a remarkable group of financially independent, middle-class women who never married, allowing them to devote their lives to art.* Traill had, like so many others in this story, trained at the National Gallery School – with Bernard Hall and Frederick McCubbin; she travelled extensively and, during the war, joined the Voluntary Aid Detachment, serving for three years as a nurse in military hospitals in Rouen, where the wounded from the Western Front were generally sent. She was there in 1917 when Rex Battarbee came through. Traill was a print-maker and an etcher as well as a painter and the works in her brilliant series of prints on the building of the Sydney Harbour Bridge are feats of visual engineering. She was also a devout Christian.

Una Sybella Teague, her companion on this second visit, was not an artist but a collector and philanthropist. She studied at Presbyterian Ladies College in Melbourne, was another inveterate traveller and could, in the early years of the twentieth century, have played hockey as centre forward for England; she went instead to India where she became an expert show-jumper. Like Traill she served in the Great War, as a section head in the Censorship Branch of Military Intelligence. This involvement was followed, intriguingly, by a brief period with the Police Force Special Branch, Scotland Yard. Una Teague joined the Save the Children Fund in 1920 when that organisation was set up in London to help those starving in the Balkans in the aftermath of the war. Back in Australia she became interested in Aboriginal artefacts and her collections of stone tools, *tjurunga* and wooden artefacts were, like her embroideries, later donated to museums.

Jessie Traill and Una Teague came up by train then travelled from Alice Springs to Hermannsburg in a buggy with Pastor Albrecht and the new missionary-teacher, Werner Peterman. It was July 1932 and during their visit they went out to see Palm Valley; their camel man on this trip was Albert and a photograph exists in the Teague family archives showing him with them in the valley. Given that Traill was a working artist and had already, four years previously, painted a view of Mt Hermannsburg, this encounter must be added to those other shadowy provocations which led the camel-man turned evangelist turned souvenir-maker to reinvent himself as an artist; but on this matter, as on so many others, Albert kept his silence.

Una Teague had a half-sister, Violet Helen Evangeline, who was eight years her senior; their father was Melbourne's first registered homeopathic physician. Violet Teague was a portrait painter with an international reputation; like her sister she had studied at Presbyterian Ladies College in Melbourne and like Traill, at the National Gallery School. She was a book-illustrator and a print-maker too, producing Japanese-style woodcuts for her two collaborations with Geraldine Rede, *Birds in the Sunny South* and *Night fall in the Ti-Tree* (both 1905). She was a Christian as well and, later in life, devoted herself to the construction and painting of altar-pieces for churches, sometimes in collaboration with Jessie Traill. Violet Teague was tiny, less than five-feet tall, with grey-blue eyes and light brown hair: *quiet of manner, yet with a surprising vitality and a more surprising sense of whimsy...she can talk on any subject from racehorses to the decline of Western culture.*

When Una Teague returned to Melbourne she told Violet about Hermannsburg and, it is said, Violet decided to go there immediately. She hired a taxi, a Studebaker, and instructed the nineteen year-old driver to take her and Una on the journey of 1800 miles over roads which were often uncertain and sometimes entirely notional. They camped out along the way and, when they arrived at Hermannsburg, Violet *filled a sketchbook with quickly executed watercolour paintings...did pencil portraits of Aboriginals as well as a number of larger oil landscapes. But the bush flowers Una had told her of had 'given way to drought and dead cattle'.* Dry times had returned to the Centre and so had the water crisis on the Mission. *Why, Pastor, this is ludicrous; you must have water!* Violet said to Albrecht. And so, on their return to Melbourne by Studebaker (the driver having waited some weeks on the Mission for them), the sisters began to execute a plan to make the Koporilya Springs water flow to Hermannsburg.

This was not a new idea. Five miles away in the hills on the other side of the Finke, the Koporilya Springs discharged 10,000 gallons of clear fresh water daily. Ever since the Mission Board, in 1924, identified tanning as a possible source of income, there had been attempts to raise the funds needed to build a pipeline. One of the reasons Albrecht had not been able to find this money was a dispute about whether the springs were above or below the Mission; a visual sight across the Finke seemed to some to suggest that Hermannsburg was on higher ground and thus that the pastor was attempting to make water run uphill.

This matter was not resolved until, in the wake of the Lasseter imbroglio, another gold prospecting expedition came through, this time from Western Australia. They quickly determined that the Petermann Ranges were not gold-bearing country at all and cut short their six-month expedition after just six weeks; but while at Hermannsburg, surveyors with the party took measurements and found the Springs were in fact 133 feet above the wireless mast on the Mission.

Nevertheless the government engineer in Alice Springs, DD Smith, remained skeptical and, late in 1931, again challenged the feasibility of the project. Albrecht was undismayed. He continued to gather information on how to do it and by early 1932 knew what was required – 25,900 feet of piping at a cost of around £3,240. He formally launched the appeal for funds; and by the end of the year had gathered, mostly *from our English friends,* donations totalling £185.

After their 1933 visit the Teague sisters got cracking, persuading a number of artists to donate works for exhibition and sale. The show, at the Athenaeum in 1934, Victoria's Centenary year, contained over a hundred works by fifty artists and included paintings by Hans Heysen and Arthur Streeton as well as Battarbee and Gardner, Violet Teague herself and the young Arthur Boyd; all proceeds went to the water fund. The exhibition and a contemporary appeal in the Melbourne *Argus* together raised £2,015, which was enough to pay for the piping (2/6 per foot) but not for its transport to Hermannsburg; the balance came from additional appeals in the *Argus* and the *Adelaide Advertiser* as well as collections among Adelaide's Lutheran congregations.

Albrecht's idea had always been that the Mission would supply the labour and that is what happened; the digging of the pipeline and the laying of the pipes took about a year to complete and at no time during this period was it certain that the scheme would actually work. In August 1934, when it was under way, Albrecht wrote: *Now we have to dig about 5 or 6 feet deep through a small hill. Our people could do it but I know from experience that it is much cheaper if a white person is there supervising…if we don't get rain soon, then we will have a very difficult time again…the day before yesterday we buried the old Emilie who also had pneumonia. Everything points to the same symptoms like before the big drought. Dast ist so bedrueckend.* Old Emilie was Albert's mother Ljukuta and this is only the second mention in the record of her Christian name; the other was when she was baptised in 1905. She is mute as the generations that predeceased her.

Battarbee and Gardner, on their fourth big trip and second visit to the Mission, had by this time been and gone from Hermannsburg. They arrived on 24 May 1934 to the shouts of children: *Here comes the house on wheels!* and found Pastor Albrecht away somewhere with Una Teague; he had been awaiting their arrival impatiently because he wanted to see Bob Croll, who was travelling with the two painters. In his absence *Mrs Albrecht gave us a very warm welcome…We also had a hot bath. The first I have had on the trip. It was very enjoyable also a nice supper and a big soft bed to sleep in.* Four days later, at Ellery Creek, Rex completed his first work on the journey: *Travelled over 1800 miles before I did a sketch, that is a record for me.*

It had not been an easy trip; the diary is full of descriptions of accidents, breakdowns and mechanical failures, as if Henrietta – now more usually Lizzie, Bessie or the bus – was at her last gasp; which she probably was. Not long after they picked up, at Stawell near Ararat, Bob Croll, *about a mile past Mt Bryan we had to cross the railway line and the bus coming around the turn quickly, skidded and… turned over on her side. It all happened so quickly that it did not seem real. I was at the bottom with the other two on top of me. We were very fortunate that nobody was injured…The trouble now was to get it off the line before the next train.*

The first car that came along did not stop but a man on a pushbike did. Then some railway gangers arrived and righted the bus; then a fellow with a truck, who pulled them off the line with a rope. *She fell over very quickly…apples were all over the place. We gave some of them to the men. After it was all over we could not help laughing because there were some funny things, such as me taking Jack's red cap off his head ready to run up the line to stop the train.*

The image of Rex Battarbee in the cab of the toppled Model T Ford with Bob Croll on top of him and a train coming is an exemplar of the incommensurability of their relationship, symbolised by Rex's invariable use of the titular 'Mr' in his diary. Mr Croll was by this time a sixty-five year-old man. He published an edition of the poems of John Shaw Neilson in that year, 1934, and would, the following year, produce a biography of Tom Roberts. This was not his first trip to the Territory; that had taken place in 1929 with psychologist Stanley Porteus, originator of the Porteus maze test, *a series of pencil-tracing mazes of increasing complexity, intended to assess forethought and planfulness.* Mr Croll had *a facetious graceful manner of unfailing pleasantness* and that probably made him a good companion on the road. *Rex is solid*, he said. *Jack is gold*. And he could shoot a pigeon as well as either of them.

He and Rex spent a lot of time on the journey fossicking: *The dingoes were howling all night. Mobs of horses would also gallop in for water. After breakfast…we went searching for Abo stones in the sandhills and found the stones everywhere, a wonderful place.* There were many meetings along the way, with old friends and new; perhaps the most intriguing occurred on 8 May on the Alberga River between Coober Pedy and Alice Springs: *We had no trouble crossing the Alberga, the new tyres proved themselves. We just flew across. We then stopped to fix up one of the wheels. While here a young fellow came across in a car loaded up, he was on his way to Arnhem Land. He is an anthropologist – Mr Stanner from the Sydney University. He was on his way to live with the blacks for 12 months. He is game and has a rough journey ahead of him.*

WEH (Bill) Stanner was then just twenty-nine years old and going to Daly River in the Northern Territory to do field work for his 1934 thesis on culture contact; in AP Elkin's words, *a work of outstanding quality*. Stanner disputed the idea that the anthropologist's task was *the naive search for uncontaminated aboriginal cultures* and was instead seeking a methodology for understanding culture contact and the resulting cultural change. The meeting seems emblematic of coming times: although Battarbee was not a man with a theoretical turn of mind, he was someone with a practical and humane approach to the problem of how best to help Indigenous communities undergoing rapid change. His contribution, though radically different in kind, is as significant as that of Stanner.

The bus ran out of petrol five miles from Alice Springs and Rex spent an anxious night sitting up by the fire waiting for Jack to come back with the petrol cans; he doesn't say what Mr Croll was doing. Jack didn't turn up until well into the morning of the next day, 18 May, a Friday, when they proceeded on to the Alice. On the Sunday evening Rex and Mr Croll went together to a service at the Methodist church – *the only Protestant church between Maree and Darwin* – and on the Tuesday a telegram arrived: *Mr Croll got a wire from the Centenary Art Committee asking him to manage the Centenary Art Exhibition beginning in Melbourne…job is for 6 months starting from July 1st…Mr Croll has accepted the position, the telegram contained 75 words.*

Later during the trip, on 6 October, when they were on their way back to Melbourne, Rex recorded: *I got a letter from home this morning saying I had won the Barrett Watercolour Prize in the Centenary Exhibition; with 'Sun-tipped MacDonnell Range Gorge'. It almost seems too good to be true.* The prize was awarded for the best watercolour painted during the previous two years and it isn't clear what say, if any, Mr Croll had in its selection. The work itself shows the blazing white trunk of a ghost gum against rocky outcrops and the sky.

Battarbee, Gardner and Mr Croll did not at first stay at Hermannsburg but went to Ellery Creek where they camped out for a couple of weeks so that Jack and Rex could establish their painting routine while Bob had a good look around; they returned to the Mission on 7 June to find it *alive with life as they were having some foot races.* Una Teague was there, and several members of the committee planning the building of the pipeline; Battarbee spent the evening in conversation with, among others, Miss Teague, whom he described as a very good business woman. *We had to have an exhibition of the work we did at Ellery Creek,* he remarked, emphasising yet again that showings of their work were not only frequent but also required.

This time he and Gardner left Croll behind on the Mission and made camp about a mile and a half away on the Alice track. On Sunday 10 June they returned to Hermannsburg to go to church. *We sat in the front of the congregation. The German Lutheran service is very like the low Church of England…a blind old Abo preached the service in Arunta, the text was Job 13–18…He seemed a fine preacher and must have spoken for at least 20 minutes without notes and he never stopped once. The singing is really wonderful…at times one would think you heard a pipe organ…but they have no instruments…When we got back we found that some of the black boys had been at our camp. They had been playing with our paints and taken some lollies and some food, had made a mess but appeared to be young boys.*

The ring leader of this spoiling party was soon identified as Claude; that is, Claude Pannka, then just six years old; he would become one of the second generation of Hermannsburg watercolourists. Others among the older boys who visited their camp can also be identified: Enos Namatjira, for instance, who used Kempe's reader to teach Battarbee the Arrernte names for birds; his brother Oscar who sold Rex a boomerang; and Herbert Raberaba: these three would also become painters. It wasn't just the boys. On the evening of 14 June *two older men came along to look at the paintings. One brought some of his own landscape sketches done on waste paper in coloured crayon. They were about the same stage as the young boys' drawings were, they were interesting and interested in our work.* It's hard to resist the thought that this was Albert experimenting with the crayons Rex had left behind in 1932; but we will never know for sure.

The visual splendour of the landscape was a constant delight: *I think Mount Hermannsburg in the afternoon is the best thing around here, it is a real plum colour with the bloom on it.* The next morning: *There was a wonderful mirage…over Goss's Range. There was a high castle at one end for a second and there were ship-like signs over the Ranges.* And later the same day: *It was a beautiful evening again and a beautiful sunset. There were a few clouds some a beautiful rich red wine colour.* Battarbee's observation of mirages, which he also tried to paint, is significant because it challenges the widely held view that his art was an attempt at plain representation of landscape; it suggests rather that he was just as interested in symbolic, illusive and anthropomorphic forms as he was in verisimilitude; and that these interests, too, were handed on to, or at least shared with, his more famous pupil.

After Rex and Jack had been camping near Hermannsburg for a week Albrecht offered them the use of four of the Mission's camels – two to ride and two as pack animals – to take a trip into the west and so, on 19 June, they set off on a three-week-long excursion that took them out to Gosses Bluff and then south into the James Range; they spent some time at Boatswains Hole near Areyonga and came back through Tempe Downs and Middleton Ponds. Their cameleer was Ezekiel and, at least at the outset of the journey, they were attended by seven or eight of the Mission children. Gosses Bluff (Tnorala) is not, as Rex thought, fault mountains but a heavily eroded impact crater from the Jurassic, left behind after a collision with a comet or some other large celestial body 140 million years ago. They rode their camels inside the ring of jagged cliffs enclosing *the finest pound for painting I have seen*.

Leaving Gosses Bluff they *saw quite a lot of Aboriginal rock carvings on rock along the creek, even without getting off the camels* and later met, at Middleton Ponds, *a real blackfellow in his native state*, a man called Andrecoona whose portrait Rex painted at least twice: *He is the finest and most unusual type I have seen. Long beard and long hair all plaited...(he) came down again this morning. He had his face covered in red ochre he looked very weird but it did not look out of place. I started another watercolour of him...this boy is so pleasant and willing, he is unspoiled but it is to be hoped he goes back to the Petermann Ranges.*

Battarbee concluded his account of the journey with some praise of Ezekiel, their guide, in terms that recall Mrs Heinrich's earlier remarks about Albert: *He carried out his job very faithfully and was always willing and never any trouble, he also did most things without being told...all this just for tucker of course.* The contrast between the *wild black* and the *mission boy* was no doubt stark but a more important point is that Battarbee was able to extend his compassion to both, as well as see how he might influence their futures. He hoped Andrecoona would go back home to his people, whose lands Pastor Albrecht had been trying for years to reserve; and when, at the Mission, he learned Ezekiel's wife was very ill and their son had died, bought the family an extra week's worth of rations. It's worth stating that Rex was often short of money and at this time had just refused a cash loan from Mr Croll.

The exhibition that Battarbee and Gardner held on the eve of their departure from Hermannsburg after the 1934 visit was different in two respects from the impromptu shows they staged elsewhere on the road: it was a formal event, inside the schoolroom; and it was open to all comers, both black and white. The show originated in an offer by the two painters to exhibit the work they had completed over the past two months to Mission staff; it was Albrecht who suggested the Aborigines might be interested as well. The seats were taken out of the schoolroom, the paintings hung around the walls, invitations issued. Rex wrote: *They all seemed interested and some came back several times.* Other accounts are rather more enthusiastic: *The exhibition was thronged for two days...some of the three hundred visitors sat for hours at a time gazing at the landscapes they knew so well.*

Mr Croll reviewed the show for the *Argus* in inflated terms, emphasising the differences between the Hermannsburg audience and that at a metropolitan gallery: *I have attended many private views at which, as a rule, you meet the whole world and his wife. You say to the artist as you go in 'Looks like a ripping show old chap' and then you spend an agreeable afternoon meeting friends and discussing others...I have at last been to an exhibition at which everyone without exception was interested in the exhibits and did not give a hoot about who was present.*

The exhibition brought forth a more considered response from one viewer. Albrecht wrote that *after looking closely at the work Albert came to me in a serious mood asking how much the artists would receive for their pictures. Upon being told that prices up to 15 guineas might be paid Albert remarked 'I can do the same.' Not unnaturally I expressed my surprise at the statement and entertained some doubts. However, Albert returned after a short while and said 'I still think I can do it.'* This encounter, and these two remarks by Albert, are usually taken to mean that the show in the schoolroom on 12 and 13 July 1934 was his Damascene moment; however, Rex had a week earlier recorded in his diary: *Albert who does the poker work would like to paint and Mr Albrecht is prepared to buy him paints and wants me to tell him what to get.*

Rather than a sudden revelation then, the 1934 exhibition has to be seen as a culmination of events and encounters, some shadowy, that go back at least to 1932 and probably some years earlier, perhaps to 1928 when Jessie Traill was painting Mt Hermannsburg. To these must be added John Gardner's account of a meeting he had while painting in 1932 or 1934 (his recall is uncertain): an Aboriginal man on horseback stopped to watch and talk with him while he worked and asked him for painting lessons. Gardner, who described this incident many years later and in contradistinction to the many accounts of Battarbee's 'discovery' of the Arrernte artist, said he believed this man to have been Albert.

Other artists visited Hermannsburg; Arthur Murch, for example, who came twice, in 1933 and 1934, with two scientific expeditions organised by Professor of Physiology at Sydney University, Whitridge Davies, who wished to learn if Aborigines living in the hot, arid conditions were adapted to water deprivation. While Davies, an alcoholic, drank, Murch spent his time measuring intake of water and output of urine and sweat as part of the endeavour to find out; he concluded there were no significant differences with European metabolism. On his second visit, which included a camel trip with Ted Strehlow to Mt Liebig in the west, Murch brought along film equipment and took many photographs and some movie footage. Strehlow remembered Arrernte people watching him painting *intently and with evident fascination.* Murch himself said, speaking of the colours of the landscape: *If I tried to paint this, people in the south would think me mad.*

Representation, especially but not simply of landscape, was thus of interest, not just to Albert, but to many among the Arrernte; but it was less a new way of seeing than a new way of describing the already seen. When Murch asked Arrernte children to draw an emu they made a picture of the bird's three-toed footprint; but some of his film footage shows young artists copying the kangaroo design off the obverse of the Australian penny then re-drawing the image from a side-elevation view. Murch was aware of differences between Mission children and the desert Aborigines: *what I did was prop [the paper] up on the easel…which was not their mode of doing things and they just didn't know how to handle it. I let them put it down on the ground. The mission children were used to things on easels and desks.* And, by implication, the habit of seeing things from the side, as it were, rather than from above looking down.

A consequence of the introduction of a side-on as opposed to a top-down view of landscape is that the sky becomes a potential element in the composition. Night skies had been shown in traditional art but only from a point of view equivalent to the top down view of landscape – what might be called bottom up; but the representation of what to Europeans since the Renaissance has been a norm – a daytime sky above the contours of the land – was unknown to the Arrernte. Serendipitously, along with the side-on view European painters also added a colour, blue, to the traditional Arrernte palette: as if giving them the gift of the sky.

Representation was a part of missionary teaching from the beginning. In the school, boys and girls were encouraged to keep diaries, writing a paragraph each day on the previous day's events; these diaries were often illustrated. Ruth Pech, who taught at Hermannsburg from 1935, recalled: *Girls usually drew flowers, following on from their mother's embroidery...boys had their own world of cowboys, horses, camels and scenes, usually along an horizon with buildings, animals or trees...before the art movement people carved kangaroos and trees on wood but mostly they just drew in the sand. They loved to do that. After the rain came then came the art, and later materials were more accessible and the atmosphere changed.*

The difference here is not between representation and some form of abstraction, nor between a side-on or top-down view, but a third, just as resonant: between images, like body or sand painting, that were ephemeral, and those with some degree of permanence. The most permanent of Arrernte artefacts were *tjurunga* which, at least notionally, were eternal, even if their invariably abstract designs sometimes needed to be renewed. The apparent permanence of the landscape images painted by Battarbee and Gardner may have been seen by Albert as a quality just as crucial as their saleability; he might have understood that the medium could also be used to express the timeless aspects of Arrernte culture in the way that *tjurunga* did.

Albert's reaction to his mother's death, just a month after Battarbee and Gardner had their show and left, is not recorded; but we know that he was deeply excited by Battarbee's promise to send him art supplies and, on his next visit, to give him painting lessons. The two painters were home by mid-October: *Between Geelong and Melbourne the rain was very heavy. We had no trouble getting through the city and got to Auburn before dark. We stayed here for the night and put the bus in the wood-yard across the street. Our trip really ends here exactly six months from the day we left. Mr Croll came over to see us this evening so we had a very interesting evening.* Battarbee's reputation was on the rise; when he and Gardner held their next exhibition, at the Athenaeum the following year, 1935, his work was praised in the *Argus* by Arthur Streeton.

The 1934 visit to Hermannsburg also resulted in a deepening of the bond between Albrecht and Battarbee, who from this time forth corresponded regularly; the basis of the relationship was their shared beliefs. *We will always be pleased to see you back again,* Albrecht wrote on 27 July. *It is not too often we have Christians with us.* Some of that bonding occurred during sing-songs in the evening at the Albrecht house; or in the Hermannsburg church, where Ted Strehlow played the organ while those assembled sang in four-part harmony. Albert was on occasion one of these singers. According to Mrs Petering, the musicologist Harold Davies said that Albert had *the finest untrained bass voice he had ever come across;* and you sense here the phantom possibility of an entirely different career.

Ted Strehlow had returned to Hermannsburg, after a ten-year absence, towards the end of 1932 to begin the fieldwork, collecting, researching and writing that would consume the rest of his life. He had already defined his task: the recording of the cultural life of the Arrernte people. He would pursue this aim with a rigour and an intensity that is terrible to behold, not least because he had formed the conviction that all that was best and most authentic amongst them must inevitably be lost as a living thing and could only survive as copies or specimens in some archive or other. Artefacts, including *tjurunga*, were on the list of things that would go and this allowed him to collect these objects along with the songs, the dances, the stories and the ceremonies with which they were associated.

He seems never to have understood that the doomed romanticism of his position was itself destructive of those things he wanted conserved; that his conviction that he was seeing the last days of a dying culture paradoxically allowed him to act in a way that was as ruinous as that of any other white souvenir hunter, finding out where the caves were and taking the sacred artefacts from them: *This is the last original cave with tjurunga in the Western MacDonnells* he wrote in his diary in November 1932, after he and his guide, Tom, had taken five of the fifteen remaining stones and Tom had declared: *I can leave this country forever now: I have nothing left in it that I have to guard.*

Over the year it took for the trenches to be dug and the pipes to be laid that would bring the water from Koporilya Springs to Hermannsburg, some of the men worked forty weeks, from Christmas 1934 until the following September, without stopping. The first pipes arrived by rail at Alice Springs in April 1935 and the ninety-ton load was carted out on a special desert train vehicle provided by the government and, stupidly, authorised only to go as far as the Mission. The pipes had to be taken the rest of the way to the springs by donkey cart, an extra month's work. The pipe-laying began in June and, as the line approached, Minna Albrecht ordered seeds from Yates in Sydney and began preparing a large garden on land beyond the cemetery.

There were still doubters. DD Smith, the government engineer, who had always been a skeptic, said in September that he thought what little water did flow would be absorbed by the fibrolite pipes. William Mattner, a farmer who first came up to Hermannsburg to build underground water tanks, and who was working on the planning and construction of the pipeline, disloyally agreed: *You can call me a flying Dutchman if that water gets to the station.* There wasn't enough piping to go the extra distance to the new garden and there wasn't any money left to buy more; Albrecht borrowed the difference and sent men out to cut desert oaks to make garden posts. He began to have doubts but his wife was adamant: *Selbstverstaendlich*, she said. *Of course it will come.* She was planting radish seeds.

In the last weeks, because of the heat, men worked by firelight at night, laying pipes deep in the sand over the bedrock of the dry Finke River. On the last day of September, with the line complete, Mattner was to divert water from the Springs at six o'clock in the evening. Albrecht thought it would take about four hours to reach the Mission and waited up; but the water did not come. He said his prayers and went to bed at 2am, only to be woken before sunrise by the shouts of women going to milk the cows: *Kwatja! Kwatja!* The valves at the end of the pipeline were not properly sealed and *kwatja*, water, was shooting twenty feet up into the air. The impossible had happened.

The anniversary of the arrival of the water is still commemorated at Hermannsburg today; and there were at the time many celebratory acts. Among them was the carving of a mulga-wood boomerang into which Albert burned a design of his own making: seven figures, alternately facing towards and away from us, engaged in the act of laying the pipeline; with Albert's signature, the red desert rose, at each end. It is a remarkable work – for its vigour and economy, its elegance, rhythm and grace. The three men behind the pipe-line, shown in full figure, wear suits and hats and look more like jazz musicians than pipe-layers; while the four in the foreground, shown only from the chest up, although they too are wearing hats and braces, seem to rise like tribal dancers from the earth below. Daniel Thomas remarked that *the upraised arms of the near side men recall the half circle symbol for man which we have learned to read in acrylic paintings from Papunya.*

The boomerang shows, among other things, the mastery Albert had attained in his handling of the medium. Albrecht tells a story that illustrates his confidence. *A visitor stood watching while Albert pokered a kangaroo onto a mulga plaque and the visitor began to point out certain improvements he thought Albert could make in the drawing. Albert did not reply and only grunted a little now and then. After the visitor left he stood up and said: 'That man wants to tell me what a kangaroo looks like. I have eaten more kangaroos than he has seen.'* The point is well made; by 1935, on the evidence of the pokered plaques, the boomerangs and the like, Albert was a sophisticated draughtsman in a difficult medium; he could draw using a hot poker as if with a pencil. There are, for example, boomerangs with exquisitely detailed images of insects upon them.

But he could not yet paint or not to his own satisfaction; by the time of the Koporilya boomerang he was clearly ready to move on to the new medium of watercolour painting while at the same time unsure exactly how to proceed. It wasn't for the want of trying: *Whenever the opportunity arose he would go to Albrecht's office and attempt to copy a Battarbee watercolour pinned to the wall above Albrecht's desk… many times apparently.*

9 May 1935, probably predating the Koporilya boomerang,

is usually given as the date of Albert's first watercolour painting, made with materials Battarbee advised Albrecht to buy. It is a double-sided work that Albert gave on that date to FCG Wallent of the Lutheran Mission Board; when shown the work again, many years later, in 1949, Namatjira authenticated both sides of the paper, inscribing the words *My First Painting* on the landscape and giving the other, more achieved work the title *The Fleeing Kangaroo*. The kangaroo, as in a number of related and near-contemporary works, is shown in profile, resembles the design on the Australian penny and seems to float eerily, as if in a membrane of discrete air, before the landscape across the face of which it flees.

However, both Albrecht and Croll record that there was another picture that preceded these two: *I well remember the very first painting he did,* Albrecht said. *It was a picture of one of the staff dwellings, with a picket fence in front. Since he had never heard of a 'vanishing line' his fence appeared nearly twice as high at the end than in the middle.* Croll's account also refers to the mis-proportioned fence but he says the subject matter included the Mission church as well as the staff dwellings; and adds that the work was actually drawn with crayons. Later Battarbee, too, mentions that Albert showed him an early painting of the church.

Again, we have to revise the standard account: Albert could already paint before he received a lesson from Rex Battarbee or anyone else: he just couldn't paint well enough to suit his own purposes, could not work to a level of skill that would satisfy his need to witness what he saw. *The Fleeing Kangaroo*, though it is a naïve work, already demonstrates something of the command of space that became Albert's signature as a painter; and on that basis it might be possible to suggest what he needed to learn next: how to move from the two-dimensional drawing of pokerwork imagery into the three (or more) dimensions of deep space that painting opens out.

In July 1934, at the same time that Battarbee and Gardner were showing their work at Hermannsburg, a Saltcoats-born, Adelaide-based doctor and surgeon called Charles Duguid was making his way north by train to Darwin to investigate for himself allegations of mistreatment of Aborigines in the Territory; events involving the rape of Yolngu women by Japanese fishermen, subsequent reprisals and clumsy police action at Caledon Bay and nearby Blue Crab Bay had helped spark his concern.

Duguid (pronounced *do-good*) was delayed in Alice Springs by the need to perform an emergency operation, missed his connection and ended up staying in the district for about three weeks, during which time he inquired into the living conditions of Aborigines in the Alice (*appalling*), visited Hermannsburg and met both Pastor Albrecht and Albert Namatjira. Duguid inspected the Mission buildings and told Albrecht some of the older dwellings had to be razed: their thick walls, poor lighting and bad ventilation made it likely they harboured the tuberculosis bacillus. There were at the time around forty people infected with TB living at Hermannsburg.

Duguid was a Presbyterian; he had been a keen sportsman and while at university in Glasgow was known, because of his red hair and his speed over the half and quarter mile, as the Scarlet Runner. Before the war he twice made the passage to Australia as a ship's doctor and during it served as a captain in the Middle East, looking after the medical needs of the Australian Light Horse. He was well-connected in Adelaide society and committed to social justice: *stubborn in defence of the rights of the under-privileged and sometimes impetuous*. He and his second wife Phyllis were early patrons of Albert's art and purchased several works, which they later donated to the Art Gallery of South Australia.

Duguid was sympathetic to Albrecht's long-term commitment to protecting the western tribes from the loss of their traditional lands by white encroachment, and so, during his 1934 visit, the Pastor suggested he inquire into conditions in the Musgrave Ranges in north-west South Australia: *Nobody knows what is going on there*, Albrecht said. In June 1935 Duguid did just that, travelling in the company of boot- and saddle-maker RM Williams to Ernabella, a pastoral lease, meeting Pitjantjatjara people and thus initiating a relationship that would last fifty years. He returned to Hermannsburg in 1936 then rode out by camel with Albrecht and others to Haasts Bluff and beyond to meet tribal peoples living there. Duguid treated some of them for yaws and noted Albrecht's passion for evangelism. *Do you think they understand what you are saying about God?* he asked, sounding, despite his Presbyterianism, like a typically skeptical Scot.

It was a moot point. However God might or might not have been understood by the Pintupi, Albrecht would, within a few years and with Ted Strehlow's help, succeed in establishing a reserve in their country north and west of Haasts Bluff; thereby, if indirectly, securing the future of the settlement at Papunya where the desert art movement arose in the 1970s. Similarly, Duguid's mission at Ernabella, where the good doctor is, at the request of the local people, buried, ensured some kind of future on their own lands for the Pitjantjatjara.

RM Williams also became involved with Albrecht's other obsession, the need to find an economic basis for life on the Hermannsburg Mission. Once the Koporilya water was flowing, a tanning industry could be properly established. Experiments began in 1933, when a part-Aboriginal man called Manasse made vats in which to soak the hides out of hollowed-out lengths of gum-tree trunks; wattle bark was used as a tanning agent and the leather turned out to be rough but strong, good for making stock-whips and for mending horse saddles and donkey collars. After the water came the tannery expanded, the quality of the leather improved and soon the Mission was producing quantities of cow and bullock hides as well as hundreds of euro and kangaroo skins, some of which were, under Minna Albrecht's supervision, cut into strips and sewn together to make decorative rugs. One of these was given as a gift of thanks to the Teague sisters.

Manasse was sent south to the RM Williams tannery at Prospect to learn boot-making; his apprenticeship in Adelaide came to a premature end because of home-sickness but he did bring some shoe- and boot-making skills back to the Mission. In the later 1930s Albrecht oversaw the construction of new workrooms next to the smithy, which had by then been in operation for half a century: adjoining spaces for tanning hides, poker-work, saddle-making, carpentry as well as a display room for showing off the products for sale. Here moccasins were manufactured, exported and sold to the Canadians.

The new garden, more than three acres in extent, also flourished; there were as many as 15,000 plants growing at any one time: cabbage, eggplant, kohlrabi, mangelwurzel, marrow, silverbeet, swede, sweet potato, tomato and much else, including some orange trees. When a plague of caterpillars descended upon the vegetables Albrecht sent in the women who *picked them off as meat*. Albrecht's letters to Battarbee invariably end with a report upon the progress of the crops; he wrote that when he walked in the garden he felt that he was *den Fuss-spuren Gottes folgt – following in the footsteps of God*. Hermannsburg after the arrival of the Koporilya water for a few brief years resembled a paradise in which the miraculous seemed commonplace; but the wonders which the return of Rex Battarbee, alone, in 1936, instigated, were unprecedented.

Rex travelled by train from Melbourne to Adelaide, which he was visiting for the first time, and stayed overnight in the Grosvenor

Hotel before continuing, also by train, to Alice Springs. Dr Duguid was aboard, going up to embark on the planned camel trip with Albrecht into the west. They were just three miles south of Alice Springs railway station when a piston on the locomotive blew and in the interim Rex started taking photographs until forbidden to continue by railway officials because, they said mysteriously, the train belonged to the Commonwealth government. The stranded passengers built campfires and had a sing-song while the engine was being repaired. Rex remarked of the journey that he found the people more interesting than the landscape but this changed when he reached the Mission: *Mt Hermannsburg was at its best and it is one of the sights of the world for beauty of colour.*

He was welcomed as an old friend and immediately admitted into the multifarious activities of the complex and exuberant family that was Hermannsburg. The children remembered him but wondered where Jack was? And the bus? He gave them lollies and saw them to bed at night, putting them to sleep with animal noises. After supper Minna Albrecht asked him to sing; but the highlight came earlier in the afternoon. *Albert gave me my biggest thrill today. He came up and spoke to me. I asked him how the painting was going. He said he could not manage it. I said I might be going out on a trip and asked him if he would like to come with me. He was very pleased and thanked me most profusely.* The planned expedition was constructed as a business agreement: *Mr Albrecht decided that I go out with Albert and 3 camels about next Tuesday. I intend to go down Palm Valley way first. I will pay 6 shillings a week for 2 camels and tucker for Albert. If we get on satisfactorily we may do a trip out Glen Helen way later on.*

In the meantime Rex inspected the new garden (*it has done wonderfully well*), began teaching the boys how to play Australian Rules football and gave them crayons and books. He was well-looked after: *The meals are very good and plenty of vegetables. I had a raw ham sandwich yesterday. They also seem to make a sausage*

of raw meat. One day there was a wailing down in the bed of the Finke: a woman called Grace, the half-caste daughter of an English Lord, died. After a period of Arrernte mourning she was buried with Lutheran rites: *They must be going to bring Grace now as I hear the bell ringing. The burial service lasted for about an hour before sunset. The bell tolling all the time, the Lutherans sing at the grave side and have a sermon.*

As always, painting was dependent upon the weather and, when the wind wasn't blowing up dust, Rex began his routine of walking out into the landscape to sketch. There was some discussion of the forthcoming trip: *I was speaking to Albert this afternoon and he showed me a watercolour he did of the Church. I think it is very good for a beginner easily up to a white beginner. Albert is very keen to go out painting with me and he was telling me a lot of good places to go. Haasts Bluff he thought was the best there are hills beyond Palm Valley that he is keen on too.*

There is an affecting sense that the putative master-pupil relationship was already morphing into a collaborative enterprise and in some respects it seems that the promised lessons had already begun: *This morning Albert came down with me to see me work. He is still very keen and stayed till I finished the picture.* Perhaps, too, the opportunity to give tuition made Rex more reflective and more analytical about his own technique: *I think that I am improving in getting my work sharper which gives a better drawn appearance. I am using the pointed brushes more now. I probably stuck too hard and fast to the flat brushes, a combination of the 2 is the thing.*

The day after this entry was written Dr Duguid and his party came back from their camel trip into the west and *told us some more sensational things about the treatment of the natives...The wild native that came in sick with Yaws has made a wonderful improvement.* It was the return of their camels that made Albert and Rex's trip possible; before they left Manasse, in exchange for a tobacco pipe, mended Rex's boots. Rex also renewed his friendship with Long Harry, took a day trip to Palm Valley – *a wonderful sunset and a wonderful sight of green shadows, I think caused by the reflection of the yellow clouds into the blue shadows* – and sold a big picture of Mt Hermannsburg for £8 8/– to a Mr and Mrs Sheard who *jumped at the price and seemed very pleased.* And then, on 7 July, he and Albert set out.

Most accounts of the lessons that Battarbee gave Namatjira at Palm Valley suggest the two spent their time in the devoted colloquy appropriate to a master-pupil relationship; in fact, as Rex's diaries make clear, it was more an experience of intense sociability mixed with, for Rex, periods of intense solitude; and this was the case whether the two men camped alone or, more typically, alongside other parties, both Aboriginal and European. The landscape Rex describes, as if in direct contradiction to Ted Strehlow's 1932 prophecy of a *vast and once populous territory…silent as the grave*, is teeming with life – human, animal, avian, insect, arboreal and also inhabited by what might be called spirits.

That first night they stayed near a cliff before the amphitheatre where Palm Valley proper begins. Battarbee had decided previously he wanted to paint this cliff. *Albert is a useful man*, he wrote, *and says the grace both before and after meals. I made a comfortable bed in the open near the fire. This is a new experience for me out on my own, just with a blackfellow as a mate.* Here a new note of equality between men is sounded; Albert is Rex's mate just as Jack Gardner had been. As their trip continues, and Albert comes and goes, Rex takes on the same role he did with Jack: the jam-maker, the bread-baker, the one who stays around the fire waiting for the other to come 'home' – which is the word he soon begins to use for their shared camp.

Next morning, 8 July, Rex started work on the cliff he wanted to paint but it took him some time to find a point of view he was happy with. Meanwhile, or subsequently, Albert told him the creation story of the place, called Unkwalkna: *The blackfellow killed the two eagle hawks and put them on two big heaps of ashes, opposite the heaps of supposed ashes are* [piles?] *composed of small stones.* This was also the day Rex *started Albert off on crayons…he can draw well but says he does not know anything about colours.* Along with their equality as mates, then, there were exchanges made, stories for lessons.

Within a couple of days Albert was ready to move on: *Albert wanted to do the subject I finished yesterday in water, he stayed on his own and working just on cardboard made a very good start. It looks as if he will do well.* Some Aboriginal stockmen were camped nearby and Albert spent the night with them, leaving Rex *all on my own in the heart of Australia.* He came back at six o'clock in the morning and re-lit the fire, which had gone out: *Albert worked on his own again today. This morning he did a small watercolour. It is not quite finished but a very good effort. This afternoon he finished the one on cardboard. It is quite a good thing considering everything.*

The following day Albert went fishing with his friends and then the two men shifted their camp into the amphitheatre itself, which held memories of different kinds for each of them. For Albert there were legendary associations: [a] *man and his family all fly up to heaven from this rock – this is what the old men say of the hill on the south side of the amphitheatre.* For Rex the matter is more personal: *This hill I painted 4 years ago and I sold the picture to WH Gill.* For the next week or so they seem to have worked independently; Rex's diary notes paintings each made but most of the salient detail is about food, hunting and stories, including one that Albert tells about the time he caught and ate a wild pussycat: *tastes good fat meat.*

On 18 July, after just eleven days, the breakthrough came: *Albert finished his sketch of the amphitheatre this morning and I am really surprised with it. Interested to buy it. He has got a colour sense and puts it on even stronger than I do and good light in his pictures too. I feel now that he will make a name for himself and for his race too. I know that I could not do anything like as good at so early a stage of watercolour painting. It even makes me sit up and take note of whether he sees better than I do. He certainly backs me up in colour because there is no doubt the Australian aboriginal has a keen eye.*

After this Albert saddled up the camels and went back to the Mission, ostensibly to get a couple of things they needed

– including tar to dress saddle sores on Jim the camel's back – but really, Rex implies, because he was excited and wanted to show the people there what he had accomplished. *Albert took three of his best pictures with him and most of the Euro and some tucker, he seemed quite happy going away.* Rex was alone again and he felt it: *Sunday evening by the campfire alone in the wilds of Central Australia, I can't remember ever before* [being like this] *without seeing or speaking to any other person than myself.*

Subsequently, after Albert's return to Palm Valley, they were joined there by a celebratory party from Hermannsburg: *This morning I found a bower bird playing under a Witchetty bush, he had a rabbit bone and cycad seeds, shells, a piece of a china cup, seeds, wild fruits…Albert says they are wonderful birds, different to any other birds and can talk in Aranda, call out like a dingo and all other birds…I got a surprise when preparing tea and heard noises. It was Mrs Albrecht and children…Mr Albrecht was very pleased with the report I gave about Albert.*

The Albrecht party, which was quite large, stayed for ten days, there was a lot of visiting between camps and several impromptu exhibitions of paintings. *Albert finished a watercolour this morning quite good considering it was only painted on the card that he got inside a shirt. This afternoon he started one of a Euro coming down off the cliff. The Euro is only small but a masterpiece of life and colour. He can draw straight.* After the Albrecht party left, Albert resumed his peripatetic ways while Rex spent quite a lot of time alone, working; his initial trepidation of solitude transformed into a preternatural awareness: *It is so quiet at times here that the small birds sound like aeroplanes when flying. There is a small bird here that sounds like a galloping horse… finished two watercolours making twelve for this camel trip…I am very pleased with the palm picture. It took four days and something different with very good colouring. Albert came home this afternoon. Had been working in the garden yesterday.*

The celebratory note was sounded again when, on 4 August, they returned to Hermannsburg: *A batch of young children came out and gave me a warm welcome and were saying in Aranda, so Mr Albrecht said, 'Battarbee you belong to us'. Mr Albrecht said he was surprised to hear it and that it was a great compliment.* He was also given a nickname, perhaps a totem: a heron, for his lankiness and his beaky nose. If the claim of ownership struck Rex as prescient he didn't say; but simply resumed the activities he had participated in before, going to church on Sunday, playing football, selling pictures, gardening: he had particular advice to give about the care of the fruit trees, about which Albrecht, he said, knew nothing.

They were only back on the Mission a week before, on 11 August, the trip into the west began. This was a party of five people, four camels and five donkeys: Rex and Albert, along with the teacher, Raatz, who was supervising two boys, Herbert and Ulkalbirya, (too closely, Rex thought); but Raatz and the boys only stayed with them for a week before returning to Hermannsburg. They went via Gilbert Springs to Gosses Bluff, through Rumbula Gorge into Glen Helen country and on to Redbank Gorge; then, with a diversion towards Haasts Bluff, back over more or less the same route: 149 miles and nearly fifty hours on camel back.

Again the expedition was highly social and full of incident. On the first night at Gosses Bluff Rex wrote that *Albert got five dingo pups this morning so that pays him for his trip as he can get three shillings for them. This afternoon he met Tom Wheeler and Billy Lang at the rock hole, they were camped on the other side and were after the dingoes but will now move on. Tom Wheeler gave Albert a Euro tail to bring to us.* When Albert was making up his bed he found a small brown snake on the groundsheet and tipped it off; it came back again so he killed it with a firestick and burnt the body in the porcupine grass; the mother dingo howled all night long. They had a shooting competition, which Albert won, the next day, and in the evening cooked the Euro tail which *Mr Raatz liked…very much.*

Over the next few days, however, things became difficult. Albert wanted to show Rex Rumbula Gorge, with its rock carvings and stone implements but, perhaps due to interference from others in the party, at first missed the way. They had further problems approaching Redbank Gorge: *Albert is very tired tonight he is not well and he has been worrying about finding Redbank. I think the boys are windy of the place and are not keen on going to bed tonight.* Evidently something about Redbank Gorge spooked the boys; while for Albert there was probably conflict between what he wanted to do for Rex and what his own people demanded of him.

Things calmed down once Raatz and the two boys left and, not long after, at Arumbara west of Rumbula, they fell in with two large parties of Haasts Bluff men. They were dingo trappers, one party, on donkeys, heading to Hermannsburg with thirty-seven scalps, the other, on camels, returning after selling theirs. Amongst the in-going party was a young man, Cudunga, whom Albert raised as a son after his parents died: Cudunga gave him three dingo scalps.

Later Titus the evangelist, who was living at Haasts Bluff, arrived – Albert had sent word that he wanted to see him. He came in the company of a boy and the next day, while they were washing up after lunch, seven emu walked into the camp. *Titus rushed for my gun and had a shot with the .22 which hit a bird but did not bring him down. Then he had a shot with a .44 and Albert had a shot with a .44. Titus then went and got his shotgun and followed their tracks.*

The following day, at Albert's instigation, Titus found honey ants for Rex to eat. *They are much bigger than I thought and I had some of the honey, it tastes the same as honey but is finer…The ants get the honey from the mulga flowers. They nest in the sand and the natives when digging for them dig below and they fall down on to the sand then. Wine can be made from the honey. Natives sometimes get a billy can full of honey from them.*

There are further detailed observations about these insects, some of which Rex preserved in formalin. At the end of the entry he writes: *I have had a variety of meat today. Rock Wallaby for breakfast, euro for dinner and emu for tea and honey ant as a tit bit in between.*

Perhaps Titus outstayed his welcome – *A good day at last Titus left for Haasts Bluff after breakfast* – but before going he and Rex had a long discussion about the fabled night parrot. *He said he would try and get one…and send it to Mr Albrecht for me. He seems to know them allright and says they can catch them but don't eat them…He also says he will get me some stone axes. I wonder if I will get the night parrot yet. This may be the man to get it. He says he can get the wild natives to get it for him. I promised him a very good present.*

There is far less detail about the painting regime on this second trip and when Rex does mention Albert's paintings, he seems to regard them pretty much as the equal of his own: *Albert started quite a good watercolour of the Haasts Bluff today* he notes on 29 August. Their relationship is in some respects unequal however: *I gave Albert my sandshoes tonight, they cost me 12 shillings and have had only two months wear of them, the canvas is going. This is very rough country on shoes.* They returned to Hermannsburg on 9 September and, the night before they arrived, Rex decided *I am going to buy the watercolour with the euro that he did at Arumbara from Albert.*

The tantalising question remains: what exactly did Rex teach Albert over these two month-long trips? It is clear from other accounts that, before Rex gave him any lessons, Albert already knew how to draw; had attempted to paint; and was a very quick learner. Once the lessons began, he occasionally made mistakes in composition but these were swiftly remedied and never repeated: *It was a blessing he had to be corrected only once. He had an unspoilt mind and had nothing to unlearn.* Rex insisted one of these botched paintings be thrown in the fire and burned; it was.

The abiding mystery remains that of colour: *I felt that colour was my strongest point and in my method I was able to take Albert right back to Nature. I was very nervous about the word 'colour'. Albert's knowledge of English was limited. His main language was Arunta and strangely enough the most freely used word in that language is the word 'colour', which occurs in almost every sentence. It has several meanings according to the way it is used, but usually means 'finish' and in some cases 'ready to start'.* This is fascinating – as if colour was, not just a central concept, but the beginning and end, the alpha and omega, of Arrernte thought.

Many years later, after Albert had died, Rex revisited the subject, saying that what he taught Albert how to do was *analyse the landscape. The breakthrough came when he learnt to see colour in a way that was sound and true. In my own handling of watercolour, during the eight years before that time I had become dissatisfied with traditional methods. I felt the need to work out a new way and to achieve luminosity... when I returned to Hermannsburg in 1936...I was uncertain how to teach him. I did not wish to divulge my new method but knew if I taught him in the traditional style he was intelligent enough to see the difference. So I decided that, for the sake of the Aborigines, I must teach my method to Albert at least.*

The key word here is *luminosity* which, in the tradition Rex came out of – that is, the nineteenth-century English watercolourists who influenced Walter Withers – had a precise meaning. There was a protracted debate amongst these painters about the relative merits of opacity and transparency in the pigments they used. Transparency was thought by some to be a superior quality and this superiority was given a perhaps specious theoretical underpinning: luminosity arises because light passes through transparent pigment particles, is reflected by the white paper, and passes back through the pigment particles a second time – as if through a stained glass window. This doubling intensified colour, which attained thereby a spiritual dimension; it became a literal product of, and a metaphoric vehicle for, illumination.

Current wisdom suggests that watercolour paints appear more vivid than acrylics or oils not because they are transparent but because actual particles of pigment are laid down in a pure form with fewer fillers obscuring their colours. Multiple layers of watercolour paint, whether mixed or simply intensified, do for this reason achieve a luminous effect – as Rex had learned at Bitter Springs Gorge and alluded to when he remarked that Albert *puts it on even stronger than I do*. It is possible however to go further and suggest that the achievement of luminosity was also a warrant of the ability to see properly, a guarantee of clarity of purpose and of execution, even a means towards a revelation of the essence of creation.

That the vehicle of this revelation was pigment, colour, had added resonance for Albert, whose own traditions valued the various ochres for their magical properties. Red ochre was used as body paint in ceremonies; mixed with animal fat, traditionally emu or kangaroo, and smeared over weapons and tools as a protective; as a healing agent. The extra-curricular uses of yellow ochre are mysterious: women employed it in sexual magic, to bring back a lost man, or to keep a desired one close by. White was for mourning; it, too, was used as body paint during ceremonies. Those ochres which contained mercury, which gave the pigment added iridescence, were especially prized.

The luminous veil of paint upon paper thus rhymes with the ochre membrane applied across bare skin in ceremony; or, infinitely renewably, upon rock faces at inscribed sites. The resultant shimmer of light, attesting to the permeability of a membrane that both reflects and allows passage, is a sign of the immanence of the divine in many understandings and these may be taken to include the ancient verities Albert had begun to learn at initiation. Pigment was thus already a revered substance; the European palette substantially increased the range of colours available to Arrernte; paint, including the blue with which the sky was rendered, was a medium for transmission of the sacred.

As for the actual lessons, there is little more to say of them. Rex does not record anything he showed Albert how to do, nor does he recount what he might have said to him about technique; many years later, however, he did suggest it might have been a mistake to have divulged his own idiosyncratic method, the one that had taken nearly a decade to evolve. A mistake, because he felt he might thereby have over-determined the kind of painter Albert would become. As if transference of the method wholesale to another had the effect of stifling whatever originality that other might have been able to discover in himself. This is a complex issue that will be revisted.

In sum, we might say that Battarbee demonstrated techniques that facilitated the depiction of the landscape with a hithertofore unprecedented degree of verisimilitude that might point toward the essence beyond appearances; while Albert reciprocated with knowledge of country that ran the gamut from simple foods to complex storytelling – it is apposite that they went to Albert's mother's and father's countries respectively. Albert's stories are particularly interesting because they disclose aspects of country that are not necessarily obvious in a pictorial view. Or not obvious unless you know they are a part of the subject and can find a way to put them into the picture.

Rex taught other painters after Albert but in doing so took special care to allow them to discover their own style; Albert too taught the techniques he had learned, for instance to his sons and other among his relatives; the tradition continues unbroken today and traces of this are recoverable. Over New Year 1971–2 George Wilson Cooper, the British-born, Queensland-based watercolourist, went on a painting trip out past Glen Helen with Albert's third son, Ewald, and another of the Hermannsburg painters, Michael Lane; and left behind this account of their methodology:

First the subject was sketched in (invariably using pencil; this is called 'getting the sketch') *and then came the application of colour. There were clouds over Mt Sonder but they were ignored…after the blue of the sky was painted in and allowed to dry, next came the purples of Mt Sonder, a light wash of yellow was applied over the mountains and then a wash of Indian red…after this wash had dried a wash of ultramarine was applied and the result was a purple Mt Sonder. Shadows from folds in the rocky structure were painted in later. The foliage colour was obtained by a judicious use of green and some blue.*

Any relation this might have to Battarbee's *new way…to achieve luminosity* is unknowable; but the Hermannsburg school is remarkably conservative and it is likely that there are here shards and glimpses of the way in which both Rex and Albert painted. Despite what Battarbee says, and despite Namatjira's clear indebtedness to his teacher, there were other, and original, qualities that Albert brought to his practice of this art; and it is these that make him the unique figure he would, over the next few short years, and miraculously, become.

5. Blind Man / New Man

When, at a group exhibition in Alice Springs in 1951, Albert Namatjira re-encountered some of his earliest paintings, he said: *I painted as a new man, like a blindman, no idea, new man couldn't see.* Olive Pink, activist, anthropologist, friend, eccentric and gardener, would not have agreed. She bought two works in 1937, treasured them all her life and made sure that, after her death, they were donated to the Tasmanian Museum and Art Gallery in Hobart. *I would not exchange them,* the redoubtable Miss Pink wrote, *for any of his later work! Those I have, have a spiritual quality that his later work lacked. And a great simplicity of treatment.*

Tentatively dated 1935, before the lessons with Rex Battarbee took place, both are views of Mt Hermannsburg: one with a large red-orange sandhill in the left foreground, the other with two tree trunks on the right. On the reverse of the painting with the sandhill is another study of the same subject – the sandhill not the mountain – which has unfortunately been written across, perhaps by Miss Pink herself. She remarked that when Namatjira sold it to her he said she was getting two for the price of one and much later persuaded him to sign this and the other watercolour (on the back) with his original signature: ALBERT. Curiously, the sandhill painting, while unfinished, looks a more sophisticated work than either of the landscapes.

But the landscapes, taken together, are fascinating, not least because they show the same subject from two different points of view. If you look at them side by side it is as if the painter's eye has slid across the face of the mountain, from the view from behind the two trees to the one partially obscured by the red sandhill, thereby highlighting another of Battarbee's lessons: how to choose a subject to paint. This is a matter at once elementary and profound; a simple case of selection that nevertheless requires deep apprehension of the variables of framing, composition and point of view itself. One commentator has suggested that the mature Namatjira's habit of choosing a slightly elevated point of view from which to paint is what gives the viewer of his work a sense of looking across and down upon an immense vista. Others remarked on his habit of framing a view through squared off fingers and thumbs, the way a cinematographer or a photographer does.

There is no doubt that early Namatjiras are different from the later works but whether it is because of a spiritual quality is open to question. They are naïve paintings, rudimentary in their drawing, with a lumpiness to the larger forms and an almost complete lack of detail at the micro level; awkwardness is their salient attribute, along with a peculiar prescience, as if something both familiar and strange is pushing up towards the surface of the image. Their attempts at perspective are clumsy so that what depth of field they manage seems illusory and, overall, a sense of patterning predominates over any real feeling of verisimilitude. Some of the early work of the second generation of Hermannsburg painters, like Richard Moketarinja and Albert's son Ewald, shares these qualities; as if the process of learning to see took the same path in different individuals.

When Battarbee realised, in Palm Valley in 1936, that he had a prodigy on his hands, it was seeing that he emphasised: *It even makes me sit up and take note of whether he sees better than I do.* Before the lessons took place Albert complained that he could not manage colour; Rex recalled later that one of the things he taught him was how to *see* the colour in the landscape. Curiously, learning to see colour might also enable you to see something beyond colour: that is, form. One of the astonishing things about Namatjira's painting after 1936 is how quickly he progressed towards the refinement of detail, on the one hand, and on the other the extension of space he learned to conjure from the landscape. His forms become intricate to a point where the proliferation of detail feels almost vertiginous; while at the same time the space he commands recedes, in the other direction, towards infinity.

These qualities, and especially the second, are not particularly characteristic of Battarbee's painting but that does not mean he was a lesser painter. Rex's work does not usually have that sense of infinite extension; but the patterning we find in early Namatjira was typical of Battarbee, who often sacrifices depth of field in favour of the rhythmic and decorative repetition of motifs across the surface of a work. Awkwardness, too, is a quality we find often in Battarbee's painting, something most commentators ascribe to the fact that he was largely self-taught and therefore, they imply, lacking in certain skills. The fact remains that, although he was an uneven painter (and what painter is not?), the best of Battarbee is equal to, though different from, the best of Namatjira. If we have not yet realised what these differences are, that is hardly the fault of the artists themselves.

Battarbee was, by the standards of the day, a successful painter in the 1930s. He showed in Melbourne virtually every year, sometimes more than once a year, from 1929 until the war broke out; in Sydney as often; and his work was seen as both practised and unusual. Of an exhibition at Tyrrell's Gallery in 1933, for instance, a *Sydney Morning Herald* reviewer wrote: *Red predominates…the scale of colour, as a whole, brings in some remarkable contrasts…The great point about the scenery is that it is absolutely distinctive. Sometimes, the views are so different from anything one has seen before that they look almost unreal.* Bob Croll, who opened the Tyrrell's show, described in his address this 'unreality' as *a brave new world…the beauty of its stark hills of naked rock, clear cut in the crystal air, its immeasurable plains…its trees with trunks of spectral whiteness…its strangely patterned cliffs and rare rock pools of shining water.*

It isn't the case, for painters, that the ability to see is all there is; rather, clear- or long- or near-sightedness enrich the possibilities available to painting. This is a crucial point when considering Battarbee, Namatjira and the Hermannsburg School which is their legacy. Much of the writing about the school emphasises exactitude as an end in itself, as if the task of painting was to reproduce, as accurately as possible, the way things look to the human eye; but there are very few painters, in this or any other tradition, who value accuracy for its own sake. It's always something else they are trying to show us: difficult to put into words precisely because it is not a linguistic quality. When Battarbee taught Namatjira, the new man who was also a blind man, how to see, the result was not, as many have thought, a series of landscapes that look exactly like the originals but something far more rich and strange: paintings in which a world not seen before manifests itself.

The question of the connection between seeing and representing is complex, contested and of some longevity: in 1859, for example, John Ruskin wrote that he was *nearly convinced, that when once we see keenly enough, there is very little difficulty in drawing what we see*; and then went on thoroughly to confuse the issue as to which is primary, the world or its representation. It's true that to paint you have to see in a detailed, analytic, even forensic, manner; and also that painting what you see changes the way things look. For Namatjira to paint as Battarbee did, he had also to learn to see differently; but, crucially, that new way of seeing seems not to have replaced, but augmented, the way he already saw. Representation was achieved upon a ground of seeing – or being – inherited from his Arrernte forebears; this may be the source of his unique contribution.

The period following Battarbee's lessons was, for Namatjira, one of growth and experimentation. Among his innovations was the replacement of pokerwork upon articles of traditional manufacture like boomerangs and woomeras with watercolour painting. These artefacts were made, specifically for the tourist trade, in large numbers at Hermannsburg; in 1943, perhaps the peak year in the trade, Albrecht recorded the sale of 711 curios (boomerangs, bullroarers, pointing bones) and an astounding 5,110 mulga articles; some of which would have been painted woomera. While woomera had sometimes previously been decorated for use in ceremonies, the idea of painting representational landscapes upon them seems to have been Albert's alone. And, as Ian Burn and Ann Stephen point out, he thereby produced objects that encoded ambivalence in a way similar to Marcel Duchamp's readymades in Paris in the previous two decades.

A woomera was a multi-functional artefact. Primarily a spear-thrower, mechanically doubling the hurling action of the arm, it was also an all-purpose carrier, a fire maker that could also be used as a digging stick and, courtesy of the flint attached to the base of the handle, a cutting tool. The woomera that Albert painted in the late 1930s and early 1940s do not, as items of manufacture, differ in any way, save one, from traditional objects: the difference is that they were never meant to be utilised for any of the purposes listed above. As tools they were inert, mere potentials, while as painted objects their actual function became decorative, aesthetic; and, to the extent that they succeeded as art or craft, they also became commercially desirable.

The mulga wood on the convex side of a woomera would be sanded and polished smooth before being painted with a landscape which, while it might have been adapted to the curved surface, also assumed it to be the kind of flat support that usually hosts watercolour painting: *On such surfaces he used a technique of underpainting light areas with opaque white, leaving other areas, like the sky, to exploit the natural colour of the wood.* Typically, if inscrutably, on the concave inner side Albert would inscribe silhouetted black figures, often in motion, of animals, birds, reptiles or insects; sometimes words; sometimes his monogram, the four-petalled red desert rose.

The painted woomera are works of strangeness, beauty and sophistication and some of the painted boomerangs are too: in 1939 Pastor Albrecht gave one to the teacher, Ruth Pech, as a Christmas present. Miss Pech's portrait, from the hips up, wearing a floral dress and with one arm extended, is painted at the apex of the curve of the convex side of the boomerang; while to the right, there is a group of seven girls and on the left, five boys. The figures are animated, balanced and realistic; it's likely that individuals among the school children could have been recognised by those who knew them. The piece of mulga out of which the boomerang has been made was a cross section of the trunk of a tree, so that most of the figures, with their black heads and white clothes, appear against a dark brown band of heart wood; but Miss Pech's head, and the figures at the extreme edges of the two groups of children, are painted upon the honey-coloured amber of the lighter outer band of sap wood. The whole is polished to an opulent, sheeny glow.

Contemporary with the painted woomera and the boomerangs are a number of paintings on small, usually oblong, blocks of wood. These, invariably landscape subjects, suggest a kind of *mise en abyme*: on a piece of mulga wood is a landscape in which mulga trees, along with other vegetation, are depicted. If, as some believe (though others doubt it), Albert occasionally painted with ochres mined from traditional Arrernte sources, then a further mirroring is implied: the hills are made out of material that was itself extracted from them to be used as a pigment in their depiction. In this way representation is both affirmed and confounded: the paintings on wood not only show a landscape, in some occulted sense they *are* that landscape.

The culmination of these experiments was about fifty paintings, from the late 1930s and early 1940s, on beanwood, a traditional material used in the making of Arrernte artefacts. During their 1938 painting trip into the west Battarbee recorded that *Albert this morning found some bean tree wood…and painted a beautiful watercolour of Mt Hermannsburg on it. It seems to be just the wood he is looking for. White and does not crack and light as a feather…It may be even better than the paper to work on. I can see it being his style line. We were talking about this wood a couple of nights ago. It is the wood that natives make their shields out of and it never seems to crack.*

Over this period, at Albert's request, Rex also taught him how to take and develop photographs; Battarbee had a travelling dark room and, while on the road, developed his own photos in creekbeds on moonless nights. At some point he gave Namatjira a camera and taught him how to use it; as a part of the painting kit. When Battarbee returned to Hermannsburg in 1939 he recorded that *Albert showed me some of his photos he took on his western trip. There are some good snaps.* The whereabouts of any Namatjira photographs, if they are still extant, is unknown but the fact that they existed at all is intriguing: like the painted artefacts and the paintings on wood, they suggest another variation upon the theme of representation of landscape – not as replica or simulacrum but as alternate creation, perhaps even, in the way of the Dreaming, ritual re-creation.

During the later years of the 1930s Rex Battarbee was, perhaps inadvertently, also re-creating himself: as agent, art supplier, dealer, impresario, in all of which roles he was aided and abetted by Pastor Albrecht. Their correspondence became more regular after Battarbee's 1936 visit and more focussed upon advancing Albert's career as a painter. Albrecht had no doubt what was happening: *You know, step by step, that is how God leads the way,* he wrote, *and he will lead to the end.* There were also examples of what might be read as judicious flattery: *You will always have a warm spot in the hearts of our people...your name is mentioned by them more than anyone else.*

In February he asked Rex to contribute an article to the *Lutheran Herald* and Rex agreed; *the fine article you wrote for our church paper* was published later in 1937, roughly contemporary with Rex's Adelaide show of July and August that year. The exhibition, titled *Central Australia Water Colours*, was held at the Royal South Australian Society of Arts Gallery. The catalogue lists forty-seven works, not all of which were painted in Central Australia (there were paintings from Murwillumbah, the Tweed River and rural Victoria), and prices ranged from seven to thirty-five guineas. The Adelaide *Advertiser* wrote: *Mr. Battarbee is perhaps not altogether conventional in his manner of work, but nevertheless is successful in his own way, with a special facility for portraying strong light with strong colour, mostly deep purples and blues and metallic orange.*

At Albrecht's suggestion three of Albert's pictures were hung as part of the show. Not included in the catalogue, and not for sale, they already belonged to Battarbee who, *inter alia*, posted a statement asserting that he had neither touched them personally nor influenced their choices of colour or composition. A Mrs Richardson started up a collection of money with which to buy Albert materials, contributions to a special collection box realised £8 and the cash went straight to Battarbee to be spent on brushes, paper and paints: *you will know best and it will be well if he gets an ample supply*. Albrecht requested in addition ten shillings' worth of the black that Albert used for the mulga pieces; he had been substituting inferior material meant for marking wool bales and thereby damaging works.

The show with Battarbee was not Albert's first in the south. In March 1937 Albrecht had taken ten paintings down to the annual Lutheran Synod at Nuriootpa, where they were offered for sale alongside craft products from the Mission. These works were priced between five and ten shillings each; four sold and Albrecht himself purchased two more, making a total of six. The two works that Miss Pink bought in 1937, plus one other sale at around the same time, realised a total of £2; for purposes of comparison, a batch of artist's materials Rex sent up from Melbourne that February cost fourteen shillings; 4/– for paper, 5/– for paint and 5/– postage.

Although it isn't clear exactly how far these materials might have gone, they were probably all used up by the time the next consignment from Battarbee arrived on 10 April, not long after Albert returned from a painting trip out towards Haasts Bluff. He came back, Albrecht said, with nineteen pictures and they were very fine work. In the same letter he remarks in passing that the reserve out at Haasts Bluff was all but secured: the present owner, a Mr Underdown, had agreed to sell for £125; notwithstanding, it would be several more years before the declaration, in 1941, actually took place. A second Mission out-station and ration depot at Areyonga was also established during these years. Like Papunya, to which in the 1950s the original Haasts Bluff community relocated, the settlement at Areyonga is still there.

What was likely the first article written on Albert's work appeared in the *Advertiser* on 28 July 1937. *An Arunta Landscapist* by a *Special Correspondent* is essentially a preview of Albert's three works in the Battarbee exhibition and gives, in outline, the inaugural version of the story of how he became a painter: the lessons with Battarbee, the extraordinary aptitude he showed, the speed with which he mastered the medium, the likelihood that he would never profit personally from sales because the money would all go to the tribe – these motifs all appear in that first piece.

The article quotes Louis McCubbin, Director of the National Gallery of South Australia, son of the more famous Fred and a painter in his own right: *It is remarkable how this aborigine has grasped so readily the European conception of art. His painting of Mount Hermannsburg is outstanding in its realism, light and form and the solidity of the hills. The drawing of the euro in the other picture is remarkable. It is full of form, and is wonderfully well observed. Altogether, the aborigine artist's knowledge of colour and tone is extraordinary.* The third picture, of the amphitheatre at Palm Valley, was the one that so impressed Battarbee when Albert painted it during their first trip in 1936.

Rex was also interviewed and in the course of his remarks makes clear how far planning had already proceeded for the launch of Albert as an artist in the southern cities: *Mr. Battarbee said it was intended to hold an exhibition of his work in Melbourne and possibly in Adelaide, next year. Efforts would be made to bring the native south for the display.* Battarbee had already written to WH Gill, Hans Heysen's Melbourne dealer and the owner of Melbourne's Fine Art Gallery, to propose Albert's first exhibition; Gill agreed to give his gallery and his time free of charge if, in Battarbee's opinion, Namatjira's work showed sufficient improvement. By the middle of the next year the two were discussing marketing strategies.

On 2 July 1938, Gill wrote: *The whole question is, would his pictures sell, would the public be sufficiently interested to buy his work…you will have to make the prices very low. I suggest you take some photos of the man…it would be best to show him purely as a Native and not wearing Any European Clothes, so as to convey to the public that he is a pure Aboriginal and not Civilised.* Battarbee declined to present Albert as some kind of noble savage, asserting his belief that the work could stand alone; there were, however, some concessions made towards this kind of marketing in the cover art for the catalogue of the show – it shows tribal dancers and traditional artefacts like *tjurunga* and woomera – which Battarbee and Namatjira designed and drew together during the last of the four painting trips they went on in 1938.

Battarbee had been on the road for ten years, travelling and painting towards exhibitions that were held in commercial galleries in Sydney, Melbourne or Adelaide; now he would induct Namatjira into that same regime. One of the aims of the 1938 painting trips was the accumulation of enough high standard work for Albert to exhibit at Gill's gallery in Melbourne. Rex stayed with Gill's son, a station owner who was re-inventing himself as a writer, on the Palmer River on his way up to Alice Springs; but things didn't look good when he arrived at Hermannsburg on 23 May. Albrecht and most of the men were away, building the tourist road to Palm Valley; there was a raging enthusiasm for marbles that kept people from playing team sports like cricket; and *Albert I believe is not too well. They say he has heart trouble and is very fat. He is down at the goat camp.*

  The two men met the next day; it turned out Albert, who'd been painting the interior of the church, had suffered a reaction to the fumes of the oil paint. He also, thought Rex, needed two teeth pulled but otherwise looked well. He was keen, as before, to get out into the landscape to do more watercolours and had arranged for his seventeen year-old son Enos to be hired to go with them as camel-man; they would share the costs. *I saw five watercolours. The only ones he has left. Three of them trees. I don't think he has altered much in the style but there is no doubt about his painting of light, a couple of them are remarkable for light.* Rex took over the painting of the pulpit and some of the seats in the church – *a real job at last* – and within a few weeks they set off, with two camels and Enos, for Glen Helen country.

This trip was as social as the others had been and among those who turned up at their camp was Charles Barrett, the journalist, naturalist and photographer, who agreed to help publicise Albert's Melbourne exhibition; and, soon after, Barrett's old friend Bob Croll, who was travelling in the company of John Gardner and another artist, William Rowell. There was an interesting moment with Croll and Gardner. *It was a pleasant change,* Rex wrote, *and being a perfect evening I had a very enjoyable time. Will Rowell…asked to see the pictures. He liked Albert's work and he liked Mt Sonder the best of mine. The light was poor when he saw them but his opinion seems similar to mine. Mr Croll and Jack did not commit themselves as usual.* Here we see Rex's native shrewdness and an implicit affirmation that he, on the other hand, *has* committed himself.

At Albert's request Rex was giving him English lessons: *He wants to improve himself and wants to learn to read English. He is clever and thinks and agrees with me that natives should be able to read and write, would find it easier to get jobs if they could. I am also learning him to tell the time. He will soon learn that. I started him on reading the New Testament in English. Albert is painting Woomeras in his spare time and has a wonderful memory.* The photography lessons had begun before they left Hermannsburg – *I developed 2 spools for Albert this morning in the tanner's shop* – and these, like the English lessons, continued for the duration of this and the three following trips.

There were, however, difficulties that culminated in an argument on 4 July, just a couple of days after Albert completed his first painting on beanwood. The cause was Albert's bringing his sons into the camp. Enos, after a journey back to Hermannsburg with some completed artefacts, returned with Ewald, a frail boy of eight. Then, after Ewald went back, Albert's second son, sixteen year-old Oscar, turned up: *Oscar put in an appearance this evening. He is out hunting but I noticed that he makes his camp here. He caused a bit of friction this evening. Enos gave him a fright and he came rushing out to where Albert and I were talking over my fire with a blood curdling howl as though he was being murdered. Albert got on to Enos for frightening him.*

Rex continues: *This morning I said to Albert is Oscar going back to the station. He flared up when I said he could not stay here. He got very hot inside and was hurt that I should get him to send his son away. I told him that Mr Albrecht said that there were to be no other men in the camp. Albert said that Mr Albrecht was always like that and repeated something out of the Bible about the Judgement Day. I said that I had to do what Mr Albrecht said as I was only a visitor in his country.*

Albert said that I was alright and patted me and then shook hands. He said he would send Oscar straight back home and that he would forget all about it right here over the fire…He said that I should have called him aside and spoken to him quietly about it as a son was just the same as a brother, my own body…I did not like all of this but it could not go on as he would have had the whole family here. Anyway Albert did two paintings today so must be feeling better.

Albert's family commitments were, to say the least, demanding. He now had seven children; the latest, his fourth son Keith, born June 1937, was just one year old. The entire family – Enos, Oscar, Maisie, Hazel, Martha, Ewald, Keith and the soon-to-be-pregnant-again Rubina – was (supposedly) still living in the small house Albert had built at Hermannsburg the previous decade. When he sought permission from Albrecht to build a larger dwelling the Pastor advised him to wait until he was more financially secure.

Beyond the plain facts of dealing with a large family, there was a cultural difference involved, one that Rex alludes to when he remarks that Albert *would have had the whole family here*. More to the point, perhaps, is the ambiguity of Rex's statement that he was *only a visitor in his country*. The context suggests that he means Pastor

Albrecht's country but whose land was it really? Surely, if anyone's, it was Albert's. Obviously, so early, Namatjira was restive under the imposition of Albrecht's authority and this restiveness, which later became an active resentment, was a major factor in the way his life unfolded over the next two decades.

The incident is also telling as an insight into the relationship between the two men and for the light it sheds on their different characters: Rex is equable, an even-tempered, even-handed man who insists upon doing what he thinks is right yet feels uneasy in his role as Albrecht's enforcer; while Albert is revealed as a highly emotional and extremely sensitive man who must, because of his circumstances, keep what he feels hidden most of the time. In an interview given the following year Battarbee remarked upon this habit of emotional restraint; Aboriginals, he said, *have the same emotions as whites, although these emotions are carefully suppressed before strangers.*

The four camel trips over six months began with the expedition to Glen Helen and beyond, which was followed by a much briefer sojourn at and around Gilbert Springs (*I only came to get the sandhill*, Rex wrote) and then by an epic trek with Pastor Albrecht to visit the Mission out-station Titus ran at Alalbi; the fourth was a smaller, intimate, final camp at Palm Valley. Rex was constantly aware of the need to select work for a strong show; the day they returned from their first trip, for example, he records: *They were all very pleased with Albert's work and think he has improved a lot. I picked out 6 of his watercolours for his exhibition collection.*

When they returned from the second trip, to Gilbert Springs, they found Lady Huntingfield, the wife of the Governor of Victoria, at the Mission. She was the daughter of a New York judge and her husband had the distinction of being both the first Australian-born State governor and the last British peer to hold such an appointment. She asked to meet Battarbee: *Said she had seen my beautiful tree pictures at the Centenary Art Exhibition and had wished to meet me but did not expect it would be in Central Australia. She has also agreed to open Namatjira Albert's art exhibition in Melbourne and is keen to do it…Lady Huntingfield is a clever woman, speaks seven languages…also a Presbyterian and does not drink and smoke or dance.* She did not, apparently, mind if others did; she was on her way to attend a cocktail party and dance in her honour at Alice Springs.

This entry, 8 August 1938, is the first recorded use of the name Namatjira and the form, the reverse of that we have come to know, was in fact a signature Albert used for a brief period in the late 1930s. Its seemingly casual occurrence here may not be accidental – it occurs again when Rex is toting up expenditure on one of the trips and, in both places, it looks as if someone has decided that, for his launch in Melbourne, Albert needed more than just the simple Christian name he had so far used.

The third trip that winter and spring took a train of seven people, twelve camels and five calves into the west. Albrecht was on his annual survey of the progress and status of the wild tribes, accompanied by a Presbyterian minister, Mr McWhirter and his wife, Rex himself and three camel boys. They had a radio with them and spoke regularly to the Mission via Cloncurry in Queensland; and also carried the equipment for putting on a magic lantern show – but the bulb in the lantern unfortunately blew before it could be properly used. Albert did not join the party until nearly three weeks had passed, in a rendezvous with Rex near Haasts Bluff at the end of August.

In the interim Rex travelled north past Papunya and west of Mt Liebig and saw things he had never before seen: *We moved camp and found more than 50 people on the plain – Pintupi, and Ngalia and maybe others. This is the most natural lot I have seen and most of them are without clothes and the children, which are numerous, look very well.*

Mr Albrecht received a wonderful welcome. He completed a number of portraits of tribal people: *I painted two watercolours of Ngalia men. All three I painted here are sons of God. Their names ending in Qulpa and come from the Quilli in the Davenport Ranges.*

When Albert arrived, he and Rex, with Enos looking after the camels, went west to Mangeraka Gorge and there hit upon a rich seam of painting. *Mangeraka looks even better the second time. There is such a variety of subjects here it is one of the best places I have ever seen... Albert is doing a lot of good work here.* By the time they decided to move on – *we have not half painted this place* – they both seem to have worked themselves to a point of exhaustion which, in each case, led to ill health. On 15 September, *Albert painted a portrait. He found it hard work but it was quite a good effort*; but the next evening he *was worried and could not think of an idea.* Then he got toothache and had to cut short the trip, heading back to Hermannsburg by donkey for an extraction.

During the fourth and last trip, to Palm Valley, Rex was constantly troubled with sore eyes, which restricted the amount of painting he could do; at one point, uncharacteristically, he says he can understand a person taking to drink in this country. Nevertheless he allows that he is pleased with the forty pictures he has completed since arriving in May. Albert's health was also up and down and at one point he returned to the Mission to have the other tooth extracted. They each painted the other's portrait: *Albert's painting of me makes me look a real bushman and tough but there is no doubt he has life in it.*

He also recorded that *Albert did a good design of an Achilpa totem corroboree for his catalogue.* It shows, on the left, eight black men in silhouette wearing conical headdresses and carrying sticks, dancing around a tall, striped ceremonial pole; while to the right a boomerang, a *tjurunga*, a bull roarer, a woomera and two crossed spears float before the undifferentiated earth and the empty sky.

At Palm Valley Rex one day became curious about two unusual stones, one big and one small, that had markings carved upon them. *Albert...says that this is an important corroboree place and there is a big story with this place. Etarratarra means two boys, one big one and one small one, who used to live between here and Koporilya Springs. They are two important markings on rocks near here and are well known. They are really Bull Roarers, one large and one small and the spring is carved out of the rock too. Albert says the stones I found must belong to the small story but does not know about it himself. Says Nathaniel could tell me.*

After he returned from having the second tooth extracted Albert did indeed fill in more of the story of the Etarratarra stones: *the small stone and the small carving on the rock is the large boy and the big one is the small boy. The small boy kept on growing. Also near the cave there are two stones with markings across their chest. They are supposed to be men. I think they have something to do with the Etarratarra story. On a rock near here there are marks where a baby has crawled over them.* One of the powerful Dreamings of this place is that of the twins and this seems to be reiterated in the fragments of this story; it is profoundly true that Albert and Rex were twinned and, as in the story, the small boy kept on growing.

Western Arrernte stories about Palm Valley sometimes feature stars that fall from the sky and, once localised on earth, become ancestral figures; they also talk about spirit children who inhabit certain localities and are serially reborn into human form; the story of the twins dreaming in Palm Valley seems to be of this second kind and, while neither man's totem was the twins (Rex was considered to be a heron), they may still be seen as bodying forth, in their work, entities from another, mythic, dimension. If so, Rex may be seen the older and bigger twin, Albert the one who started small then outgrew his sibling.

Whatever eternal verities may have pertained, there was still real life to negotiate. Other news came back from Hermannsburg:

Albert had a fight at the station yesterday. He gave Conrad a hiding because he stood at the girl's house window with Maisie half the night. The other young men sided with Conrad and there was a real fight and spears and boomerangs were flying everywhere. Albert told Mr Albrecht about it and he said Albert was right and since has spoken to Conrad. Albert…thinks also that they are too closely related to get married. I think Conrad and Maisie are cousins. Maisie, Albert's eldest daughter, was then fifteen or sixteen years old. Conrad Raberaba went on to be ordained in 1964 as one of the first Lutheran Aboriginal pastors.

On 14 October they packed up and returned to the Mission, where Rex gave Albert what was left of his paints, paper and brushes – *a good load of things to take away.* Rex also intended to donate his clothes as prizes in a series of foot races but the craze for playing marbles was so intense he could only interest three competitors, one of whom was Edwin Pareroultja and another a one-eyed man from the west. *Albert…remained faithful so he got some more presents. He has scored but he seems to be the most worthy. I always find it hard leaving a place when I have been there for a good while.*

At Jay Creek Ted Strehlow was disappointed that Rex had already bought what he considered the best of Albert's Mangeraka pictures – *a wonderful study in purples* – for two guineas, a record at that time. There were a number of impromptu showings of pictures by both painters in Alice Springs and on 24 October Rex went down to the post office and there *posted to Mr Battarbee, 95 Puckle Street, Moonie Ponds, Victoria. 18 watercolours of Albert Namatjira for his exhibition.* The two elements of Albert's name are here reversed from the order of their previous appearances in Rex's diary; this is perhaps the first time his name was written in its familiar form – the way it will be appear on the exhibition catalogue, in future publications and as his signature on subsequent pictures.

These eighteen were not the only paintings of Albert's that Rex had; there were others he showed around Adelaide after a train journey down during which, near Oodnadatta, according to Rex's diary the following occurred: *Miss Rose Quigley at the Black Bull Hotel Adelaide* [is] *travelling down with us in the same compartment. She has been staying with Mrs Hayes at Undoolya. Mrs Hayes has no time for the natives and says she would like to put them all in the Alice Springs jail and burn them. She told Miss Quigley that she would gladly put a match to them. Strong talk. Mr Rumball* [another passenger] *has no time for them so it was just as well I did not have Albert with me on the train. It would have been a job to get him to Melbourne without any unpleasantness.*

Those he showed pictures to in Adelaide included Henry Earnest Fuller, church historian and secretary of the South Australian Royal Art Society, at whose gallery Albert would show the following year; the Duguids, who bought two on the spot; Pastor and Mrs Reidel; the Adelaide *Advertiser*, which ran an article on Albert with a reproduction of a watercolour and a photograph of him painting at Alalbi that Rex took; the artist Max Ragless, who also bought; and Louis McCubbin, Director of the National Gallery of South Australia: *He thought they were remarkable and said they would cause a stir in Melbourne. He did not want to buy any but that may come later. I had a good yarn to him and he showed me around the gallery.*

After a hectic week in Adelaide, on 2–3 November Rex caught the overnight train to Melbourne: *I had a sleep so here ends the trip. I am staying in the city for the present. Met John and Mr Croll at the Athenaeum, so seems like old times again. Took some of our Albert's pictures to Mr Gill and he is pleased with them.*

Opening Albert Namatjira's first one-man show on 5 December 1938, under the auspices of the Victorian Anthropological Society at the Fine Arts Gallery in Melbourne, *Lady Huntingfield carried a sheaf of lavender and deep purple iris, and wore a frock of black silken crepe and a close-fitting hat across the front of which were bird's wings,* and was accompanied by Miss Hermione Pott, whose black frock was worn with a black velvet hat. *We must realise,* Lady Huntingfield said, *that these people are worthy of recognition when they respond in such a wonderful way to tuition and sympathy.* There were forty-one watercolours on exhibition and within three days every one had sold, adding to a total yield from painting sales in 1938 of £204.

The *Age* reported: *It may be out of place to review this exhibition from the usual critical standpoint; yet there are qualities in the work of the 'native' artist that command respect. He is clearly a careful observer of the scene he sets out to portray.* Not everyone agreed upon the standard of the work. Harold Herbert, watercolourist and sometime teacher of John Gardner, said that there was *no need for a fanfare of trumpets. I do not accept his paintings as outstanding art.* Another critic was of the opinion that *the special note that ought to be Albert's is missing. In watercolour he is a white man.*

Bob Croll, by contrast, in his catalogue introduction pointed to the continuity between what Namatjira was doing and the many forms of traditional decorative art that were his inheritance. But he too thought accuracy was a salient quality: *the most remarkable feature is the invariably fine selection of subject matter. The clarity of the sunlight in the arid Centre is excellently conveyed and the strange and startling hues of those remarkable ranges, the MacDonnells, have been faithfully observed and just as faithfully portrayed.*

Albert's own reaction to this prodigious and unprecedented success is harder to gauge. According to his first biographer, Joyce Batty: *That's good, he said. Now I paint more pictures, earn more money. Buy nice things for everybody. Build myself a nice house.* Pastor Albrecht's response was more disenchanted. Writing on 12 January 1939 to thank Battarbee for his efforts, he said that Albert had opened an account with the Commonwealth Bank in Adelaide and was buying goods from the Mission store on credit. He had the raw materials to do more mulga work but was disinclined to utilise them: *It almost*

seems he has to go through the lot before he will think earnestly of work again...my only consolation is he does not gamble or drink, that it all goes to the tribe...otherwise one could become quite disgusted with the whole affair.

In fact, Albert re-invested the bulk of the money in art materials and took his family on a painting trip out west from which he returned, Battarbee reported on 1 July 1939, with about thirty watercolours as well as the aforementioned photographic prints: *He has done a lot of big ones and has made an advance, some of the work is quite different to anything before. Mr Albrecht bought a beauty of Haasts Bluff, the most even work but not quite as strong as some of the others. His portraits are quite good and give a new angle. Have no doubt that he is a big artist.*

Rex arrived a few days after Albert's return from this trip and was met at Alice Springs by Albert and Pastor Albrecht, who was in town to preach (in Arrernte) in the new church the Lutherans had built there; while Albert had been commissioned to make a painting of the church; which was presented, during a service which included communion and a christening, to the new pastor.

Albrecht tried hard to persuade Battarbee to accompany himself and Ted Strehlow on an expedition to the Petermann Ranges but Rex refused.

He went instead to Palm Valley on a painting trip that was, however, rather bleak at first because Ukalbi, his camel boy, was miserable and dull; he was, it turned out, coming down with the flu that was epidemic at Hermannsburg, and was soon replaced by the more ebullient Otto Pareroultja. Otto had been working for a builder in Alice Springs and now received his first painting lessons; with his brothers Edwin and Reuben he would go on to become one of the shining lights of the second wave of Hermannsburg watercolourists.

Albert missed Rex; he confessed that *when it was raining when I was up at the Warraba he was thinking of me all the time*. The reason he had not gone with him was because he was awaiting the birth of his tenth and last child, Maurice, who came into the world on 14 August; three days later, with Terence as their camel man, three camels, a calf and Albert's horse, they set off for Glen Helen country. The season was wet, the land lush and green and there were wild flowers, which both men painted at different times, everywhere. Albert and Terence got on well and Rex's diary of this trip, which was happy and productive, is full of tales of their high jinks together. Sometimes when playing marbles in the evening they shot them right over the fire.

This is also, of all the 1930s diaries, the one that contains the most traditional stories of the landscapes they were passing through. Rex recorded these stories assiduously, usually without comment, and made other notations, for instance writing out Rubina's tribal name, Ilkalita, and a list of all her and Albert's living children, along with their birth years. He also wrote down, in both Arrernte and English, the graces Albert continued to say before and after meals.

There were other innovations. On 26 August *Albert painted a good picture of Achilpa (wild cat) corroboree. There is no doubt he can do them. He got an old man to give him a few points on the colours. I told Albert this morning that he should do some corroboree pictures.* And interruptions: on the last day of the month Rex received his National Register forms, filled them out and gave them to Enos to take back to Hermannsburg. The Register was in essence a census, which none among the Arrernte had to complete; this exemption from census-taking was the legal device that denied Aboriginal people Australian citizenship: for if you did not exist to be counted, how then could you claim any other rights or privileges?

They visited Ormiston Gorge, where Rex had not been before; and the Pound beyond: *This is a wonderful Gorge. I think it beats everything else in the MacDonnells. It has got everything, good gums and Illumbas* (ghost gums), *plenty of water and several pools. Just as good colour as Redbank and Mangeraka also a good view of Mt Giles through the Gap. It is a wonder I have not heard of this place before…The only trouble there seems to be too much to paint and time is fleeting.*

The valedictory note was appropriate; a couple of days later, on 13 September, Terence returned from a trip to Glen Helen station for rations with *a note from Mr Bowman saying that England and Germany had declared war. He did not know any more. Mr Albrecht had sent him a note. It is strange to be out here and a war to start it makes one restless but I suppose I may as well stay here a while longer and put in a miserable afternoon and evening. Strange to say this morning I was thinking about the situation and I thought to myself it would be just as well to have a war and get it over because things seem to be impossible with some nations the way they feel at present.*

In fact they stayed out for the rest of the month: *I have painted 18 pictures on this camel trip. The most I have done on one trip like this and most of them large pictures. Albert has painted 23…So this ends the best camel trip I have had, six weeks and two days, two very good men to be with no rain every day fit for painting. I never raised the tent once on the whole trip.* Not long before they left Ormiston Gorge, on 19 September, Rex wrote that *Albert piled a tin with wild flowers and put it on our stone table;* and suddenly there is before us an image of rare beauty, felicity and fraternity. The 1939 painting trip was remarkable enough for Rex to rough out a sequence of events, places, stories which he thought might provide the basis for a book; which, alas, remained unwritten.

Like the trip the previous year, this one was made with the intention of gathering work for an exhibition: Albert's second one-man show at the South Australian Royal Arts Society Gallery in Adelaide in November. Within days of their return to Hermannsburg Rex was preparing the catalogue, naming and pricing the pictures, working out sizes in preparation for framing, making lists of names and addresses for invitations, writing business letters and, finally, packing up the paintings and sending them to Alice Springs to be railed south. Both men developed the photographs they had taken and, the day Rex left for Alice Springs, Albert also departed, going into the west on another painting trip.

On a beautiful day in Alice Springs *we decided to hold an exhibition in the ping pong hall behind the church. It was ideal because we could regulate the light as there was no glass window. It was a surprise the number of people who came along, we had all classes...Mrs Carrington brought along Frank Clune the author who left this evening for Ayres Rock with Mr Tullock. Clune was more interested in me than the pictures and took several snaps of me holding a picture.*

Frank Clune was at that time a peripatetic tax accountant who used his travels as the basis for speedily-written accounts combining historical detail, narratives of explorers and contemporary political observations; but this meeting in the early days of the war was ominous rather than auspicious. Clune, who never let the truth get in the way of a good story, claimed later to have met Namatjira already, at Hermannsburg in 1935, when he was researching the story of Lasseter's Reef. He would, in the 1950s, have a decisive and largely pernicious effect upon the way Albert's life unravelled over that calamitous decade.

By 27 October Rex was in Adelaide and events were gathering pace: *Albert's pictures have arrived and Mr Speirs had them nearly all framed. I met Dr Duguid and Mr Fuller and we have decided to open a show next Thursday afternoon.* A week later, on 2 November: *Albert's show was opened by Dr Charles Duguid this afternoon. It was a great success and a wonderful attendance. Some of the pictures were rushed as many as 3 people wanting the same picture. 17 pictures gone first day 75 catalogues sold at 1 shilling and 6 pence sales 90 pounds.*

Half-a-dozen more pictures were sent down from Hermannsburg, hastily framed and also offered for sale. One of the buyers was Louis McCubbin for the National Gallery of South Australia, who bought *a distant view of a lavender blue Haasts Bluff across a green plain*; this first institutional purchase of a Namatjira painting was made, Dr Duguid said, with slight exaggeration, only three years after the artist first picked up a brush.

Rex had shown at the same gallery earlier in the year: while noting that the scenes could appear *unreal* to those who had not seen the country, the *Advertiser* wrote on 19 May *that Mr. Battarbee has improved in technique since his last show here, and this exhibition will no doubt prove especially attractive to those who have visited the north. He has included a portrait of Albert Namatjira.* The same paper reported on 3 November that *the culture and intelligence of the Australian aborigine and his amazing facility for drawing and writing was nowhere better exemplified than in the art of Albert Namatjira.*

A week later His Excellency the Governor visited the exhibition and a week after that one Edward Lucas of Medindie in Adelaide wrote to the paper: *Sir – The watercolour sketches of this native artist are simply wonderful...I regard them as a complete refutation of the slanderous misrepresentation under which our native tribes have suffered ever since the advent of the white man among them...Albert Namatjira's paintings are a revelation.*

Rex's 1939 diary concludes with a list of the forty-one catalogued paintings; next to each title he noted the name of the buyer, the purchase price and also the size of the mount. Most of the works were landscapes but there were several tribal portraits. Intriguingly, it appears that among the forty-one, or perhaps among the uncatalogued pictures that arrived later, was the aforementioned corroboree picture, about which Rex wrote: *Painting of Corroboree by Albert Namatjira 1939. Achilpa (wild cat) Arunta Corroboree. Big College Corroboree. After this main man dances around the pole other men can dance around as well. The young men hold Corroboree pole with both hands before they have their final operation which makes them real men. Men standing and sitting at the side of the pole sing afterwards. The new men receive a present of one of the Nama-tuna (bull roarers).* Albert had apparently painted an image of an event from his own initiation.

The whereabouts of the corroboree picture, which may be unique, is unknown; unless a version of it appeared on the dust cover of CP Mountford's *The Art of Albert Namatjira* (1944): *a border design made up of sacred churunga, shields, boomerangs and spears...the group of senior men with their totem pole or nurtunja...in the distance is Haast Bluff*. Most of Namatjira's other portraits, which were amongst the most sought after pictures at the Adelaide opening, have also disappeared and, further, he does not seem to have painted any more after 1939, just as he is not known to have taken photographs after this date.

This resiling from portraiture is usually explained as the result of an interdiction against the making of images handed down by tribal elders. Battarbee in 1971 wrote that the Hermannsburg painters were, in the main, landscape artists because the genre freed them from taboos: *One of these was that no tribesman might represent any creature or object of the Dreamtime in its actual form, but must use symbolism.* He recounts the story of the portrait that Albert began in Palm Valley in 1938, the one that made him *look a real bushman*, but with an addition that is not in the diary: *on the next day he turned up empty-handed...an old tribesman had seen the work and said in effect, 'You can't do that!' So Albert destroyed the unfinished portrait and did not attempt another.* The old tribesman in question may have been Albert's father Jonathon.

Some years later, in the 1950s, Namatjira gave his own explanation of the matter to Rex's wife Bernice, who asked if he ever painted a portrait of his own wife, Rubina. He had: *One day I was sitting in camp watching Rubina talking to an old lady...and I started to paint Rubina and I was enjoying it and the painting would have been good but...my wife was well trained in tribal ways and when she saw I had painted a portrait of her and therefore there were two Rubinas she was so cross that she destroyed the portrait. I was not allowed to finish it. It would have broken tribal taboo and grieved a spirit.*

The matter is not simple. Images of people, animals and birds are common in Albert's watercolours of the 1930s, as they are on the wooden artefacts he continued to paint into the 1940s. He represented many creatures in their actual forms and, presumably, thereby grieved many spirits. Further, his own attitude to such transgressions, if that's what they were, was

ambivalent. In both stories, the one Rex tells about the fate of his portrait, and his wife's version of what happened to Rubina's picture, Albert appears as a man who will transgress until actively forbidden to do so. He obeys the interdiction but it seems that, had it not been made, he would have continued with his portrait painting. Perhaps this is best understood as a commitment to artistic freedom above tribal law, allied with a pragmatic sense of where to draw the line when the two came into conflict.

There is another, more important point to make. The landscape of the Western MacDonnells, even to a casual view, is easily anthropomorphised. The human propensity to find faces in stones, as we see shapes in clouds, water, fire or elsewhere, called *pareidolia*, needs little encouragement here. One explanation, then, for Namatjira's abandonment of portraiture might be this: he ceased to paint images of people, and of animals too, because he had found a way to represent their entities as a part of the landscape itself.

In this he was following, or more likely rediscovering, ancient traditions in representational painting. Art historian Daniel Thomas: *The human faces which so often become visible in the rocks painted by Namatjira, and the tree trunks like wrinkled arms and elbows, are a reminder that semi-hidden humans and dragons are a conventional presence in rocks and stumps in Persian and Chinese painting, two art traditions which, like the Australian Aboriginal, place little emphasis on innovation and are content with repetitious refinements.*

This anthropomorphising tendency surfaced early. One of the paintings hung in that first one-man show in Melbourne, Sand Drift, Central Australia (1938), is delicately ambiguous. It is a simple composition, sparse green shrubs and their purple shadows scattered across the gentle rise and fall of a brick-orange dune before a pale, cloudless, egg-shell blue sky; yet the whole can morph, like a figure–ground ambiguity, into a view of human buttocks and thighs, and suddenly you are looking across the declivities of the reclining form of the torso of a woman lying prone before you. A sand maiden rather than an earth mother perhaps.

Battarbee, it will be recalled, on the second of their 1938 painting trips, said he went to Gilbert Springs specifically *to get the sandhill* and, while his 1938 painting has not been traced there is another, Sand Dunes at Henbury (1936), a strong work, made two years before Sand Drift, Central Australia. It is an example of the way the two painters often shared subject matter or at least painted the same subjects. However, the anthropomorphic quality, though it is not entirely absent, is far less pronounced in the Battarbee and a case can be made for this quality, or ability, to have been one of the things that the older man, the older painter, learned from the younger.

It is anyway crucial to an understanding of both painters' works: they encode in their representation of landscape entities that might be described as imaginary if they were not so present; fanciful, if they were not so actual; illusory if they were not so real. Verisimilitude is, after all, a convention, a means, by which other realities, which are primarily emotional, can be revealed. When Albert said he painted like a blind man, he perhaps meant that he could not then yet see a way of depicting those qualities, or entities, immanent in the landscape; when he became a new man, he called himself that because that's precisely what he became: a conduit, unprecedented and unforeseen, for ancient verities to make themselves known in a contemporary form.

6. The Offerings of War

At Christmas 1939, the Centralian Lutherans found themselves catering for a thousand souls: all those at Hermannsburg as well as their people at Haasts Bluff in the west, Alice Springs in the east, the cattle ranches to the south and the Jay Creek reserve halfway between the Mission and Alice; where, after five years' service with the Commonwealth Government, Patrol Officer Ted Strehlow was about to be relieved by Hermann Vogelsang. Traditionally there were three celebrations: the German–European one on Christmas Eve, Christmas Day itself, when church services were held, and then Boxing Day or Third Christmas Day as it was known, which was given over to sporting contests of various kinds.

After the summer camel loading arrived, the goods were unpacked, weighed, inventoried, then the gift parcels made up – one for each person at the station, one for every visitor and one for any Aboriginal person who was in contact with the Mission. Native pines were sought out, cut, brought in and decorated as Christmas trees; the craft store made last-minute purchases of leather goods, fancywork and mulga-wood artefacts so that people had cash in hand; there was choir practice every evening and a gradual build-up of excited anticipation, especially among the children.

Albrecht, who now had the use of a Chevrolet truck, took a service on Christmas Eve morning at the new church in Alice Springs and afterwards red handkerchiefs tied up with lollies, dried fruit and honey biscuits inside them were given out, along with cake (bread dough baked with dried fruit), salted beef and servings of a mixture of sugar and tea. There was a similar distribution of food and gifts at Jay Creek and then, on the afternoon of Christmas Eve, 382 parcels were distributed at Hermannsburg; at the same time a collection was held which raised a little over £3 towards the printing, by the British and Foreign Bible Society, of the whole of the New Testament in Arrernte.

Following the Christmas Day services, the Boxing Day events featured dozens of contests, including archaic activities like spear throwing and spear dodging along with more modern sports: shot putting, tugs of war, obstacle courses; the high-, the long-, and the hop-step-and-jump; billycan racing (you had to run with a can of water on your head without spilling any); as well as the more conventional foot races. Some of the young men, such as Edwin Pareroultja, were fine athletes and, under the stringent and committed coaching of Rex Battarbee, would go on to compete in regional and national competitions. Edwin and his brothers Otto and Reuben, who were relatives of Albert Namatjira (they shared a grandfather), would also learn the techniques of watercolour painting from their athletics coach.

Another tradition had grown up alongside the Hermannsburg Christmas; or perhaps it was the other way round. In 1939, as in previous years, in the week leading up to the Christmas festival, initiation ceremonies were held, with singing and dancing every night. Albrecht was aware of these circumcision corroborees, which included ritual transformation of adolescent boys – but also of the politics of tolerance, lest he alienate potential or actual members of his flock. *They had Christmas with a sideshow*, he wrote in his newsletter; though that too should probably be the other way round. *He wasn't interested in those stories!! That's only rubbish!!* Pastor Eli Rubuntja remarked in 1986. *Only one way, he preach to people God's way, he didn't know about this Aboriginal culture. He wasn't interested, so we didn't talk about it to him. Kept that part by ourselves.*

As in World War One, the German affiliations of the Lutherans led to suspicions of complicity with the enemy. Adair Macalister Blain, Member for the Northern Territory, alleged in Federal Parliament that some people on the mission were Nazis, or at the very least, Nazi sympathisers. The accusations were taken seriously and the Army ordered to look into them. When the investigating officer, Captain Balfe, arrived at the Mission – on the day after Albrecht returned from his annual winter trip into the west – it turned out the two had met before: in the editor's offices at the Melbourne *Argus* in 1935. Balfe, a journalist in civil life, had contributed articles in support of the scheme to bring Koporilya water to Hermannsburg.

He inspected the gardens, with interest, given that he had helped raise the money to build the irrigation system that made them possible; and the wireless room where, as instructed, he disabled the pedal-driven short-wave radio transmitter by removing the key with which Morse code messages were tapped out; but when Albrecht invited him into his study to look through his papers, Balfe declined: *I didn't think*, he said, *that a man who spent his vacation working for the Aborigines would be a Nazi.* He was interested in Namatjira's paintings and bought one, plus some mulga work, before he left.

There were other slurs against the Mission, including a threat from a man with an interest in the Haasts Bluff lease, who advocated *burning down that bloody German Mission*; but in the short term the demand that Hermannsburg be closed was countered or at least delayed through the appointment of Rex Battarbee as Liaison Officer. This course of action was acceptable to the Army because of Rex's record in the previous conflict. The outbreak of war had not varied Rex's rhythm; he had made his usual annual winter trips to the Centre in 1940 and 1941; nor did the official appointment change anything else for him; or not at first.

The war had other ramifications. It has been said that, with the exception of Darwin, no Australian town was more affected by the war than Alice Springs, which became a major supply base for thousands of Australian and American troops stationed in the north and, after the bombing of Darwin in early 1942, the only means by which they could be supplied. Alice Springs became the capital of the Northern Territory for a period from 1942 and it was proposed that, after the war was over, this change become permanent. People and records were evacuated south from Darwin and, while many civilians remained in Alice Springs, they were outnumbered by servicemen and women; subject to restrictions, including curfew; and living in what was, in many respects, a military camp.

The first soldiers arrived in September, 1940, around the time of Captain Balfe's inspection. They were officially called the Darwin Overland Military Force (DOMF) and under the command of Lieutenant-Colonel, later Brigadier, Noel Medway Loutit. Loutit, universally known as Tommy, was a Gallipoli veteran who landed on the peninsula on 25 April 1915 and spent the entire nine-month long campaign ashore; he is said to have been one of only three Australians who actually saw their objective, the sea of the Dardanelles. He had been an oil company executive between the wars, possessed the instincts of a Napoleon and ruled as a despot, which led to frequent conflict with the Administrator, Charles Abbott, and with the free-living citizens of Alice Springs, who resented any restrictions placed upon them; but, despite the fact that many of them did not want to be there and sometimes showed it, Tommy remained popular with his men.

By mid-1942 there was a huge military presence in Alice Springs, at its peak about 8,000 men and women in various roles and occupations. There were transport companies, supply companies, engineers (both electrical and mechanical), a works department, a garrison, infantry and salvage units, ordnance and fuel companies, a hospital, a graves registration and inquiries unit, a censorship unit, army education personnel, the canteens service (including butchers), a pay corps, a postal unit and a signals unit. There was also the Allied Works Council, which employed 140 men, many of them locals and some Aboriginal; while out at the new Seven Mile Aerodrome south of the town, the No 57 Operational Base Unit of the RAAF was stationed alongside two USAAF units for which they were logistical support: the 4th Air Depot Group and the Weather Observer and Forecaster Unit. Later No 87 Squadron was also based at the aerodrome for a period while undertaking aerial topographic survey work.

There were sometimes sixty trains a week arriving at the Alice Springs railhead, to be unloaded into the ubiquitous three-ton Fords and Chevrolets and trucked north; between 1940 and 1944 as many as 200,000 soldiers passed through the town which, partly as a consequence, gained several large new items of infrastructure: a much bigger and better reticulated water supply; a new power station that was built in the Sadadeen Range. The military airport, south of Heavitree Gap, would become in time the present Alice Springs airport. And the 109 Australian General Hospital, which arrived in August 1942, established itself around, and greatly augmented, the existing hospital.

All of these developments had consequences for Hermannsburg. Albrecht was concerned, as ever, at the effect upon Mission

Aborigines of opportunities in Alice Springs, where some of the men went to work, and especially their exposure to alcohol, prostitution and other pleasures and dangers that trail in the wake of an army. Battarbee, by contrast, saw the concentration of troops as an opportunity: *The boomerang makers and painters have had a harvest and there is still just as big a demand for them as ever. Several of the young men are very keen to be artists…and are showing a great improvement in their work. In fact some have advanced so much in the last few weeks that there seems to be no doubt that this place will become known for its Aboriginal artists. They are not going to let Albert Namatjira have it all his own way.*

The presence of so many military personnel in Alice Springs, including those from the United States, who were enthusiastic souvenir hunters, transformed the trade at Hermannsburg while at the same time obviating the need for Namatjira – or any other artist – to exhibit his work for sale in the southern capitals. The Americans from the air base were fascinated to find an Aboriginal artist painting such accomplished pictures in a European manner and anything Albert cared to produce was snapped up by a buyer – which was good for the artist but not necessarily good for his work. His paintings were now selling for between one and five guineas each and were so much in demand that he was, according to Joyce Batty, overwhelmed with orders.

This burgeoning trade had unanticipated local effects. *Strangely*, Battarbee wrote, *Alice Springs people were not interested in Albert's pictures until the Army personnel showed their appreciation*. There was concern however that the quality of Albert's work might suffer from this degree of popularity and that, even if it did not, he would not have any paintings left over to exhibit in the metropolitan capitals when the war was over and normal activities resumed. These concerns led to the establishment on the Mission of three bodies whose function it became to regularise the production and sale of paintings.

The Arts Advisory Council, later the Aranda Arts Council, first convened in 1941, was chaired by Pastor Albrecht and comprised the white representatives on the subsidiary Artists' Committees; subsequently Manasse, the leather-worker, joined the council as a non-artist Aboriginal representative. The two committees reported to the council: the Namatjira Artists' Committee was made up of Battarbee; Hilda Wurst, the headmistress of the Mission school; Pastor Gross, the newly appointed Assistant Superintendent; and Art Latz from the Mission staff along with Albert himself, his son Oscar and his uncle Walter Ebatarinja; while the Pareroultja Artists' Committee, which was founded somewhat later, had as its white members Battarbee, Mission accountant Oswald Wallent, teacher Ruth Latz and teacher's assistant Mona Kennedy; and as its artist members Edwin, Otto and Reuben Pareroultja, Henoch Raberaba, Richard Moketarinja, Enos and Ewald Namatjira.

The committees priced all paintings produced by their members while the council arranged the sales. Albert's work, for example, after the establishment of the council, was offered at higher prices than formerly: between three and fifteen guineas per painting. There was also an informal agreement that he would restrict his output to fifty paintings a year while at the same time reserving certain works from sale so that they could go towards his next exhibition. In this way an attempt was made to balance present needs against future possibilities.

Those ten artist's names, those ten committee men, make up the core of the Hermannsburg School in its early days; they were all students of Rex Battarbee's and they would all go on to exhibit, with or without Albert, in the cities. In 1951 Battarbee enlarged upon the way the school was founded: *First the natives started painting on boomerangs and woomeras, which had a ready sale while the* war lasted. *Through this experience they had practice in drawing and acquired technique in using watercolours. By the time the war was finished the demand for curios ended; but several of these men had established themselves as watercolourists and have continued to make a good living.*

He also described the way the council and the committees were meant to operate: *The aim...is to protect the artists by making the disposal of their pictures as foolproof as possible so that they may get the benefit of their work, and be enabled to save something for lean times and their old age.* But the bureaucratisation of their art practice, however well-intentioned, was not easy for them. Albert was prevailed upon to empower, *as a means of protecting him from unscrupulous people,* Pastor Gross as the counter-signatory of his cheques; but neither he nor Gross felt comfortable with this arrangement and it was soon allowed to lapse. Mission attempts to protect Namatjira from himself, or at least from the alleged deleterious effects of his fame and fortune, become a constant theme from this point on and would lead to tension, acrimony and finally rupture.

There was tension also amongst the constellation of satellite artists revolving about the superstar. Battarbee remarked, with an asperity that is rare for him, *the missionaries also took the view that, if Albert was such a great artist, his must be the true art, so that men whose work bore most resemblance to his were encouraged.* This is an important point. Battarbee continued to feel that, through inexperience, he had taught Albert in the wrong way, so that the younger man's work was too like his own; and when it came to teaching other artists, rather than facilitating an imitation of his manner, he made a conscious effort to help them develop what he considered to be their own individual style.

Another, more serious, attempt was made to close the Mission down in 1942. The background to this move, initiated by Brigadier Loutit, was Albrecht's absence on leave in the south. He and his family departed for Adelaide at the end of 1941, around the time of the bombing of Pearl Harbour and the entry of the Japanese into the war; before he left, Albrecht, always mindful of the threat of famine, ordered extra large quantities of flour and brown rice and also solicited from the army bags of sugar and crates of raisins that were slightly water-damaged. He was undoubtedly acting innocently but, following the shock of Japanese bombing attacks on Darwin, rumours began to circulate that the stockpiles of food at Hermannsburg were a depot meant to feed the enemy when they invaded and advanced down the continent.

One day, without warning, a group of officers and men arrived by military transport to search the Mission. They investigated the staff houses and the main buildings but found nothing untoward apart from the caches of rice and flour. Glen Helen station owner Bryan Bowman, who was buying supplies at the Mission store, was questioned about the allegiance of the Albrechts and remarked that as far as he knew they were *pro-German and anti-Nazi*. The military authorities, however, persisted in their plan to close the Mission down. They wanted to transfer all staff to Alice Springs and disperse the so-called full-bloods into the bush to live off the land; while the half-caste population, then housed at the Alice Springs Government Home, would be sent to Hermannsburg to live.

Albrecht had a personal meeting with the Director of the Department of Native Affairs, EWP Chinnery, at Parliament House in Adelaide at which he was told the final power of decision rested with the federal Minister in Canberra. Albrecht's response was to suggest that Rex Battarbee's position as Liaison Officer be upgraded to that of Residential Inspector for the duration of the war, with the duty of reporting fortnightly to the Northern Territory Administrator on the activities of the Mission. This suggestion was accepted and, in the compromise worked out between the Army and Chinnery, Battarbee was described as *a returned soldier and well-known artist who has an intimate knowledge of Central Australia and its natives.* A consequence was that he would have to move permanently to Hermannsburg.

During the decade and a half (1928–1942) he was on the road Battarbee kept a room in his brother Malpas' house in Melbourne, first at Bakers Road, Blackburn, latterly at Puckle Street in Moonee Ponds, where Malpas' pharmacy was; and, similarly, a room in the Albrechts' house which he used when visiting Hermannsburg. Now that he held an official position, he relinquished that room and established an independent camp on the other side of the Finke, which he'd cross in the evenings to join the Albrechts at their table for meals. He was an honoured guest who had come home, a pilgrim who'd found his place; he would live the rest of his life in Centralia.

There is no doubt that he received a call. It was compounded of several elements: his Christian duty; his feeling about service in war; his affection for the people; and, perhaps most of all, his love of painting and the ambitions he still possessed in that area, both for himself and for those he taught. It's probable too that Pastor Albrecht issued a direct plea that he come; certainly, around the same time Jack Gardner wrote to him in the rueful tones of another who had been summoned: he had been manpowered onto the family farm, which is where, as an adolescent boy, he had spent World War One. His letter can be read as a farewell to a way of life and begins: *Bat, my darling*.

Albrecht, meanwhile, was still in Adelaide. As a civilian he needed a permit to return to the war zone, of which Alice Springs and Hermannsburg were a part, and in May 1942 received a letter saying that he and his family had been denied such a permit. It took him three more months of wrangling with officialdom before one was granted; it was made conditional on Battarbee's appointment, which became official on 27 July. Even so, Albrecht was forced to leave his wife and children behind and return to the Mission alone. He arrived early in September, after eight months away – his longest absence in sixteen years. His flock surrounded the truck in jubilant welcome as it drove into the compound.

Most weekends parties of soldiers, four or five trucks strong, would make their way out to Palm Valley for Sunday picnics, usually stopping at the Mission on the way there or back to patronise the craft store. At the same time, men from Hermannsburg were going into town. Albrecht, on his return from Adelaide, had been required to take a census, the purpose of which was the mobilisation of Aboriginal men in the Territory into labour gangs for semi-military service. Tasks included cleaning, cutting firewood, kitchen work and so on; and by November 1942 forty men from Hermannsburg, including two of Albert's sons, Enos and Oscar, were working in Alice Springs.

The co-option of Mission Aborigines into the war effort was not without its difficulties. There were complaints: the men were paid 5/– a week, women's wages, half what white soldiers and workers earned; they were given giggle hats, made of green cotton with floppy brims, not regular soldier's hats; were expected to work barefoot. A few became homesick and ran away while others identified so strongly with their new masters that they began to reject Mission ways. Some took to gambling and visiting town prostitutes; wives who followed their men to town became prostitutes themselves; one woman was sent north to Tennant Creek hospital to be treated for a venereal infection.

Albrecht and Battarbee initiated a series of discussions with the colonel in charge of the labour gangs in order to address these matters. They managed to persuade him to issue boots for the men but he refused to raise their wages to 10/– a week and equivocated on the question of tunics and regular army hats. He did however agree that the military would provide for the families of men working on the labour gangs.

Battarbee was by this stage fully employed in Mission work and in many ways had become Albrecht's right-hand man. When, towards the end of 1942, the Pastor went out to inspect the depot at Haasts Bluff, Rex went with him. Because summer rains had washed out the road around the Mereeni Range, they had to drive the northern route via Alice Springs, a trip of 500 miles there and back. Similarly when Albrecht, looking for a site for a new depot, twice investigated the abandoned cattle station at Boatswains Hole to the south-west, both times Battarbee went with him. Subsequently, under the direction of the extremely capable Manasse, a new road was built out to Haasts Bluff; and another constructed into the springs at Areyonga, near Boatswains Hole; and that, as mentioned, did in time become the second of the Mission's western depots.

Another of Albrecht's and Battarbee's initiatives was the Hermannsburg Aboriginal Pastoral Scheme, conceived during the war years as a means of local employment. Aboriginal men had proved themselves preternaturally skilled horsemen and generally expert in all kinds of work with animals; the war had also seen an expansion of the cattle industry. The idea was to set men up with stock and equipment on land of their own and, with sensible business advice, give them the chance to become independently self-employed. One of the beneficiaries, Ephraim Wheeler, in 1984 recalled: *Pastor Albrecht...give me twenty cows, and a bull and few horses, packs and saddles and I bin grow 'em up, all that bullock, sell 'em back again, get 'em money all the time sell 'em, branding, take 'em Alice Springs, good work that time.*

There were legal and taxation issues, particularly focussed on the registration of separate brands for the men; Albrecht rejected the idea of using the Mission brand with a different serial number because *officials would be led to think it is only a branch of our Mission undertaking...also the Natives might not gain that feeling of pride of ownership*. Battarbee was characteristically more direct: *Work is the only salvation for these people...so far all the artists and pastoralists are Arunta men; but in this area there are Loritja, Pintupi, Pitjentjara and Ngalia tribes who are still intact but living in a more primitive state...they too want to become artists and cattlemen*. And, presciently, given the Desert Art movements that arose from the 1970s on: *who knows but some of these men may show us a new form of art?*

Meanwhile, what of Albert? What was his war like? All the indications are that he spent the majority of his time following the pattern established in the immediate pre-war years: long sojourns into the landscape looking for subjects to paint then a return to the Mission with the works, so like hunting trophies, for sale. His surviving paintings of the 1940s are the most various, resonant, elegant and striking of his career; the sophistication he achieved in works like *Alumbaura Haasts Bluff* became, as it were, second nature to him and he applied the new-found confidence in his skills to a variety of landscape subjects to produce a body of work that remains astonishingly good.

Namatjira almost never dated his works and rarely titled them either; on most there is just the signature, in printed capitals, down in the bottom right hand corner of the painting. Battarbee also signed his paintings using printed capitals, more usually in the bottom left hand corner; and it was Rex, in his role as agent, who most often supplied Albert's works with titles. Some of these titles are self-consciously poetic and seem awkward now; others are descriptive of the subject of the painting or simply name the place that has been painted. Given that Namatjira, like many artists, returned again and again to the same subjects, this makes it difficult, if not impossible, to construct an accurate chronology for the progress of the work. Most dates have to be inferred from secondary evidence like exhibition catalogues or other contemporary documents which mention a painting that can be otherwise identified.

Namatjira's reluctance to date or title his paintings can be read as ignorance of, or lack of interest in, the procedures by which an artist over time constructs an oeuvre which may then, after death, be interpreted by others as a way of reconstructing their career. It might mean he wasn't concerned with the posterity of his works,

only their present utility as objects for sale. But there is another way of looking at this: perhaps, rather than seeing his works as ephemeral, he actually regarded them as enduring in a way that obviated the need to provide them with particular identifications. Perhaps he saw them as artefacts which carried the imprint of the eternal and it was this, not their ephemeral nature, which made it unnecessary to name or date them.

When Albert spoke about Rubina's refusal to allow her portrait to be painted, it was the dread spectre of duplication of image, and the consequent compromised authenticity of soul, that he gave as the reason for the prohibition; but the same fear does not seem to have applied to the duplication of images of the landscape. Indeed, it looks as if the opposite is the case: if every painting of a particular place in some sense *is* that place, perhaps by painting it you thereby increase its resonance, its power, and what might be called its purchase upon eternity. Many commentators have noted the lack of representation in traditional Arrernte art; some have identified Namatjira's primary innovation as an espousal of representation; a few have gone further and suggested that his art somehow melds the representational and the abstract into a new form that is both traditional and contemporary; but no-one has yet said exactly how this was done.

All forms of conventional representation of people and most animals disappear from Namatjira's art towards the end of the 1930s; his landscapes after that date are unpeopled. Yet they are not in any sense empty of presences; in fact the reverse is the case. He gives up the habit of placing figures in his landscapes only to resurrect them, if that is the term, as ambiguous presences within the forms he paints. In this way his paintings, and especially the paintings of the 1940s, function like *tjurunga*, those objects of painted or inscribed wood or stone that do not just embody totemic beings, but in some sense *are* those beings. In the same way, a Namatjira painting can be representational of a landscape, an actual simulacrum of it and also embody equivocal presences that resemble – and perhaps are – totemic beings who are neither representations nor simulacra but partake of the essence.

The point can be made clearer from a consideration of some of the paintings that were shown in Melbourne in his third one-man show in 1944; these were works reserved by Battarbee from casual sale precisely for this purpose. That exhibition featured at least eight paintings of trees, mostly ghost gums, and a similar number of pictures of the rocky faces of bluffs or gorges. *The Ghost Gum of*

Palm Valley, dated 1942, is a startlingly anthropomorphic picture of a twin-trunked tree before a landscape that features one of the Palm Valley monoliths recognisable from other paintings. The tree is set slightly to the left of frame and is, as it were, truncated: you cannot see its top branches and most of the foliage is also absent. However the two divisions of the trunk recall legs in the air and the placing of a genital slit below a dark, wrinkled hole at the groin where they meet irresistibly reinforces this analogy; while, on the right hand fork, not far up, a bole that resembles the glans of a penis protrudes from the wood as if in the process of erection. The tree, then, is not just anthropomorphic but hermaphroditic as well: a totem of sexual potency in which both male and female genitalia appear.

Particular trees were considered to be living, indeed timeless entities, among the Arrernte; the death of an individual tree did not interrupt its being, which would migrate to a nearby sapling and so continue its existence. Trees were also, in the metamorphosed form of *tnatantja* poles – which were constructed out of actual trees – intermediary between earth and sky. In this sense they were both living creatures and beings that partook of eternity. Namatjira's trees, and especially those he made in the 1940s, embody human forms, sometimes as single individuals, sometimes as groups of people erotically or fatally or tragically entwined together, sometimes as body parts that inevitably recall the manifold wounds suffered by the Arrernte during the enforced colonisation of their land. And, insofar as they take human form, they are also pictures of ancestors, whether or not those ancestors can be named or otherwise identified.

In the same 1944 Melbourne show there were a number of remarkable paintings of rock faces: particularly because of the way Namatjira has framed the works in what might be called extra close up. One, *The Fish Hole, Jay Creek*, has water at the base but no sky at all; another, *Quarraitnama, Finke River*, shows a more generous firmament above the red-orange complexity of the bluff at Glen Helen otherwise known as the Organ Pipes. An undated third lies somewhere in between: there is a blue triangle of sky in the top left of the image, which is otherwise made up, in the foreground, of the complexities of a rock-face and in the mid-ground a fall of scree, with another rock-face behind that; while at the base of the picture lies the limpid mystery of a pool of still dark water.

In this painting the rocky cliff in the foreground reveals a series of stepped-down faces in profile, like the generations of men succeeding one another through the years. You can count these generations: there are four, but within those four are other, subsidiary beings, just as within any predominant family there will be subsidiary groupings. These faces in profile are indistinct, anonymous, archetypal, as if their real meaning is to be found, not in any individual features they may possess, but in their relationship with each other; while above and beyond them, behind the fall of scree like jets of blood, another figure, unmistakably European, is picked out in profile along the reddish cliff: a harbinger of the eclipse of generations.

The Organ Pipes are in Alice Springs; the cliff painting left these shores some time ago and, mis-titled *Hammersley Gorge*, is now in a private collection in England; the whereabouts of *The Ghost Gum at Palm Valley* is unknown but it is likely still in Australia. It was bought by Charles Mountford and is reproduced in his book, *The Art of Albert Namatjira*, published by the Bread and Cheese Club in Melbourne in 1944. Mountford first encountered Namatjira in Palm Valley in 1942: *He was seated with his companions around a fire. It was just an ordinary native camp, such as I have seen many hundreds of times – a low windbreak of boughs, a line of smouldering fires with hollows between them where the men had slept the night before, spears and shields leaning against the bushes and pieces of cooked euro meat in the forks of trees nearby...from the low windbreak Albert took a parcel of beautiful water colours, wrapped in a clean cloth, to show me...no studio whatever, and only the simplest of equipment: a box of watercolours, a bundle of brushes tied up with string, a parcel of drawing-paper wrapped in clean linen. That was all.*

Charles Mountford was at this time fifty-two years old and, on leave from his job with the post office, studying Arrernte *tjurunga* under the auspices of the Board of Aboriginal Research and the University of Adelaide. He was an excellent photographer, using both colour and black and white, and on this expedition carried with him a movie camera with which he made a film, his second, completed under the title *Brown Men and Red Sand*, which is also what he called the book of his travels published in 1948.

Mountford was the son of farming folk from Peterborough, South Australia, who helped his father, also Charles, on the farm from the age of ten. He was mechanically-minded and, when the family moved to Adelaide, worked as a tram conductor while taking correspondence courses in mechanics and engineering at the South Australian School of Mines and Industries; he became an electrical mechanic with the Municipal Tramways Trust before, in 1913, joining the Postmaster-General's Department.

In 1920 Mountford was promoted and sent to Darwin as senior mechanic in the Post Office and it was here that he first became interested in Aboriginal people. His lodgings were near the famous – or notorious – Kahlin Compound and he used to visit in his leisure time, hearing the stories the men told and attending some of their ceremonies; in later life he profoundly regretted not having documented these early encounters: some of what he observed was unique, unrepeatable and is now lost.

In 1925 the death of his first wife, with whom he had two children, caused a crisis and Mountford returned to the family farm at Peterborough where, with his father, he began to record

Aboriginal rock carvings in the local area. In 1926, with Norman Tindale of the South Australian Museum, he published a paper on these rock engravings and, the same year, father and son became foundation members of the Anthropological Society of South Australia. This became his life's work: the seeking out and recording of the artistic practices of Aboriginal peoples, most often, but not always, those of the central desert. He continued working as a public servant until his retirement in 1955; his prodigious anthropological and art recording activities until that time were all accomplished while on unpaid leave or during holidays.

Mountford's 1942 meeting with Namatjira was not a chance encounter. His friend and colleague, Harold Sheard, had commissioned him to buy four of Albert's paintings and he subsequently purchased two more for himself. Then, on Mountford's second visit to Albert's camp, something unprecedented occurred: *He knew that I was collecting tjurunga drawings and offered to make one for me of his own totemic area, which is about two miles up the gorge. It is a yelka nut totem place and this was the subject of the myth he drew...in the primitive symbols...inherited from his mother.* Albert's crayon drawing of the design was reproduced, with a detailed explanation of its symbolism, in black and white in Mountford's book: *all the objects shown in this drawing were later miraculously transformed into the curiously marked rocks that can be seen today at this place.*

There are several points of interest here. Mountford was an experienced collector of Indigenous art who had, since the 1930s and perhaps earlier, always travelled with paper and crayon which he would offer to people he met in order that they might set down their traditional designs. In this sense what he was doing with Namatjira was no different to what he had done previously with many others. As far as *tjurunga* themselves were concerned, they had been an item of trade between Europeans and Arrernte for the whole of the century thus far and, as objects for sale, their secret-sacred status had been severely if not completely compromised. Most *tjurunga* offered for sale were as a matter of course accompanied by some version, however vestigial, of the story represented in the designs upon them. Nevertheless, Namatjira's act in communicating the yelka nut design to Mountford has usually been seen as profoundly transgressive.

His motivation for doing so is unclear: was he simply helping Mountford with his research? Was he offering something in return for the sale of six works at one time? Or was he making another kind of statement, of ownership of, or at least managerial rights over, the country they were in? He wasn't alone in Palm Valley and there is no suggestion that his companions, whoever they were, objected to what he was doing or that he faced sanctions for revealing the designs. All the indications are that Namatjira felt that he had a perfect right to give the knowledge – which may not of course have been the whole story – that he did to Mountford.

It has to be said that, in the literature, most of the criticism of Namatjira's alleged transgression has come, not from his own people, but from European commentators; it's also the case that Mountford, later in his career, was responsible for at least two violent controversies as a result of his own transgressions. He would twice publish material deemed unsuitable, by its traditional custodians, for wide circulation. One of those controversies involved his magnum opus, his *Nomads of the Australian Desert* (1976), which contained images of restricted Aboriginal subjects and was withdrawn from sale soon after publication and is now extremely rare. The other came about as a result of his inclusion of footage of secret-sacred ceremonies in the documentary film he would make about Namatjira for the Department of Information in the immediate post-war years; but before the film came the book.

Its publisher, the Bread and Cheese Club, was inaugurated in Melbourne in June 1938 as an all-male fellowship devoted to *Mateship, Art and Letters*; or, in another formulation, *to serve literature, luminous conversation and good fellowship*. Over the twenty years of its existence it issued around forty books as well as its own magazine, *Bohemia*. Poet John Shaw Neilson, prose writer Miles Franklin, and Tom Collins also known as Joseph Furphy were among those honoured. In 1943 the club brought out Bob Croll's and Charles Barrett's *Art of the Australian Aboriginal* and Mountford's *The Art of Albert Namatjira* formed a kind of sequel to that. Melbourne book collector JK Moir, the Knight Grand Cheese, was the central figure in the club and Mountford's book includes a facsimile of a dedication to him hand-written in Arrernte by Albert: *Aa ngana Dankilama Alnamea* it reads. *I thank you sincerely.*

A 1942 photograph of Namatjira by Mountford, presumably taken at Palm Valley, is reproduced opposite the title page. He is in extra close-up and half profile, wearing an open-necked shirt with a frayed collar and a hat that looks like a black turban; his eyes are hooded, unseen, and the overall effect is of some desert, not necessarily Aboriginal, wise man. Other photographs in the book show a full-faced, rather plump, young-looking forty year-old; in one he is sitting on the ground painting, with his paper balanced on his drawn-up knees and a dog lying companionably at his feet. Mountford's short, biographical account of Namatjira's coming-to-be as a painter is introduced by Hon Trencherman Bob Croll, who on the first page quotes an audacious speculation from the *Antiquity of Man* by Sir Arthur Keith: *Of all the races of mankind alive, the aboriginal race of Australia is the only one which, in my opinion, would serve as a common ancestor for all modern races...*[including] *the fair-haired native of north-west Europe.*

There are ten watercolours reproduced in the book, all but one already in private hands – Croll, Duguid, Mountford, Sheard,

Strehlow; the exception is the work bought by the Adelaide Gallery in 1939. Also featured is some children's art: a pencil drawing of a dog chasing kangaroos drawn by Enos Namatjira, another by Clod (Claude Pannka) of horses being mustered. One of the photographs shows Albert in the act of drawing the totemic design of his family group; the actual drawing is also reproduced; a third shows the veritable *churinga of the yelka nut totem place of Nuamana in Palm Valley...the personal property of Namatjira's family*. It is an oval stone incised with concentric designs which are connected each to each by lines like the spokes of multi-valent wheels.

The presentation of Albert Namatjira as an un-alienated tribal Aboriginal was emphasised by the book's dust jacket which showed a group of naked, bearded, painted men gathered around a *tnatantja* pole before a desert landscape and inside a decorative border made up of woomera, boomerangs, bull-roarers and *tjurunga*; the piece is signed, prominently, *Albert Namatjira* in the bottom right-hand corner. Daniel Thomas suggests that this cover design, which could be seen as both transgressive and a perpetuation of kitsch stereotypes, might in fact constitute a land-rights claim. Whatever it may have been, the book itself was extremely popular. It went through five editions between 1944 and 1949 and two more in the 1950s; all up about 20,000 copies were sold. Through its agency both the name Albert Namatjira and the way his art looked in reproduction became familiar to thousands who had never seen, and never would see, any of his actual works.

This somewhat schizoid marketing of Namatjira, with the apparently conventional, European-style watercolours wrapped around with images of the archaic, was not just successful, it was in accord with a vogue for the primitive that already possessed a respectable genealogy, in Australia as elsewhere. European modernism espoused tribal and prehistoric art from the beginning of the twentieth century; the Dadaists and Surrealists, likewise: three Arrernte songs, collected by Carl Strehlow, had been translated into French and sung by Tristan Tzara at the Cabaret Voltaire in Zurich in 1917 as part of his cycle *Poèmes Nègres*, later published in the journal *Dada*.

There had been a major exhibition of Australian Aboriginal Art in Melbourne in 1929, to which two Arrernte men, Jack Noorywauke and Stan Loycurrie, had gone and performed ceremonial dances, built *mia mia*, made tools. The exhibition was popular, the opening so crowded it was difficult to move amongst the press of people. Anthropologist AP Elkin gave the opening address, in which he said it was a chance to explore the psychic as well as the physical condition of primitive man and thereby to discover the true motive underlying his art. The catalogue cover doesn't do much to advance this ambitious agenda: it shows a naked man, sitting and drawing animal figures onto a piece of bark propped up against a tree trunk before him.

Namatjira exhibited in a group show of Aboriginal art at the Lower Town Hall in Melbourne in 1938; and his work was recognised as an example of contemporary Indigenous art in anthropologist Leonhard Adam's 1940 book *Primitive Art*; but the higher echelons of the art world denigrated when they did not ignore him. He was not, for instance, represented in the *Exhibition of Australian Aboriginal Art and its Applications* organised by Frederick McCarthy at the Australian Museum and held in 1941 in the exhibition gallery at the Sydney department store, David Jones.

The David Jones exhibition was arranged in three groups – one showing the art of the Aboriginals, one demonstrating the application of Aboriginal motifs in such media as pottery and fabrics, and one including the works of a number of artists illustrating Aboriginal life. In other words, it included Aboriginal paintings and artefacts alongside examples of European arts and crafts that showed some influence from, or connection with, Indigenous styles; but, with the notable exception of Margaret Preston, the works of art by Europeans were depictions of Aboriginal people or subjects rather than emulations of their style. This exhibition was also popular; it ran for eleven days and an estimated 3,000 people saw it.

Also in 1941, under the auspices of the Carnegie Foundation, an exhibition of Australian art toured the United States and Canada. It was constructed to show a national art tradition that began, prehistorically, with bark paintings and then progressed on to the work of contemporary white artists, represented by their more overtly 'Aboriginal' work; Hans Heysen, Arthur Murch and Margaret Preston were all included and Preston contributed a catalogue essay on Aboriginal art *that was advanced in its thinking about primitive art, emphasising its contemporary practice and complexity... 'every tribe has its own characteristic of expression'.* She did not however mention Namatjira in this essay, nor did she do so in any of her other writings; nor was his work included in the Carnegie show. He was unassimilable; neither authentically primitive, typically Aboriginal, or recognisably contemporary.

But still eminently saleable. His April 1944 exhibition of thirty-eight paintings at the Myer Mural Hall in Bourke Street, Melbourne was, like his two previous one-man shows, a sell-out; as was his first show in Sydney, in March 1945, of forty-four works at the Fine Arts Exhibition Gallery at another department store, Anthony Hordern's; which netted him about £1,000 including several international sales. The Melbourne show was opened by Mr AW Cole, MP and in Sydney the now Professor AP Elkin did the honours. Entry was by donation of a silver coin and the money thereby raised went to the Red Cross. Between these two openings Namatjira became the first Aboriginal to be given an entry in *Who's Who*; it was pro forma, a bare biographical outline, but included this unbecoming remark, apparently from Pastor Albrecht: *is happiest if sitting in sand or around a campfire playing marbles like others of his tribe.*

In fact, rather than walking about in the bush, in 1945 Albert was buying a car and building a house. It was a two room cottage with provision for the addition of more rooms in the future, built on land a few kilometres from the Mission. Construction was out of blocks of local sandstone, which Albert himself cut into bricks;

the walls were plastered with cement then white-washed; and the timbered roof clad with corrugated iron. A contractor was employed to sink a bore, run water pipes to the house and erect a windmill. Within brushwood fences, flower and vegetable gardens were established. One of Namatjira's most poignant and unusual paintings shows a glimpse of the roof of this house nestled between round green hills, with the red cliffs at the entrance to Palm Valley beyond: a somehow heartbreaking picture of home.

Albert had previously, in 1944, when the military presence in Alice Springs was beginning to decline, asked the Mission for permission to buy a truck but this had been refused; now, with the war over and vast amounts of military hardware being disposed of, the same request was granted and Pastor Gross on his behalf bought a thirty hundredweight Chevrolet truck for £140 at an Army Disposal sale in Alice Springs, the first of a number of vehicles Albert would own. He learned to drive it and so did his sons. He had always been a big man, with a tendency to put on weight when living a sedentary life; and at times weighed over eighteen stone, making journeys on camel-back arduous and uncomfortable. Now, he could go on painting trips by truck.

According to Joyce Batty, Namatjira in the war years lived largely independently of the Mission, visiting only when he needed supplies, had work to drop off or a meeting of his art committee to attend; since 1943 he had been paying a commission of ten per cent on all sales. Relations with Mission staff were cordial but not necessarily close; however, he made a point of attending church if he was at Hermannsburg on a Sunday because he loved to sing.

Rex Battarbee was by now effectively himself one of the Mission staff, with responsibilities far beyond the work he did as Albert's de facto agent and dealer; in mid-1945, for instance, he spent a month at Haasts Bluff distributing sulphanilamide tablets to those suffering from the eye disease, trachoma. And his diaries of the war years are full of detail of numbers and movements of stock: almost as if he had at last become the farmer he had wanted to be.

Rex had fallen ill in 1944 and while he was hospitalised Albert wrote to him: *Dear Mr Rex Battarbee, I am sorry to hear your in bed, I am still rememberens your all my tribe would forget your in my prayer thank God our father in haven.* There are other similar letters, usually in black ink in running writing on lined note-paper; often they conclude, like one written in January 1946, when Rex was down south visiting family in the aftermath of his sister Florinda's death on Boxing Day 1945, with requests for materials: *and another thing I am short a painting bruches can you find 2 painting bruches for me art* [hard?] *to get now from Sydney this time...I am your friend Mr Albert Namatjira.*

Also in 1944, at Easter, Battarbee had taken his best athletes, including Eli Rubuntja and Edwin Pareroultja, into Alice Springs to compete in the annual sports day events. Edwin Pareroultja, who spent hours practising leaping the stockyard rails, was an exceptional high-jumper; Eli Rubuntja excelled at the long-jump, the hop-step-and-jump and in the sprint events. It was the first time Aboriginals had competed in any sporting fixture in Alice Springs and both young men came home with prize money. Later, controversially, Battarbee would take Edwin and Eli to Victoria to compete in Australia's most famous foot race, the Stawell Gift.

He was a far more confident man than he had once been and when Daryl Lindsay, Director of the Melbourne National Gallery and himself a watercolour painter, publically criticised Namatjira, Battarbee leapt to his defence. Lindsay said he thought Namatjira's art was too Westernised; he had abandoned his own, allegedly authentic Indigenous art tradition in favour of a second-hand European one; his works had little to commend them apart from the superficial technical ability they showed and some slight degree of topographical interest.

Battarbee's response was robust: *The outlook of 90 percent of Australians was to keep the black man where he was,* he wrote. *White men could be influenced by any art school in the world so why shouldn't the black man. When Australian painters adopted French styles, no-one criticised them for doing this. Therefore his highbrow critics would be well advised to regard Namatjira as a watercolourist and not an aborigine.*

The *Sunday Sun & Guardian* agreed: *Mr Albert Namatjira has had to submit to some impertinences of criticism à la mode because he is an aboriginal,* the paper wrote. *But all the bunkum showered upon our Aranda artist need not disturb him. The public which prefers pictorial observation and good technique in its pictures has so far responded by buying Albert Namatjira's paintings. The truth is that Mr Namatjira's landscapings of Central Australia are convincing because they represent the ranges and plains as the aboriginal as well as the white man sees them and record them with a competence that infuriates the critics...*[he] *is a very good artist indeed.*

This is astute, especially in its perception that Namatjira painted landscapes the way they were seen by the Aboriginal as well as the white man; even if the writer meant, as he may have done, that there was no difference between the two views. That there *was* a difference no one can any longer doubt; sixty years ago, moreover, it was unlikely that anyone would have said that Battarbee's painting, superficially so like Namatjira's, represented an Aboriginal view of the land.

Nevertheless the forces unleashed by Namatjira's sudden and excessive fame were powerful and unpredictable; so much so that it became apparent that in the commonality the two men possessed as artists and as men, and in the apparently harmonious, if distant, relationship between Namatjira and the Lutherans on the Mission, there were fault lines which the pressure of events over the next few years would force to shift – seismically and, as it turned out, irrevocably.

7. High National Policy

When, in the middle of July 1946, Charles Mountford went out to Hermannsburg to seek approvals for the film he was making for the Department of Information in Canberra, neither Battarbee nor Namatjira was there. *I had quite a job to find Namatjira,* Mountford wrote to the Director-General, EG Bonney. *With the aid of his newly acquired truck, he had forced a track into the rough gorges of the MacDonnells, and we tried to follow his wheel marks in a utility truck, finally getting well and truly bogged in a sandy creek. We walked the rest. Namatjira is willing to help, he really is a nice chap.* Mountford had to make *another 80 mile journey over foul tracks* to locate Battarbee, who was out at Areyonga painting; like Albert, Rex agreed to be involved. Mountford, who'd already secured the co-operation of Pastor Albrecht, made arrangements for both men to rendezvous with the crew at the Mission on 28 July.

It was to be a small, three-man unit: Mountford himself; Lee Robinson, a nascent writer–director, later producer, formerly of the Military History branch of the Army, recently de-mobbed, *whose work…reflected a rapidly growing understanding of the essentials of film production*; and Anglo-Swedish photographer Axel Poignant as both

stills and movie cameraman. From the outset the demarcation of roles between Mountford and Robinson was unclear and this in time led to conflict. *Mountford was on the picture for two, three weeks*, Robinson recalled, *and we were on it for three to four months*.

Mountford was however the more experienced film-maker and in the early stages of the planning it was intended that Robinson work under his guidance. In the event, and after some acrimonious exchanges, ex-pat Canadian Ralph Foster, the Film Commissioner, who was never on set, was credited as Producer–Director, Mountford as Associate Producer and Robinson as Assistant Director: a list of credits that is wrong in almost every particular.

Quite whose idea the movie was in the first place is unclear but it may have been Foster's, who was certainly a film-maker; insofar as the Ministry of Information was concerned the motivation seems to have been to take advantage of Namatjira's potential to publicise, both at home and abroad, what could be represented as an outstanding success of the Commonwealth Government's Aboriginal policies. Bonney on 9 July wrote to Foster at the Sydney office of the National Film Board that *high national policy is involved in any film approach to so delicate a topic as the Australian aborigine. Mr Mountford, having lived among these natives, is a safe man.* Foster in his reply acknowledged that he shared Bonney's *concern over the dangers of exploiting the curiosity value of Australia's aborigines.*

Mountford was more than safe; he was a rising star who had just made two successful trips to the United States during which he showed his films and gave lectures on 'primitive man'. In the course of the first, in early 1945, after a lecture–screening at the Cosmo Club in Philadelphia, one of Mountford's sponsors, Melville Grosvenor, suggested that he apply for a grant from the National Geographic Society to undertake ethnological research in Australia. By May, before the tour was completed, the application had been written, tendered and the proposal accepted. *It is certainly a big thing*, Mountford wrote, with some understatement, in his diary – *the first National Geographic expedition to Australia.*

Mountford's second American trip took place over seven months in late 1945 and early 1946; it was a national tour that began in Milwaukee and concluded in Santa Barbara, visiting both coasts as well as the mid-west; the thirty-nine events drew a total of around 40,000 people. Afterwards Mountford returned to Australia by ship, leaving San Francisco on the *Mariposa* on 13 May. Pre-production for *Namatjira the Painter* had already begun and, concurrently, Mountford was also organising the far bigger, far more complex, National Geographic Expedition. After a great deal of meticulous planning, and several setbacks, caused either by bureaucratic meddling or obstruction from vested interests within the Australian anthropological community, the expedition to Arnhem Land went ahead in 1948.

It's no wonder that, during the making of the Namatjira film, Mountford sometimes seemed distracted and eventually fell ill and had to return to Adelaide; but Robinson's recall of his presence on the set for just two or three weeks is parsimonious. Mountford was still there on 19 August, when he was anticipating taking over the camera work because Poignant had contracted sandy blight (conjunctivitis) and had to be hospitalised in Alice Springs.

The major and most difficult part of the film is complete, Mountford wrote to Bonney. *We only have now to photograph the primitive people and I can do that.* The basic problem might have been generational: *Mountford told us nothing!* Lee Robinson recalled: *Alex and I got off on the wrong foot...he was a much older man. He was the technical advisor on aboriginal matters. Mountford knew a bit about aborigines. The aborigines themselves felt he tended to make up what he didn't know.*

There were other problems. Albrecht wrote that the *Mountford Film Party has gone to Areyonga. We shall be pleased to have them off our district again. The other two men he has with him are quite nice people, but from occasional remarks made to Battarbee, he is a snake in the grass...his attitude is definitely antichristian and that explains everything.* Battarbee thought the same: *I hardly believe Mr Mountford is a suitable person to make a film of these men...he has shown little consideration for the natives...Albert complains about the time lost quite apart from the substantial quantities of petrol he has used travelling to places where Mr Mountford wanted to photograph...his criticism and antagonism to the mission and the work they are doing has not been at all helpful.*

Helene Burns, Pastor Albrecht's daughter, some years later offered another perspective on these antagonisms. *The underlying factor,* she said, *was Ted Strehlow who was there as well and he couldn't tolerate Mountford...and poor old Dad was the meat in the sandwich because Ted wanted exclusive rights to any filming because he was the Archangel Gabriel, wasn't he? And he painted Mountford as black as you could get. Strehlow spoke first to Rex and then to Dad and got their backs up, and nobody looked beyond it.*

Robinson and Poignant were working on several projects

concurrently: by 11 November Robinson estimated they had material for four 16mm colour films, with footage that included two corroborees, a newsreel item about the traditional Koporilya Day celebrations, coverage of an election campaign in Darwin, scenic shots for a Northern Territory tourism promotion called *Top End* and another newsreel item about Mirror Finish Mica, a mining enterprise east of Alice Springs.

The Namatjira film, shot in Kodachrome, was sent to Melbourne to be processed and then to Sydney to be edited; a commentary was written and comprehensively vetted before being approved by the Department of Information; an orchestral score was composed by J McKerras and recorded using a forty-piece orchestra. It was, wrote Minister of Information Arthur Calwell, *one of the most costly ventures the Department has ever undertaken.*

Despite discussions with MGM, 20th Century Fox and Warner Brothers, American sales did not eventuate; the presence of naked men in the film was a problem. There was however a theatrical release in Australia, with a 35mm blow-up of *Namatjira the Painter* opening before the Howard Hughes film *The Outlaw* at the State Theatre in Sydney and going on to have a long run. *It played all over the place*, said Lee Robinson. *It was the first post war documentary to go out into theatrical release.*

When it played in Alice Springs there was all hell to pay because there were a lot of aborigines in the audience and when the segment with the corroboree came on, men began belting up women and knocking them unconscious with anything they could find because it was sacred material. Robinson continues: *The fault was not ours. Alex and I had permission to use an emu dance. Mountford...made the decision to use another that we had filmed, the Wild Dog corroboree, which was very sacred.*

Ralph Foster was replaced as Commissioner halfway through the filming, allegedly because the Prime Minister, Ben Chifley, refused to renew the contract of a man who was earning more money than he was; he went back to Canada and later worked for the United Nations. Subsequently both Foster and his replacement, his own nominee, Englishman Stanley Hawes, were investigated by the Australian Security Intelligence Organisation on the suspicion that they were communists. But Foster was that rare thing, in Lee Robinson's words, *a visionary*, and responsible for making a timely, innovative, controversial and fascinating documentary film.

Unfortunately it was re-cut – mutilated might say it better – in the early 1970s. The score was excised completely, the secret–sacred material too; what survives seems disconnected and this is emphasised by the fact that neither Battarbee nor Namatjira speaks; it is all silent action. Nevertheless it remains a valuable document, largely because of the on-screen presences: Albert's massive, stoic calm; Battarbee's tensile, lean grace of person; shots of Namatjira's family accompanying him on a painting expedition; a priceless glimpse of his father Jonathon amongst those crowding in to the school house to see an exhibition of paintings.

Two days after Battarbee, Namatjira and the crew met at Hermannsburg to begin filming, solicitor John Reed, from the Melbourne office of the Contemporary Art Society of Australia, wrote to Minister Calwell. Reed, who with his wife Sunday was a committed patron of the arts and a particular sponsor of Sidney Nolan, at that very time painting his Ned Kelly paintings on the dining room floor of the Reeds' country house at Heide, had seen a press release announcing the making of *Namatjira the Painter*. He was furious.

In the opinion of myself and of many artists and others deeply interested in art in the country, he wrote, *the use and publicising of the talents of this particular aboriginal…has been a serious dis-service to the cause of the development of culture in this country. In the art of the Australian aboriginal we have a genuine cultural field of considerable richness and value...the so-called 'art' of Namatjira...has however nothing to do with aboriginal art but is only the clever aping of an alien art form.*

Reed went on to say that any Namatjira film would be *definitely harmful locally* and, overseas, *detrimental advertising for Australia.* On the other hand, he continued, *a documentary film covering the true artistic activities of the aboriginals would be of inestimable value both here and abroad.* Reed's letter was put before the National Film Board but no action was taken. A reply came from the Minister's office on 19 August and, in early October, Reed again wrote to Calwell. The tone of this second letter is more conciliatory, no doubt because the Film Board had declared an intention in future projects to publicise other aspects of Australian painting and suggested that Reed might like to act as an adviser to such projects; but he cannot entirely leave the subject of Namatjira behind: *the painting he is doing is entirely false to his own culture and is merely a clever aping of a completely different one.*

Reed must have been aware that his efforts to prevent the making of the film would prove futile; whether he had read Battarbee's robust defence of Namatjira against similar attacks is unknown; had he been aware that the crew had already begun shooting a second film, this time dealing with the activities, both athletic and artistic, of the three Pareroultja brothers, he might have been less incensed. The footage for this film, which was shot but never edited, disappeared some time after the negatives were sent to Sydney and has not been found again; but the paintings of the Pareroultja brothers, always less naturalistic than Namatjira's, proved to be more popular with those espousing the cause of modernist painting in Australia: the Pareroultjas were perhaps not so obvious in their aping of alien forms.

This arcane debate between the virtues of Australian modernism, with its love of primitivism, and the apparently mimetic art of the

burgeoning Hermannsburg School, meant very little, if anything, to Albert who, in the recollection of Lee Robinson, had *a little concrete home just out from the mission. The only time that he spent in it was when he was painting, he would lock himself away in there for hours and paint Mt Sonder twenty, thirty miles away...and you could take that painting back to where it was supposed to be painted from and compare it...and every tree tussock or blade of grass seems to be in the right place. He had this wonderful capacity to totally memorise every aspect of country.*

The film mimicked this process: *We shot Albert painting – and then later revisited and shot what he was painting, days or weeks later. As far as possible we shot early morning and late afternoon...Albert was such an intelligent person that you simply had to explain the scene and the reason for the scene – and leave him to it.* Robinson continues, describing the way Albert conceived a painting: *He framed the view with his hands like a modern cameraman – he squared it off – decided what the start and finish of his ends were going to be – how high he would take his sky – and from where he would take his foreground. Once he had that he could go somewhere else and paint it...it seemed to be a natural thing with him.*

The analogy with the way a film- or camera-person works is explicit and can be traced back to Battarbee's own methodology. Rex had been taking black and white photographs with his Pocket Kodak No 1 folding camera at least since 1928 and, as mentioned, in the late 1930s taught Albert how to photograph and develop film. Battarbee was a fine photographer who used the medium not just to record people he met and things that happened, but as a means of documenting his painting as well; now, in the immediate post-war years, he began experimenting with colour film. Philip Jones writes *he soon became proficient with it. He visited several of his favourite painting sites...securing photographic proof of his own artistry... Battarbee used the colour film to convince the remaining sceptics who questioned the vivid colours in his paintings.*

The relationship of the painting of both Battarbee and Namatjira to photography serves to clarify Reed's disdain: it was the apparent verisimilitude of Namatjira's work that he objected to, and its assumed debt to what was already considered, in avant-garde circles, an out-moded genre: that is, realism, the landscape tradition and its attendant commitment to a nationalist agenda. If, however, the alien art form that Namatjira was allegedly aping was indeed film, what then? His ready adaptation to the medium, as attested by Lee Robinson, and his long acquaintance, through Battarbee, with the aesthetics and mechanics of stills photography, suggest an entirely different perspective: rather than an imitator of a defunct tradition, Namatjira was an innovator, using techniques derived principally (but not only) from photography to frame aspects of the landscape that allowed him to re-present it in a way not seen before.

For example, some of the paintings from his 1946 one-man show at the Royal South Australian Society of Arts Gallery in

Adelaide, opened by Alick Downer, lawyer, grazier, former prisoner at Changi and future Minister of Immigration, suggest a filmic perspective upon the landscape. *Grass trees at Gosses Bluff* (1945) shows four of the plants, actually a member of the lily family, with their flower spikes black and seeding, like a group of dancers before the distant walls of the ancient crater. The framing is exquisite: the tallest of the grass trees, second from left, rises from its roots in the red earth the height of the picture so that its spike just touches the top of the sky and its skirt falls gracefully before the blue that takes up two thirds of the painting; while the three smaller trees stand attendant on either hand and the littlest, which has not yet flowered, starts up in the right foreground like a growing child. In the middle distance other grass trees can be seen, members of different families of the same tribe.

There is nothing explicit in the symbolism of the picture – and yet the figures of the grass trees remain powerfully anthropomorphic. Namatjira's paintings of palm trees, *arrangkeye*, have a similar presence: as if a preternatural degree of verisimilitude should reveal something more than mere resemblance. A second work from the 1946 Adelaide show, *Palm Valley, James Range* (1945) shows a stand of palms to right of frame, another tribal family, while protruding into the picture from the left is a massive, purple-red rock outcrop like an ancestral lizard-being in profile. Once again, with great subtlety, Namatjira has managed simultaneously to reveal and conceal entities within what otherwise appears to be a plain scenic view. And as with the grass trees, framing is all.

In 1951 Rex wrote that although he had been out with Albert on later painting trips he had *never given him lessons because I felt that he already knew enough and I wanted him to show something of his own outlook and personality in his work.* He took the same approach with younger painters like the Pareroultja brothers, Richard

Moketarinja and Henoch Raberaba; while Albert continued to offer practical advice to his three elder sons Enos, Oscar and Ewald and his classificatory uncle Walter Ebatarinja. Later his younger sons Keith and Maurice would also become fine painters.

Rex's and Albert's teaching activities during the latter part of the war and in the immediate post-war years laid the foundations of the Hermannsburg School of watercolour painters, the first tangible sign of the emergence of which was an exhibition in Melbourne by Edwin Pareroultja towards the end of 1946. Edwin had been painting for just three years at that point and Battarbee mentions that his tuition, such as it was, simply consisted on the one hand of the reiterated advice not to copy Namatjira, and on the other, a single lesson about how to keep his washes clean. Edwin Pareroultja's first ever painting, a stark, intense, abstracted vision of Mt Sonder, was chosen for the cover of Battarbee's book *Modern Australian Aboriginal Art* (1951); *the picture,* he wrote, *is remarkable for its strong drawing and colouring, although it is really only in three primary colours.*

At Edwin's show in Melbourne's Athenaeum in November 1946 forty paintings were snapped up on the first afternoon and within three days the entire fifty pictures had sold, netting him over £400; among the buyers were the Melbourne National Gallery, who were never, while he lived, to buy a Namatjira painting. At the same time Albert's first show in Perth also sold well and he received a cheque for just under £1,000. These were large amounts of money and their receipt caused concern on the Mission. *More and more of our men take to painting,* Albrecht wrote, *the latest being Henoch* [Raberaba]. *Walter* [Ebatarinja] *sent 30 pounds to the bank the other day...we all regret that Albert has so much freedom with his money, which enables him to feed more and more loafers.* It wasn't unusual for Albert to take ten or twelve people in his truck into Alice Springs to go shopping or to the movies.

Rex had a different attitude to worldly matters, taking Edwin via Adelaide to Melbourne for the opening of his exhibition and entering him in the Stawell Gift in 1946; they stayed with Rex's cousins, Mr and Mrs JK Moreton, at Lake Bolac for six weeks but unfortunately Edwin injured his leg a week before the race and broke down during it. His companion Eli Rubuntja was more successful, running six times for three firsts and three seconds. Both men went on to compete at a second meeting in Bendigo before returning to Hermannsburg. *Rex Battarbee take me that exhibition, enjoyed that*, Edwin recalled in 1984. *Have a look your exhibition, with the frame…I was really happy that time. Everybody come up and shake my hand, paper, pencil, sign my name.*

Albrecht however was not impressed and told Rex that a request for a repeat performance at the Stawell Gift the following year was unlikely to be granted by the Department of Native Affairs. *He was very bitter when I told him he had little chance of getting permission*, the Pastor wrote to his superior in Adelaide. Adverse publicity seems to have been the reason behind this lack of support. Newspapers had sensationalised the matter with headlines such as: *Aborigines train at secret camp! Aborigine sprinters put on weight! Native runners shy but not nervous!* and Albrecht, as always, was extremely sensitive to any publicity about the Mission that might have negative consequences.

Both Albert and Rex earned well in the war and in the immediate post-war period but the effects upon them were very different. One result for Albert was that, now he had a truck, he tended to drive to places to which he would once have walked or ridden. Always a big man, his weight blew out, with a concomitant decline in his health. In March 1947, he complained of chest pains and was admitted to Alice Springs hospital for observation. Angina pectoris was diagnosed and he was advised it was imperative that he lose some weight. Leaving the truck behind, but taking Rubina with him, Albert went bush, living for some months on kangaroo and goanna, witchetty grubs and honey ants; when they returned he was slimmer, fitter and said he felt much better.

Another consequence of his wealth and fame was that the Tax Office became interested in him; he received a demand for back taxes on his income to the amount of £417. The Namatjira Council on the Mission objected, pointing out that Albert was not a citizen of Australia but, like all so-called full-bloods, a ward of the state: why then should he pay tax? The matter went so far as to be debated in Federal Parliament but the assessment of monies owing stood and Namatjira, who was selling out at least one and sometimes two shows a year in the cities, in the end wrote out a cheque for the full amount.

Rex's job, and therefore his salary, terminated in October 1945, ending the only substantial period he spent in regular paid employment since his service in the AIF; he would remain self-employed for the rest of his life, continuing to take commissions for commercial art when and if they became available or necessary. Both production and sales of his art had dipped during the war years but, he records, a year later in October 1946 he had completed thirty-eight watercolours. The progressive sub-division and sale, by Rex's uncle David, brother of his mother Mary, of the family farm in Warrnambool had over the years helped support George and Mary's children; in 1945 Rex used some of his money to buy land on the eastern bank of the Todd River in Alice Springs. By mid-1947 he was impatiently awaiting the arrival of his house plans so he could forward them on to the builder, a Mr Bennett, who sourced some of the concrete he used from supplies meant for the Rocket Range then being built at Woomera. There were war shortages; other materials were obtained from Pastor Albrecht.

Modernist architect Jack Cheesman was contracted to design the house, which was to double as an art gallery and included a flat, rooftop studio where Rex could paint *en plein air*. Cheesman was educated in Adelaide and studied in New York between 1929–31, where he observed the construction of the Empire State Building; then spent a period travelling in Europe before returning to Adelaide. He was innovative and up-to-date, a pioneer, and his own 1949 residence at Port Noarlunga was *energy efficient,* [with] *low thermal inertia, cross ventilations, cool in summer, solar gains in winter.* Rex's house was the first in Alice Springs to have solar panels for hot water heating on the carport roof; it also featured a porthole window, a round glass panel next to the front door through which the Todd River and Mt Gillen beyond could be seen; he was in the habit of looking through it every morning when he got up.

Namatjira was by now himself a tourist attraction and among those who sought him out were His Royal Highness the Duke of Gloucester, then Governor General of Australia, and his wife the Duchess. Albert was painting at Standley Chasm on that day in August 1946 and, although the visit was informal, it was also tightly choreographed; in the event the official who was meant to make the introductions went astray in the rough terrain and Alice, the Duchess, walked up alone, shook hands and then introduced her husband Henry, younger brother of King George VI, to Namatjira.

Albert was, in Pastor Gross's recollection, *unperturbed* and continued painting while he talked to the Royals; or, more likely, they talked to him. The photographs show him in his typical working position: sitting on the ground with the board to which the paper is pinned propped up on his knees and held stable with the left hand; the brush in the right hand, the paint box and the water container precariously placed on the ground. After the picnic lunch was over and the vice-regal party departed Albert said, when asked, that *it was all right.*

Not long afterwards a letter arrived from Buckingham Palace:

The Lady-in-Waiting to the Princess Elizabeth is desired by her Royal Highness to thank the members of the Aranda tribe for so kindly sending the three watercolours painted by Albert Namatjira, Edwin Pareroultja and Otto Pareroultja for the Princess' acceptance. Her Royal Highness much admires these paintings and has been graciously pleased to accept them. The idea to offer the heir to the throne a twenty-first birthday gift came from the accountant at Hermannsburg, Oswald Wallent, and is another example of the way in which the Mission actively sought good publicity for its causes.

Another painting was offered as a gift to the warship HMAS *Arunta*, commissioned in 1942 as one of the navy's tribal class destroyers. The *Arunta* was a well-known ship in World War Two, serving with distinction in New Guinea and the Pacific and taking part in the Battle of Leyte Gulf (1944) and that of Lingayen Gulf (1945), both in the Philippines. Namatjira gave the *Arunta* a painting of Mt Sonder, which was presented to the ship's officers by Battarbee in a brief ceremony on board ship at Port Melbourne in November 1948. It hung in the wardroom until the *Arunta* was decommissioned in 1956, after which the picture was transferred to HMAS *Creswell*; with the commissioning of the second *Arunta* in 1999, Namatjira's Mt Sonder was again transferred and now hangs in the commanding officer's cabin.

At around the same time Albert donated the proceeds from the sales of two of his paintings to the fund that had been established to provide the Mission with an electric power plant. Much of the money had been raised by Lou Borgelt, a Lutheran garage proprietor from Adelaide, who had been soliciting donations while showing home movies of Centralia to congregations in the south. Once a generator had been purchased, the wiring was installed free of charge during the winter of 1947 and the power was switched on by Borgelt himself.

A separate ceremony was held in the church: *Last Tuesday night we had electric light for the first time in our church,* Albrecht wrote. *We had a hymn, a scripture reading, a prayer and a short address. Then Albert was asked to switch on the lights, which he did, as he considers the church lights his contribution.* Some of those living on the Mission subsequently acquired gramophones; in 1949, Battarbee, who also gave a record player to Richard Moketarinja, noted that *Edwin Pareroultja has bought the complete record set of the Messiah recordings.*

Amid so much that was positive, if sometimes remote, came a development that was both troubling in the present and ominous for the future. From December 1947, advertisements began appearing in the *Centralian Advocate* offering Aboriginal watercolours for sale: *fit for the Duke of Edinburgh's drawing room and more than fit for his duck house,* one of the early ones said. By May 1948 the notices were appearing weekly and naming names: *Tourists and Visitors: CALL at my domicile at Jail Corner if wanting WATERCOLOURS done – under my personal supervision by Edwin and Otto Pareroultja, also by Walter Ebatarinja. Pictures also by the junior Namatjiras.* They were placed by one W Austin, a contentious and eccentric white man who lived in a tent on the outskirts of town. Austin dealt in mulga wood souvenirs and semi-precious stones as well as paintings and had already attempted to involve the senior Namatjira in his dealings.

One day a crate addressed to Albert arrived at the Mission. He took delivery and the crate, when opened, was found to contain a very large number of sheets of an inferior grade of paper. It had been ordered by Austin on Albert's behalf and there was the extravagant sum of £42 owing upon it. Initially it seemed that Namatjira, having taken receipt of the crate, was obliged to pay and he did in fact write out a cheque for the amount and send it off to the suppliers in Adelaide – who were, not coincidentally, also the firm from which he purchased the much higher quality sheets of paper he usually painted on.

It turned out that Namatjira had, along with the other artists named in the newspaper advertisement, been making work available to Austin, cheaply, for cash; Austin would mark the paintings up by several hundred percent (1.5 guineas to 6 guineas for an Ebatarinja is an example) then pocket the difference. Further, as a quid pro quo, he had promised to obtain cheap paper for the artists and this shipment to Namatjira was the result. Later, after the matter had gone to the Crown Solicitor in Darwin, it was determined that Namatjira could not in fact be forced to buy inferior paper he had not ordered and Mission staff began an attempt to get the cheque returned.

Pastor Gross, on a visit to Adelaide, went to the suppliers and spoke to the woman who had filled the original order. It was, she said, cheap drawing paper usually sold to schools at threepence a sheet and that she had been surprised at both the quantity and the name of the addressee – yet had despatched it anyway. The cheque was at length returned uncashed and Albert promised that he would have no more dealings with Austin. Some of the other artists, however, did continue trading with him.

Battarbee decided to investigate: *I bought some of W Austin's paintings…works mainly by Walter Ebatarinja, Edwin and Otto and they were cheap…Austin gets these boys to paint the pictures in his camp from memory and pays them for the day.* He reported back: *This evening we had a meeting of the Namatjira Council. Walter and Oscar came along for the first time. All the white men there attended. It was quite an important meeting and we gave Walter a good talking to for selling his pictures to Blackmarketeer Austin. Walter also consented to destroy those of his pictures…that he had painted.*

There are several issues here. One was that Austin, whether or not he acted illegally, had challenged the Mission's monopoly on the sale of Hermannsburg watercolours; another was the possible flooding of the market with cheap, inferior works; a third, which became much more troubling later on, was the question of the authenticity of works painted from memory; fourth, and of most concern to Albrecht, was the old spectre of the corrupting influences that existed in Alice Springs: *with regard to Austin, he wrote, our artists, more under Albert's guidance, have now all decided no longer to patronise him but leave him alone. Let's hope they will. Unfortunately the natives, ours included, have a great tendency to link up with the lowest type every time. I have reported the matter to Native Affairs...it remains to be seen what* [they] *will do.*

Taking Austin to court was not an option, Albrecht thought, *as he is a very unscrupulous man and would have loved to invent lies and throw dirt about.* Later, when Battarbee named him as a crooked dealer, Austin did bring an action against him for defamation. That there was a degree of self-righteousness in the position the Lutherans took is undeniable but this wasn't something they could be expected to be able to see for themselves. The accountant, Wallent, wrote: *The man who poses as a friend of the Aranda artists is definitely not an agent for the Hermannsburg Mission and his attempts at encouraging the artists are nothing short of an effort to wreck the honest intentions of the Mission to help the Arandas into a life of usefulness.*

Nor were Mission staff always entirely straight in their dealings, as this diary entry from Battarbee, made while he was on a painting trip, shows: *I have been disappointed in Otto's work lately and today found out the main reason. I felt he was probably using poor colours, so I asked to see his paints. Well I have never seen such a poor collection...and would not give them to a child. So I burnt most of them and gave him some of mine. He told me that Pastor Gross said that there were no good colours in the store. But Otto said they seemed to keep them for Albert, only Albert gets good paints. This business of trying to keep the Pareroultjas out of it is beyond a joke. Somebody is looking for trouble.*

Insofar as Namatjira was concerned, in 1948 he began another attempt to help himself into a life of usefulness. On 11 October Battarbee recorded in his diary: *A cool clear day. The mail plane arrived this morning. We had a meeting of the Namatjira council. Albert had a lot of things to put before the council. One was that he was to take out a lease at Haasts Bluff and had already spoken to Mr McCoy about it. Albert called the meeting and it was a long one.* This was Namatjira, on his own initiative, planning an extension of Albrecht's policy of establishing Mission Aborigines on cattle runs over untenanted lands to the west.

Battarbee supported the plan, for various reasons. The following year he wrote, echoing Albrecht, that *Albert is becoming very difficult mainly because he has his truck running. Also because Alice Springs seems to hold more for him than ever. Albert demanded his cheque book and to do as he wished...I feel that Alice Springs would be Albert's downfall – the townspeople are his greatest trouble and no doubt are urging him on...I am also all for Albert buying cattle and renting the land north of Mt Liebig. I feel this is the lesser of two evils.*

On 4 October 1949, then, Namatjira, with Battarbee and Gross, went to the Department of Lands in Alice Springs and made an application for a grazing licence; the sum of £38 10/– was tendered as payment for the lease of 750 square miles of land. The block in question took in the Siddeley Ranges north of Papunya and west of Central Mount Wedge; it included an area known as the Salt Marshes. *The Lands Office in Alice Springs,* wrote Albrecht, *was agreeable, especially after Albert pointed out unless the Siddeley Ranges were included he would not be interested, as otherwise the country is just sandhills and mostly useless desert. He has been out there.* Native Affairs initially seemed positive; a senior official commented that *the granting of a licence was another step forward in the policy of assisting natives to full civic rights.*

Yet when, a month later, a letter arrived from the Administrator granting the grazing licence, the lease was described as just 460 square miles; and the sum of £14 10/–, payment for the missing 300-odd square miles, was refunded by cheque. The area excised from the lease was that part consisting of the Siddeley Ranges, which Albert had specifically asked for because it was the only well-watered country therein. Without it, in Albrecht's words, the lease was *cut down to a proposition that never can succeed*. District Officer William McCoy, the Department of Native Affairs man in Alice Springs, allowed that he was surprised and asked Albrecht to comment. Albrecht himself wondered why Darwin had overruled the recommendation of the local Lands Officer. What had happened?

McCoy, sounding duplicitous, wrote to his Director: *Namatjira had previously mentioned to me his desire to obtain a block north of Haasts Bluff, but, as a result of a discussion with TGH Strehlow and others concerning the area, I did not encourage him to do so…Namatjira called at this office on 30 November, 1949 and was informed of the extent of land granted to him and expressed his disappointment. He was advised not to purchase any cattle.* Albert had in the interim been out to the Salt Marshes and dug a well ten feet deep in a soakage near the south-east corner of his putative block; but the water was adjudged to belong to the neighbouring Haasts Bluff Reserve. Further, it was the protection, and possible extension, of that reserve that appears to have been behind the advice of Strehlow and the anonymous others: a misguided and high-minded attempt to protect *tribal blacks' need of access to soaks, ceremonial sites and the like that may be on such a lease.*

Albrecht was furious. *A native knows best how to refrain from offending another Aborigine*, he wrote, *occupation of tribal areas for stock raising purposes by another Aborigine is certainly preferable to a white man. It is impossible to imagine how an Aranda native could ever attempt to prevent another native whose tribal country he uses for stock from visiting sacred caves...our Aranda cattle men have been operating now for five years, we have never heard of any illegal killings...the assumption that through the occupation of a section of tribal country by Albert Namatjira ill feelings would be caused...is not based on facts.*

It was, he went on to say, not just a kick in the teeth for Albert personally, but also a setback for his people as a whole. *It is not a matter of not offending tribal owners who have left their hunting grounds, but of finding ways of re-populating the areas they have left...since pastoral pursuits would be nearest to them, it is of the greatest importance that we should try and encourage every aborigine who is prepared to launch out as a cattleman...the lead* [Albert] *would give in this respect to other aborigines is so valuable he should receive every possible encouragement.* It made no difference; the policy of the Lands Department *to recognise the principle of the aborigine as a human being with civil rights* was contrary to the programmes of the Native Affairs branch, which announced, hypocritically, that the land excised from Albert's proposed lease was *subject to the policy of developing the Haasts Bluff Reserve as a Native Affairs Branch cattle station.*

On 24 April 1950 the grazing licence was formally cancelled and the licence fee, less the £14 10/– that had already been refunded, was returned to Albert. His brand, issued on 15 November 1949 and consisting of the letters ANT – perhaps standing for Albert Northern Territory or, less plausibly, Albert Namatjira Territory – was never used although the certificate attesting to it remains in the Lutheran Archives in Adelaide. As to the effect the debacle had upon him personally, it is likely to have been profound. He at first refused to accept it and planned to drive his truck to Darwin to reapply personally at the Department of Lands; but in the event changed his mind and, after getting the requisite permission, made the thousand mile journey by bus in the company of local identity, the author and adventurer, Bill Harney.

It was July 1950. The first thing he did in Darwin was go to visit the two government offices concerned, the Departments of Native Affairs and of Lands, to reapply for his grazier's licence. Predictably enough, although the Administrator, AR Driver, promised to give the matter full consideration, there was no change in the government's position and therefore no grant of a viable pastoral lease. Thus the compelling image of Albert as a rancher, with his five sons riding the range as if in a black *Bonanza*, fades from view.

There were compensations. It was his first visit to a big town and his first view of the sea; also his inauguration as a media star; and it's likely that he enjoyed every moment of it. He dined at the exclusive Darwin Hotel, where many prominent local citizens lined up to meet him and where distraught officials of the Native Affairs Department made comical attempts to intervene lest he dare to take a drink; which, as a ward of the state, he was not entitled to do. He was invited on board HMAS *Koala*, then in port, and was shown over the ship by the captain himself; the engine room in particular interested him. He went shopping, buying gifts for his family and thereby exhausting his funds; but a local author, Douglas Lockwood, lent him the money for the bus fare back to Alice Springs and, upon his return, Albert repaid him by cheque.

A tangible outcome of the visit was a series of four Namatjira watercolours of the sea, two of which were sold to the *Australian Women's Weekly*, a third bought by a Darwin resident and the last taken back to Alice Springs. One of these paintings resurfaced at a Manly dealership in the early years of the twenty-first century; it is accomplished but undistinguished and, like another seascape Namatjira painted a few years later in Sydney, lacks the powerful aura possessed by the best of his central Australian works.

In the year previous to the debacle over the lease, the Namatjira family suffered a series of personal tragedies. In May 1949 Albert and Rubina's second surviving daughter, Hazel, then in her mid-twenties, died giving while giving birth to her first child at Hermannsburg; the boy lived and grew up on the Mission. Then, the following January, Martha, their youngest daughter, also died during childbirth at Haasts Bluff. Her daughter, Biddy, survived too and became a much-loved favourite of Albert and Rubina, who brought her up.

Between these two deaths, in July 1949, while on a painting trip out past Areyonga, Albert and Rubina's third son, Ewald, had a serious shooting accident. Ewald never said exactly what happened; he told his father he didn't know. In one version he was out hunting and the gun went off by mistake as he was chasing a kangaroo; in another, the accident happened while he was playing with the rifle at camp. Albert, who was painting, was close enough to hear the shot, which he at first thought inconsequential; then he heard voices calling out and came to see what the matter was. The bullet, a .22 calibre, entered Ewald's right eye then lodged in his brain.

They had gone out on camels, not by truck, so had to improvise a litter in order to carry the wounded man back to Hermannsburg; one of the boys ran ahead to sound the alarm and along the way the stretcher party was met by Enos, riding on horseback from the Mission with medical supplies. After emergency treatment Ewald emerged from bloody unconsciousness and began to sing Lutheran hymns. Then the Mission truck met with the party and took them back to Hermannsburg, where a plane of the Flying Doctor service flew the wounded man to the hospital at Alice Springs.

He lost the eye and the bullet never was extracted; in later life he sometimes suffered bad headaches or was afflicted by a loss of balance which the ignorant attributed to drunkenness. Remarkably, however, he continued to paint; he was already the most unusual, the most individual, the most distinctively naïve, of the younger

HIGH NATIONAL POLICY

Namatjira painters. A roguish boy around whom, one who knew him in later life said, things were always happening. Once out of hospital Ewald returned to the site of the accident and painted it; the work, *Flame-Like Mountains, James Range*, is reproduced in Battarbee's second, 1971, book.

After these events some thought they saw signs of an increasing restlessness in Albert. He had previously sold the house he built at Hermannsburg to one of the Pareroultja brothers and purchased instead an army hut which he placed nearer the Mission; now, he decided he wanted a caravan and, with the permission and the help of the missionaries, and using some of the proceeds of his second Sydney show at Anthony Hordern's – 1500 guineas from the sale of thirty-five paintings – did so. When it arrived in September 1950, he immediately attached it behind his truck, loaded up with supplies, and he and Rubina headed out west *en famille* on yet another painting trip. They didn't come back until it was time for Rex Battarbee's wedding.

Rex had always wanted to marry but, in that old-fashioned way, felt that he could not do so until he had a home to offer his bride; now that he had one he found her in, of all places, Yuendumu. With advice and practical help from Pastor Albrecht, the Baptist Church had begun a Mission among the Warlpiri at the new Ration Depot settlement that the Department of Native Affairs established at Rock Hill Bore, subsequently renamed Yuendumu, in the Mt Doreen area out on the Tanami Track. Two missionaries, with their families, arrived there in February 1947 and immediately began taking regular church services.

Yuendumu was a government settlement and the missionaries there thus had to operate within the bounds of the government's assimilative policies; they were however involved in more than just well-meaning attempts to meet the Warlpiri's alleged spiritual needs. The Baptist Church donated clothing and medical supplies and their missionaries and helpers taught craft skills, ran a store, helped to build and sometimes staffed the hospital, began a kindergarten and inaugurated the first school. One of the earliest of the teachers was a young woman from Exton near Launceston in Tasmania called Bernice Loone. She had attended Melbourne Bible College in Melbourne and then, in January 1949, took up the position as kindergarten teacher at Yuendumu.

Rex and Bernice first met when he visited Yuendumu where she, living in atrocious conditions in a dirt-walled hut, still managed to serve tea in china cups on a white table cloth she ironed using a square kerosene tin as a board; but the later stages of their courtship took place in Alice Springs. Bernice was under pressure from the Baptist Church because of her lack of a formal teaching qualification; and, ill with rheumatic fever, moved into town to recuperate. She was staying with friends near the site of the house Rex was building and would walk past it several times a week on her regular visits to the doctor. He would look out for her and invite her in for tea.

The house was blue and Rex himself like one of the birds he loved so much: a bower bird, attracting females to his court that was strewn with precious things. On 19 February 1950 he recorded: *A hot day again. I had a visit from Miss Bernice Loone and spent quite a time with her.* And, further on that year, in the middle of August: *I had lunch with Bernice Loone and later made my proposal to her in Todd St. in broad daylight. She is considering it. Says it was a complete surprise.*

He was fifty-seven years old and she just thirty but the age difference seemed not to matter: *This morning I pruned. Bernice came along and spent the day here. We are still making progress. She seems to be the ideal mate for me. We will probably get married in a couple of months... our love has grown. This week has given us a chance to settle down and become natural.* They were painting the kitchen together and Rex had shown her his household things. When she went south in September they kept in touch: *I spoke to Bernice in Adelaide on the phone. It was very clear. She was in good form.* And, on the 9th: *I had a beautiful letter from Bernice. She has laid her heart bare.*

The wedding took place in the church at Hermannsburg on 7 October 1950, with Pastor Albrecht officiating. Rex described events in some detail: *Rain through the night. And the Todd in flood this morning. The big day. Our wedding day. D called in his taxi at 8.30am for us to go to Hermannsburg...where we arrived at 12.45...Bernice and I had dinner with Albrecht. The wedding was for 3pm...the church was packed inside and out. Pastor Albrecht gave a simple service and a wonderful address. I was sure this was the right place for the wedding. The simplicity of the final mission farewell was marvellous.*

After the service we went to the natives' dining room where we held a reception with the natives. I said a few words. The people were interested in the bride and how she looked – beautiful. She had a large train…51 telegrams…there was more water on the road than this morning. The other taxi gave a lot of trouble. Back in Alice Springs at 11.15 pm that night the Todd was running bankers and we could not get accommodation at the hotel. So we camped at the Lutheran mission. We had no blankets. But had rest and protection.

There may have been a previous family connection between the Tasmanian Loones and the branch of the Battarbee family, represented by Rex's older sister Florinda, who settled there. The wedding of Rex and Bernice was certainly considered a matter of local interest and the Launceston *Examiner* reported upon it in some detail under the headline *Novel Wedding Reception*. A Mrs AH McCormack, the paper noted, gave a pre-wedding party in Adelaide to which thirty friends of Miss Loone were invited; and the *hosts at the reception were the aboriginal painter Albert Namatjira and his sons, who are also painters*.

Albert and his sons were indeed present at the wedding reception, but only just. He told Bernice later: *We went to Mangeraka Gorge especially that I might paint the scene as a wedding gift. We knew that rain was coming when we left the gorge and by the time we got to the creek my wife Rubina was complaining, she kept saying we should have left the day before, then when we saw that the creek was running at knee depth she was really upset and Biddy my little granddaughter began to cry. 'You knew it was the wedding tomorrow and now we won't be there.' The boys were cross and excited, they also had paintings for their friend Rex Battarbee.*

Enos, who was in charge of the truck at the time, thought we should chance on crossing the creek, so we put the truck into low gear and slowly moved through the water, only to find there was a deep hole in the middle of the creek and the truck lurched forward and stopped. We jumped out into the water and now found it waist high. The boys carried Biddy across. I grabbed my paint boxes and brushes and called to Rubina to bring the sugar and flour. By this time Rubina was already in the water and when I looked down there she was in the water with the painting on her head. 'You've got to get this to Battarbee,' she said.

In the event the truck was pushed out of the creek and restarted and the entire family did make it back to Hermannsburg in time for the wedding and the reception that followed. Rex recorded that *Albert, Enos and Oscar Namatjira gave us beautiful watercolours while Edwin, Reuben* [Pareroultja], *Richard* [Moketarinja] *and the Albrecht family gave us kangaroo mats.*

Because of the rain most of the wedding photographs were taken inside the church but there was at least one outside. The couple stand together between the two old gum trees that grew in front of the church; he bare-headed, gaunt, a bit hunched, wearing a dark suit; she radiant in white with her arms full of flowers, perhaps lilies; confetti, or fractured light, or perhaps rain drops, lies like dust on the shoulders of his suit jacket. There is another couple smiling behind, two Aboriginal girls wearing hats with bands and white shoes stand on the church steps and, in the immediate left foreground, is a widely grinning boy.

Battarbee's marriage gave him a new legitimacy among those he represented: he was a proper man after all. And, because he was no longer single, women painters were now permitted to join the movement. And the relocation to Alice Springs meant a shift in the epicentre of the Hermannsburg School, for whose members he was now both agent and dealer; from this point on the Mission, albeit reluctantly, began to relinquish the control, particularly the financial control, it had tried to maintain over the activities of the artists. Albert, as the most successful and also the most ungovernable of these artists, was clearly chafing at the restrictions placed upon him. The disappointment over his failure to obtain a workable grazing lease only exacerbated these feelings and he soon arrived at another money-making scheme, another attempt to achieve financial independence.

On 9 November 1950 the Administrator, AR Driver, minuted: *The Director of Lands informed me today, and the Director of Native Affairs also, that Albert Namatjira has reported a find of copper at Areyonga...if this discovery shows promise, then a decision must be reached as to whether it can be mined, because in all probability it will be on a native reserve.* Albert had in fact taken a sample in to Alice Springs *without*, Albrecht complained, *saying a word to us*. The Director of Mines and a Patrol Officer went out to investigate and found the ore to be about forty-five per cent copper and worth about £90 a ton. Albrecht continued: *our minds were considerably agitated by this, as a mine, worked by white miners, would be the last thing we would want here...Thereupon we made investigations, trying to find out whether we could do something to prevent the developing of the mine.*

The legal position was thus: all minerals on Reserves and Mission Leases in the Territory remained the property of the Crown except for a ten per cent royalty payable to whoever worked a mine. Not the Lutherans: *I have told them we shall have nothing to do with it.* Albert, however, with the help of the Department of Mines, persisted in attempting to develop his claim over the next seven years and did in fact earn some money from it in the mid-1950s, although not much. His ability to work the claim was constrained by various factors, some physical, some legal. Access to water was difficult and Territory laws restrictive: Aborigines were not allowed to possess or use dynamite and were prohibited from working underground.

The Areyonga copper claim, which generated voluminous correspondence over the next half decade, was an example of Albert's entrepreneurial spirit but the Mission did not see it that way. *What we regret so much is that Albert more and more gets into the habit of trying to make more and more money...one would say nothing if he knew how to handle it...it becomes more and more a curse to him and those who associate with him.* They must have felt they had created a monster and that, in some respects, the copper claim was the least of the problems.

A greater issue surfaced towards the end of the year, when newspaper headlines in the south shouted *Forgeries!* The chief of the Adelaide CIB said, ominously, that he didn't think *there is really a flourishing trade in these forgeries yet...but I think there are about 30 or 40 paintings of doubtful origin in Adelaide.* They seem to have been genuine watercolours by other hands that had been signed with Namatjira's characteristic, and easily forgeable, capital-letter signature; perhaps unsigned works 'commissioned' by Austin before he was chased out of town late in 1949. Albrecht thought they had most likely been painted by Walter Ebatarinja and Oscar Namatjira. Some, however, could have been genuine: *Albert Namatjira informs me*, McCoy wrote, *he has at various times given away to various of his friends paintings which he has not been satisfied with but will now burn all such paintings. It is possible some of these might have found their way to Austin.* It has even been alleged that Austin offered to prostitute his own wife in exchange for signatures on sheets of paper upon which he then painted himself.

Austin was not the only dubious character trading on Albert's reputation. There was another, by the name of Jack Harris, operating in Alice Springs during 1950; a man, Battarbee wrote, who made Austin look like a child. Quite what Harris was doing isn't clear from the documentary evidence – it had something to do with pipes or a pipeline – but Rex's diaries record a number of conversations he had with Albert during which he reiterated the insistence that he have nothing more to do with Harris. McCoy became involved in these conversations, as did Pastor Gross and Albrecht himself. There is a sense of exasperation in the writings of all these men at this time as they struggle, and seemingly fail, to protect Albert from himself; he did not seem to want their protection.

The culmination of this series of events, the third act in the drama, as it were, after the pastoral lease and the copper claim, came at the end of 1950 when Albert told Mission staff that he had bought a block of land in Alice Springs upon which he intended to build a house. The land, on the western side of town, had been owned by a Mr Kenna and Albert was already consulting with a local builder over what kind of dwelling he would have: *like Mr Battarbee's house but a little smaller*. It was, wrote McCoy, *a condition of the lease of the block he wants to purchase that it will be developed as a poultry run. It has a good well on it, and has been fenced by Namatjira. Whether...the Lands branch would consent to it being used for residential purposes is not known.*

For the course of action Albert proposed was in conflict with the law. The main problem was both simple and profound: under the Ordinance, which classified so-called full-bloods as wards of the state, such Aboriginals were subject to a curfew. They were not permitted to stay within the borough limits of the town of Alice Springs after dark. How then could Namatjira build a house there and live in it? Most people who commented at the time assumed that Albert's plan was an act of naivety, that Namatjira didn't really know what he was doing. From today's vantage, however, it looks a little different: perhaps, rather than behaving unwittingly he was, like any other man, simply assuming the right to act with perfect freedom in the pursuit of his desires.

It would not have surprised anyone following the story, which had been picked up by the national press, when Albert was refused permission to build. Battarbee, who supported him in the plan, wrote in May 1951: *Albert is not allowed to build on his block of land. He was quiet for a while but is not going to give up trying. He does not like paying income tax without getting any privileges. He says he would pay his tax – but income tax will not help.* Namatjira would continue to live on and off in Alice Springs for the rest of his life; but not in a house he'd built and not upon land he owned either; he became a fringe dweller on the outskirts of town, in a humpy at a camp near the cattle yards and the railway station at a place called Morris Soak.

8. Tmara Mara

When Rex and Bernice asked Albert to give them a name for their new house he offered *Tmara Mara*; adding that when Arrernte people were travelling and found a good place to sit down and rest, that was what they called it: an oasis of sorts. And so it became. Over the years Rex had collected seeds from trees he painted and some of these he now germinated and planted around the house and in Prickle Park across the road from it, so that in time they would form a grove of trees of unique character. In the bed of the Todd River, upon whose eastern bank Tmara Mara was built, numbers of ancient gum trees, named and addressed as individual beings, were already growing; when an old tree died its spirit was believed to re-incarnate into a nearby younger tree; and so Rex's plantings can be understood as a way of adding new members to an existing pantheon.

All sorts of people found Tmara Mara a good place to sit down. For example, during 1950, visitors included HC (Nugget) Coombs, Governor of the Commonwealth Bank, in those days the most important post in the regulation of the Australian economy, and his wife Lallie; Clem Christensen, the founding editor of the literary magazine *Meanjin*; the British philosopher Bertrand Russell. *A white frost and a beautiful day to follow,* Rex recorded in his diary for 6 August. *I had a visit from Lord Bertrand Russell. Lord Russell is very human and interesting. We got on well together. He was interested in my place and keenly interested in the native art movement. He bought two Oscar Namatjiras and one Enoch Raberaba.*

Subsequently a press report that Russell had bought a number of Albert Namatjira paintings while in Alice Springs was denied by Hermannsburg: *There was a long waiting list already for pictures by Albert Namatjira, a spokesman said, and he wished to make it clear that Lord Russell would have to wait in line.* The stiff tone of the rejoinder suggests some degree of disenchantment with the exigencies of dealing, not just with *the apostle of free love and socialism,* but with Namatjira himself; people at the Mission were becoming weary of the complexities attendant upon Albert's fame and fortune. Persistent accusations that the Lutherans were lining their pockets with excessive commissions from sales, although incorrect, were widely believed; while Albert's own profligacy with money continued to worry Albrecht, especially now he was spending more time in town than he was at the Mission.

Dear Brother Reuther, he wrote in the autumn of 1951, *last Monday we had a meeting…at Battarbee's place and tried to clarify Albert's position. From having over 1200 pounds six months ago he is down to about 200 and soon will be at bedrock. Of course we will be blamed for not stopping him but as he resents our control, it has reached a stage that he seldom stays here…the whole atmosphere was unpleasant.* One of the suggestions was that the artists' business, and their money, should be handed over for Native Affairs to administer but Battarbee felt that this would most likely mean the end of the art movement; in the event another meeting was scheduled to take place in two weeks' time, with both Albert himself and representatives of Native Affairs present.

After that second meeting Albrecht again wrote to Reuther: *the outcome was that the council accepted in broad outlines a proposal by Battarbee...to form a new council in Alice Springs...I...relinquished the position of chairman of the old council and shall not be a member of the new either.* The new body, called The Aranda Arts Council, was chaired by Battarbee, had a paid secretary (Bernice Battarbee was elected) and was, like the old, responsible for the pricing and the sale of all paintings; a commission would be charged and payments would be made to the artists by cheque. Native Affairs would oversee arrangements and if any paintings were to be sold at Hermannsburg, they would have to go there via Alice Springs. The Aranda Arts Council hoped to end the trade in forgeries, and in inferior works, by authenticating all genuine paintings with its official stamp on the back. The stamp was oval, with *Hermannsburg–Aranda Artists* on the border and a boomerang crossed with a paint-brush within; and it needed to be confirmed with a signature written across it.

Albrecht's report to Reuther of these new arrangements concluded by repeating a remark Albert allegedly made to Rex after the meeting: *I was happier when I had no money at all than I am today.* Many years later, in 2001, Joyce Batty said that *both Pastors Albrecht and Gross told me how Rex Battarbee was individually responsible for influencing Namatjira to move to Alice Springs where he alone would have control over Namatjira's paintings, which by that time represented a lucrative income from resale plus charging for commissions.*

Battarbee was never a profitable artist, she went on, *his major source of income was from the sale of Namatjira and other Arrernte artists' paintings.* This calumny is cognate with previous accusations that the Mission was lining its pockets with commissions. It is indicative not of Battarbee's practice – for most of his life his bread and butter came from commercial art, with fine art sales as a bonus; and he was always an honest broker for those he represented – but of a sundering between him and Albrecht. The two, who had worked so closely together for a decade and a half, had reached a parting of the ways.

Albrecht relieved some of his feelings by going into print. He had been asked by the Aborigines' Friends' Association in Adelaide to write a pamphlet on Albert Namatjira for publication and agreed, requesting the printing of a thousand extra copies for sale at Hermannsburg. His *Albert Namatjira: Native Artist* is dated October 1950, but wasn't published until mid-way through the following year; it concludes with the phrase that has come to haunt all subsequent writings on Namatjira, with its reference to Mark 8:36. Namatjira *would gain very little,* Albrecht wrote, *if through the dazzling lights of publicity and wealth he should lose himself – a wanderer between worlds.*

Of more interest, perhaps, is this passage from the pamphlet: *A well-known pastoralist of the district, who knows him well, remarked: 'Albert is the only aboriginal I know who is proud to be one.' That is a fact which, incidentally, also has certain disadvantages. He makes no attempt to keep up an appearance similar to white people, shaves seldom, washes when he feels like it, and his clothing at times is anything but representative of a famous and wealthy artist. In all of these matters he shows clearly that wealth and fame have meant little to him…essentially, he has remained a restless nomad; his greatest contentment comes to him when he is on the move, 'walkabout,' even if this means riding, as he usually does, right at the back of his truck, sitting hard on the boards of the tray over the back axle.*

Albrecht's strictures reveal a profound disappointment in Namatjira's failure to be the kind of person the Mission wanted; and ignore or belittle the kind of person he in fact was. His attempts to reinvent himself as a pastoralist and a property owner are dismissed as misguided and bound to fail; while his achievements and his character as an artist are held to have been somehow compromised by what Albrecht calls his *spenditis*. This in despite of the fact that everybody knew how Albert spent his money:

not on himself but, proudly and generously, upon the support, the provisioning and the entertaining of his relatives and friends.

Namatjira was by now a national figure and Sydney newspaper *The Sun* picked up the story of Albrecht's pamphlet and asked several artists for their opinions. *Most landscape artists I know are restless wanderers*, painter Norman Lindsay remarked. Cartoonist Eric Jolliffe, who had lived in the Territory, observed that the *colour bar was more rigidly imposed in the Northern Territory than in the southern states*; while fellow cartoonist and watercolourist, New Zealand-born Cecil (Unk) White said, poignantly given what was going to happen, that *Namatjira's wanderings and behaviour were those of a true landscape artist. After all if he was kept in a cage he would only be able to paint the cage.*

In a long article in the *Sunday Telegraph* of 21 July journalist Larry Boys, who on his visit to Darwin had rescued Albert from a Native Affairs imposed limbo in a camp outside town and taken him to the Darwin Hotel, was so scathing about Albrecht's pamphlet in particular, and Lutheran paternalism in general, that the missionary considered suing him for libel. Reporting on the imbroglio, the *Centralian Advocate* paraphrased the main points of Albrecht's pamphlet without ever mentioning his name; then exacerbated matters by regaling comments upon it, and upon Boys' allegations, from what it called *the southern press*. These comments tended to reflect negatively upon the unnamed Albrecht's views.

Albert was asked to comment. *I have read all this*, he said. *It is utter nonsense. If they do not leave me alone I shall be too unhappy to paint. Surely it is my own business as to what I do with the money I earn for myself.* This was what he had been saying to Mission staff for years; it was as incontrovertible as it was unacceptable to those who had elected themselves his guardians. Unfortunately it seems also to have been lost on his burgeoning crowd of well-meaning supporters in the cities that their support, too, was unhelpful to Albert.

It wasn't just Albert who was under scrutiny; a journalist from the *Argus* managed to track down Rubina and subjected her to an interview that was written up and published on 3 October 1951 under the title *Meet Mrs Namatjira*. *Albert's subsequent successes in the field of art haven't made any big difference to Rubina's social status. When I saw her in Alice Springs this week she looked no different from any other native. Her hair was lank and grimy with dust, and she wore a plain floral print frock and a vivid red cardigan which had seen better days. She was squatting on her haunches in a circle of 10 other women, all talking at the same time. There were several groups, and it looked like 'gossip day.' One woman who was doing the washing on an outdoor stove called to her, 'Namatjira, you come longa here.' She walked slowly over holding the hand of Biddy, her inseparable companion.*

Battarbee organised an inaugural show for his new gallery, an exhibition of thirty-seven pictures that would juxtapose Aboriginal and white interpretations of the Central Australian scene. *Art Show Will Be Unique* reported the *Advocate* on 4 May 1951. *Thirteen aboriginal artists from the famous Hermannsburg colony, and six white painters will be represented. All works to go on show will depict Centralian scenes, and with the division of aboriginals and whites, an unrivalled opportunity for comparison will arise. It is hoped that some of the southern art critics will be present to see the exhibition, because it is unlikely that such a gathering of work will be available again for a very long time. Entrance…will be free.*

The black artists were Albert and his three sons Enos, Oscar and Ewald; the Pareroultja brothers Edwin, Otto and Reuben; the two Raberabas, Henoch and Herbert; Richard Moketarinja and Walter Ebatarinja; and newcomers the Inkamala brothers, Adolf and Gerhardt, who were the sons of Albert's half sister Clara. The white painters were Sidney Nolan, John Gardiner, John Eldershaw, David Chittleborough, WS Carroll and Rex Battarbee himself, who would be showing *paintings of the type which have already won him a world-wide reputation as an exponent of Central Australian colour.* But Nolan was the star: *Mr. Nolan has recently held a most successful exhibition in London,* the *Advocate* reported, *and one of his pictures was bought for the famous Tate Gallery.*

Battarbee wrote on 19 April: *Mild and warmer. Mr and Mrs E Connellan brought along the Sid Nolan painting…the painting will cause a lot of discussion at the Exhibition.* And, a week or so later: *Cool and mild…Albert came, Ewald and Enos also, and they had a good look at the Sid Nolan picture. Albert said that it did not make him feel lively and Ewald said it was no good.* After some further discussion the Namatjiras decided it was, at most, a five pound picture; Albert thought the hill looked funny sitting on its side, it made him laugh. It's a pity that John Reed was not there to overhear their prognostications.

As to what the painting was, that remains unknown; but it was almost certainly one of the series of Central Australian desert paintings Nolan did, many from aerial photographs, after his trip to the inland with his wife Cynthia in the winter of 1949; most of them are very red, with the landscape contorting expressionistically beneath cerulean skies. They also, ironically, and perhaps also unconsciously, revert to using the top-down perspective of traditional Arrernte painting; most of them were done with the board lying flat on a table and the artist standing above it looking down.

Eddy Connellan, who brought the painting down to Tmara Mara, was a schoolteacher who became the pioneer aviator in the Northern Territory. From the late 1930s he had a government subsidised mail run going from Alice Springs to Wyndham in Western Australia and for twenty years hired out planes to the Flying Doctor service. It was Eddy Connellan who, in his pre-war Beechcraft bi-plane, flew the Nolans over the landscape out to Hermannsburg and then all the way on to the Indian Ocean during that 1949 excursion; it's likely that the painting was one that Nolan had given the Connellans, or that they had bought from him.

They are raw, violent and confronting paintings, beside which Namatjira's watercolours, and indeed the less naturalistic work of his younger contemporaries, look quiet, contemplative, even numinous. Yet on a second look Albert had more to say about the Nolan: *High here up to heaven*, he remarked. *Like a corroboree stone*. Nolan was also aware of complementaries: *People have to become gentler, more like the aborigines, to live in this country,* he said. *They must learn from it, otherwise it will inevitably bring them to their knees…that's doubly true for a painter.*

The exhibition was an outstanding success; over 500 attended the opening, and in the three days following a large number of works were sold. There was more excitement to come. A matter of weeks afterwards, on 21 July, Rex wrote: *This is a historic day. The author's copy of my 'Modern Australian Aboriginal Art' arrived by air. 19/– postage from Angus & Robertson. Though it has a different cover to the one I expected, it is a wonderful production.* On 23 July, he continues: *We have had a crowd of visitors all day. 36 copies arrived by post. Rabbi Dr Brasch called in and bought the first one. I gave a copy to the Alice Springs library…I had a letter from Frank Clune and he congratulated me on the book. He is sending me one of his. Also offers 15 of his books to me and also wants to buy one of my paintings.*

Modern Australian Aboriginal Art has a foreword by TGH Strehlow, an introduction by Battarbee and then nine chapters on ten individual Hermannsburg painters (Enos and Oscar Namatjira share a chapter), also by Battarbee; each painter is given a brief biography followed by a discussion of his work. The text is illustrated with twelve fine black-and-white photographs of the artists, usually in the landscape, and there are twenty-one coloured plates in the back of the book. Although his writing is occasionally awkward and sometimes formulaic, Rex's generosity and his passion nevertheless shine through; perhaps too much so. The Melbourne *Age*'s art critic reckoned that *Mr Battarbee tells an interesting and often moving story. Howbeit, due to the author's excessive enthusiasm for his protégés, while gaining as a human document it loses as an authoritative art book.*

The *Sunday Telegraph* agreed, but gave the book's deficits a different spin: *He is no writer,* wrote BC, *and perhaps he would be the first to admit it; neither is he an art critic, which perhaps is a good thing, since he remains largely untroubled by intellectual misgivings as to the value of the work of his protégés. I believe this book, with its faithful reproductions, makes the value of that work as Art with a capital A clear beyond the doubts of those who see no merit in any contemporary movement that remains uninfluenced by the School of Paris. What emerges is this: To Albert Namatjira, the Arunta tribesman who in two months mastered the difficult and alien technique of watercolour, belongs the credit for a movement of exceptional interest. But there are now other Aborigines in the Alice Springs area who, though they do not always match him in skill, are greater artists than he.*

This is not BC's last word on Namatjira: *It is as easy to underrate him as it has been to overpraise him extravagantly. Despite the opinions of members of the Plastic Arts Committee who saw fit to omit his work from the recent Jubilee Art Exhibition, his painting is more than just technique.* As for Battarbee, *he does not shirk any of the unpleasant issues connected with the Hermannsburg Aborigines that have forced themselves upon the public attention since Namatjira's rise to fame…but he does nothing to… modify one's view that taxation of these men without representation, and official denial to them of all civil rights, together constitute a monstrous violation of human liberties.*

Looking at the colour plates now, sixty years on, it is apparent that there is indeed a gap, not so much in quality as in emotional resonance, between Albert Namatjira's work and that of the other nine artists, including his sons, in the book; and, although he is not represented therein, the painting of Battarbee as well. At the time this divergence was usually explained by saying that Albert was more naturalistic, technically proficient and westernised; while his colleagues were more spontaneous, expressive and decorative in intent. (Decorative was not a pejorative term in the Battarbee lexicon.) Now it seems obvious that there is a monumental, even epic, quality to Albert's work, a grandeur and a solemnity that is largely lacking in the others'. The younger Hermannsburg painters' work is delicate, subtle, often beautiful, sometimes very unusual, frequently charming but always somehow ephemeral; whereas Albert was painting for the ages.

In this regard Battarbee's extravagant claims for the school he was promoting do not seem so much grandiloquent as naïve; and his contention that this was *one of the greatest art movements in history* bound to raise the hackles on the necks of metropolitan critics. His own reputation as a painter was already, and unjustly, on the wane; the pre-war notices that praised the startling originality of his sense of colour in particular had been replaced by more measured, sometimes actively disenchanted, reflections, partly no doubt because the novelty of his work had faded now that many more people had seen the Centre for themselves; or at least had seen colour photographs of it.

The *Argus* in 1947 reported: *Among present-day painters, Mr Rex Battarbee is in the uncommonly happy position of having found a subject to work on which is distinctive, well suited to his style, and apparently inexhaustible. His present show...repeats a formula which he has already made familiar, but which shows no trace of repetitive dullness. Perhaps this is due to the honesty of Mr Battarbee's painting...his work is not completely free from clumsiness, but he shows many well organised pictures of strength and originality.*

Two years later, in 1949, the *Sydney Morning Herald* critic was much harsher, if not entirely lucid: *Battarbee has travelled further, has gained more technique, and, in his stately works, has lost much of the joy of living…There is little to distinguish this manner of presentation from that of Namatjira save in the element of design. The aboriginal has much the surer touch, otherwise all is calm and deep colours rather monotonous in repetition…There is little underneath it all, and one's sensibilities are not really touched. One may admire the scenery, but one does not think of art.*

It is difficult now to understand how Battarbee's work could have been mistaken for Namatjira's, or vice versa, unless it was because of their shared subject matter; they are, even to a casual eye, very different painters. Namatjira's habit of working from the edges of the picture into the centre, his inclusion of multiple points of view, his always nascent anthropomorphism, the extraordinary depth of his pictures, their vertiginous display of detail at the micro-level, are distinct from Battarbee's preference for a flat picture plane, a rhythmic design, a fascination with light and shadow, a love of decorative patterning.

Battarbee is also, like many naïve painters, someone whose work did not really change over time: he produced strong paintings throughout the four decades during which he was active and, if they were not so assiduously dated, it wouldn't be easy to say which are late, which early; whereas the almost always undated Namatjiras fall distinctly into three periods, corresponding with the three decades during which he painted.

So that, and paradoxically, many of the painters in *Modern Australian Aboriginal Art* now look to have been influenced more by Battarbee than by Namatjira. This may be simply an artefact of selection but it may be something more: Battarbee's notes to the plates emphasise qualities he himself admired and which are characteristic of his own work: an Otto Pareroultja is *full of rhythm…and looks like a piece of tapestry*; one by his brother Reuben is *decorative, mural like*; a gorge in the James Range painted by Henoch Raberaba has *a sense of decoration, good drawing, strong light, beautiful colour harmony and free handling*; and so on. There is again a sense that the set of attributes Battarbee celebrates, while engaging, is also somehow transient; while the painting that Namatjira would go on to do in his last decade attains sometimes to a tragic majesty.

One painting from 1952 is a case in point: *Heavitree Gap* is observed from a point of view near where Albert's block of land was, and thus where the house he wanted to build upon it would have stood. It is a picture of the Todd River running through the gap south of Alice Springs, seen from the north and slightly to the west and, in typical Namatjira fashion, shows successive ranges of hills apparently drawing back to disclose more distant hills behind; with a soft blue curve gracing the far reaches. However, untypically, in the left middle ground of the picture there is a house; and, to the left of that, on the rising slope of a low hill, a windsock; with the fragmentary posts of a fence line running diagonally along before them.

Human traces in Namatjira paintings are rare after about 1939; there is the idyllic 1945 painting of his house at Hermannsburg; there is a portrait of a tree, undated, that has the word *Salaam* inscribed in the trunk; a notable painting of Mt Hermannsburg with the Mission below; one of the homestead at Glen Helen; a superb work, also from 1945, showing intricately painted red bluffs at Illara Creek in the James Range behind a fence line that runs across the river; and there is this. The house has been retained in the picture of Heavitree Gap even though other signs of human activity – the road that runs through the gap, the railway – have not. It was not an invention, the small cottage belonged to Eddy Connellan and the accompanying windsock seems like an acknowledgment of that; but it's hard not to see it also as a symbol of flight, or perhaps the desire to flee; while the house itself, with its two mournful dark apertures looking back towards us like empty eyes, seems to be a sign not of presence but of absence.

In this it is the exact opposite of the Hermannsburg house in the 1945 picture which, nestled in the landscape between two trees, looks away from us into the soft, round, green hills beyond. Where the earlier painting is a picture of home, more precisely of a house at home in a beloved landscape, the later work brings to mind thoughts of exile, of a house without a soul at home: a place that could have been inhabited, perhaps once was, might be again, but at the present moment represents an impossible dream. An ironic grimace on the face that can be glimpsed in the bluff at the far right of the picture only exacerbates this sense of exile, even expulsion; and the painting overall has a bleached, dry, parched atmosphere, like a heart full of dust.

One day in June 1952 Albert was painting a favourite group of trees at Heavitree Gap when he was joined, by pre-arrangement, by artist and entrepreneur John Brackenreg. Brackenreg, who grew up in Western Australia, later rehearsed his own credentials as a companion to, and agent for, an Aboriginal artist: he had previously painted in the Kimberley, in the Porongurups and in the Stirling Ranges and included in his work were *studies of full-blooded black trackers*. Brackenreg was secretary of the Society of Artists in Perth in the mid-1930s, during which period he also wrote art reviews for the newspapers; his father had been a printer and publisher. At Christmas, 1937 he had, in a development that prefigured his economic activities in later decades, produced for sale an edition of Christmas cards showing paintings of Australian landscapes.

On 11 March 1938 the *West Australian* reported that *Mr John Brackenreg, the West Australian artist, left Fremantle yesterday by the motorship Kanimbla to spend seven months in the Eastern States. In*

Melbourne he will meet Mr Robert Johnson, and with him will go on a three months' painting tour by caravan in Victoria and New South Wales. Although he continued to travel and to paint, from this period on the focus of Brackenreg's activities lay in the east and especially in Sydney where, in the early 1940s, he founded Legend Press; and where, after the war, during which he served as a cartographer, he studied at the Julian Ashton school. Then, in 1955, he established the Artlovers Gallery (later Artarmon Galleries) which in its day showed artists as diverse as the Lindsay brothers, Desiderius Orban, Lloyd Rees and Jeffrey Smart; both gallery and press remain in the Brackenreg family and both are still in operation today.

Brackenreg recalled his personal friendship with Namatjira in these terms: *I first met Albert early in 1952. I remember the feeling of acceptance from him as one often does when interests are the same. I felt there existed a mutual trust and understanding that would be difficult to explain.* Brackenreg was already acquainted with Charles Mountford and in the introduction to his 1983 book on Namatjira speaks affectionately of Fred and Minna Albrecht, Philipp and Avis Scherer and Gary and Liz Stoll, all Lutherans active on the Mission or in town whom he met on this his first foray into the centre. But the most important relationship was the one he established with Rex Battarbee, the man he would, in some respects, replace.

It was Rex who facilitated the meeting with Albert. On 17 June he wrote: *Another frost and a beautiful day. We decided to go to Simpson's Gap to do some painting. On our way out we called in to J Brackenreg who wired in yesterday. When we arrived home we found JB and his friends waiting* [to go] *down to the mission to meet Albert. This party will need a car to get them there. Will have to see who perhaps might lend them one.* Brackenreg gave some sheets of high-quality Arches paper to both Albert and Rex and, on 20 June 1952, over dinner at the Battarbee house, discussed *special publishing prospects.* A few days later the project had firmed up: *He talked about the book he wants to make for me early next year – 16 colour plates and the size of Art in Australia...probably to cost two guineas.* Legend Press's book on Battarbee, text by Ted Strehlow, would be published in 1956.

At the same time Rex was recording in his diary early sales of sets of cards with reproductions of Namatjira paintings on them: *Murray Neck sold eight dozen sets of Namatjira cards in eight days*, he writes on 4 July. And, ten days later: *We got a big lot of Namatjira Xmas cards in today and Murray Neck bought 91 pounds. It is surprising to me how well they are selling.* In fact, the beginnings of the reproduction of Namatjira paintings by Legend Press go back to mid-1949. On 23 May that year Rex, out at Hermannsburg, wrote: *A cloudy day, calm. The mail plane arrived at 8am. This afternoon I bought 2 stone tjurungas, one at £4 and one at 25/– , from Albert. This evening we had a special meeting of the Aranda Arts Committee. It was to decide about a ghost gum of Albert's that Legend Press wanted to publish – to go into a book of Australian Art. We've decided to agree.*

By July 1952, then, and probably earlier, sets of cards had been printed and were selling well. A month later, in August, Rex writes that *we have not sold an original painting for several days, only prints and books*; around the same time he wonders how many houses in Alice Springs already had a Namatjira on the wall. The sale of reproductions was becoming a lucrative business, not simply from sets of cards but from prints of Namatjira's work, from card-size to actual size which, especially in the 1950s and 1960s, proliferated to the point of ubiquity: you could be forgiven for thinking there was one, framed and behind glass, on the wall of not just every sitting room in Alice but upon that of every dwelling in the land.

Namatjira was already a household name; as reproductions of his work became widely available, his paintings too became intensely familiar; this despite the fact that, like poetry in translation, something essential is lost in their transmission through the lens of the camera: their luminosity and their textural qualities, as well as their character as objects both humble and miraculous. What survives is a picture of an image with some of its unique qualities subtracted. Brackenreg's arrival in the centre was coincident with the burgeoning of this trade in reproductions; within a few years, Legend Press would become the owner of all copyright in the works of Albert Namatjira.

In 1952 Namatjira painted one of his biggest paintings (34x18 inches), and sold several others for the highest price he had yet commanded (100 guineas). Joyce Batty rehearsed the circumstances under which the big picture was painted: *Albert had gone to the Mission at the request of the Superintendent* [i.e. Albrecht], *who was worried about the artist's abandoned caravan at Haasts Bluff Native Reserve. Since his break with the Mission his visits there had been rare...It was of Mt Hermannsburg with the Mission nestling below its vividly coloured contours.* Mt Hermannsburg was among Namatjira's principal subjects, one he returned to again and again over the years; this picture, which may have been the last, like the others chooses a point of view that shows the oddly concave scoop along the southern face of the mountain as a mass of dark shadow: both a fact of observation and a motif replete with associations.

Sidney Nolan spoke of the empty eyes of dead animals he painted in his drought pictures of the early 1950s as a *window to unmoving space*; such windows are common, though relatively unremarked, in Namatjira paintings: the boles of trees, for instance, where a branch has dropped off; or the yawning, usually triangular, aperture at the base of his ghost and river gum portraits; or the darknesses in the crevasses of rock piles that foreground so many of his pictures. Or, as in this case, the shadow that lies along the side of a hill in the afternoon light. In Namatjira's case, the window seems to lead, not to Nolan's *unmoving space* but to the protean darkness of the Everywhen; and, in metaphorical terms, to repositories like those secret–sacred caves where *tjurunga* were kept.

This late, perhaps last, picture of Hermannsburg carries within it all of the earlier ones and in particular the earliest, from 1936, which also shows the hopeful, somehow animate, small huddle of buildings on the Mission, each with their square or oblong windows, like eyes, spread out in a line across the mid-ground of the composition. The 1936 painting has three black horsemen on the red plain in the foreground; the 1952 painting, a wide greeny-yellow expanse upon which stand two trees and in which there are two vertical shapes, one to the left of frame, one in the centre, which may represent isolated humans accompanied only by their shadows. Mt Hermannsburg is mostly blue: not the blue of distance but, mixed in with purples and reds, of naked stone or even adamant. The scooped-out portion of darkness dominates the picture and is, on closer inspection, also made of reds and purples and blues; and leads, you cannot help but suppose, into another world.

Manangananga, the cave ritually desacralised by Albrecht and his Aboriginal evangelists in 1930, is up there somewhere; it survived its Christianisation and, for many of the Arrernte, in time resumed a ceremonial, even sacramental function in their lives – though whether *tjurunga* are still kept there is unknown to outisders. In this painting you feel the imposing weight of ancient tradition, not just in the scooped-out darkness of the bluff but also in the strangely triangular, pyramidal hill to the left and, most powerfully, in the eminence behind and directly above the dark aperture: here are age-old faces, as of tribal elders, gazing imperiously off towards the north where Namatjira's father's country was.

The painting is, like so many of Namatjira's works, a picture of home – this was after all where he was born and grew up and lived the best part of his life – but home was for him, as for so many people now, always a paradoxical concept, made up as much of things that are lost and gone as of things that remain; or else of the intertwining of both. The mission buildings, for example, have a fragility that suggests it would not take much, perhaps just a big flood coming down the Finke, to sweep them away forever; while the mountain behind, with its complex patterning and its evocation, simultaneously, of the leonine and the reptilian, seems enduring but at the same time remote: a home to presences, perhaps deities, who belong to an old dispensation which has been dishonoured and continues in despite of, not because of, human activity. And so it seems that there is at once a way back and no way back; a home but not a home; a place that is, under the enormous, cloud-streaked, sheltering sky, both here and not here.

After one of the early meetings of the new Aranda Arts Council, McCoy of Native Affairs wrote that he *was considerably surprised, and somewhat shocked, at the underlying venom with which certain artists criticised the Finke River Mission…which had failed to realise the artists as a body were quite capable of formulating and expressing such opinions.* Nevertheless when, towards the end of 1951, the Albrechts were leaving to go to Europe on long-service leave *most of the dozen-odd Aboriginal artists appeared on the veranda…with a painting or two… Albrecht felt embarrassed, remembering the many times he had reprimanded these men. But they appeared to hold no grudges. Albert Namatjira also came with a painting wrapped in a hessian sugar bag. Albrecht hesitated, feeling he should not accept such a valuable gift…Namatjira insisted, saying he had not forgotten how much the pastor had done for him.*

We don't know what the painting in the sugar bag was but that big picture of Mt Hermannsburg did become the property of the Finke River Mission. It was shown in Albert's one-man exhibition at Tmara Mara in October 1952, a show which, in Battarbee's view, included some of his strongest work yet. *Albert came in with 14 new paintings – north of Glen Helen – some very good ones,* Rex wrote on 24 July. *He came in by taxi and is going to the dentist.* There is a certain amount of relief associated with this entry because, in the weeks previous, Albert had been troublesome. *He can't wait a minute for anything,* Rex observed, *and wants everything he sees. The latest is that he wants to buy a Holden.* Albert had some War Bonds that he was trying to cash in to buy the new saloon car but, between them, Battarbee and McCoy talked him out of it. On 28 July it was his

fiftieth birthday. Arthur Calwell was in town, there was a meeting of the Aranda Arts Council and Albert *did not stay for supper and he was going to. Bernice gave him a present.*

It's salutary to recall that, whatever else may have been going on, the painting, registering, cataloguing, packaging, freighting, exhibiting and selling of work continued unabated and at a pace that still astonishes: an enormous amount of work that was mostly accomplished by Battarbee alone. Albert's first show in Alice Springs did not take place until 1947, after the wartime interest of soldiers and other foreigners sparked the locals' curiosity. Subsequently, he exhibited in Perth and Brisbane and continued thereafter to exhibit regularly in five of Australia's state capital cities (the exceptions are Darwin and Hobart) until his death. However, from the late 1940s on, solo shows became less common and Namatjira's work was more likely to be seen in the context of group exhibitions of the Hermannsburg painters.

At Tye's Art Gallery in Bourke Street, Melbourne, for instance, in July 1951, he showed five watercolours and the only oil painting he ever exhibited in a group show with, among others, the Pareroultja brothers. The next year, in April, at Anthony Hordern's

Fine Art Gallery in Sydney, he had eight watercolours in a similar exhibition of *The Aranda Group*, in which he was joined by his son Ewald, Edwin, Otto and Reuben Pareroultja, Richard Moketarinja and Cordula Ebatarinja. Cordula, who had been taught to paint by her husband Walter, who had himself been taught by his nephew Albert, with this showing became the first woman artist to be recognised as a Hermannsburg painter and also the first to exhibit in the metropolis. Rex records a visit from her on 14 May 1952, perhaps after the cheque had arrived from the Sydney show: *Cordula returned here on her own today by taxi. She was all dressed up and looked marvellous though she is just about due.*

Not all of the artists painted with the degree of commitment and intensity that Albert showed and not all of them continued to paint. Adolf Inkamala, a painter Battarbee considered one of the most interesting and unusual of the younger group, was after the war assigned his own brand and given his own herd of cattle, which he ran on the reserve west of Areyonga and Haasts Bluff. Adolf became a successful rancher, so much so that in 1956, when the Native Welfare Branch's own western herds became depleted, they bought bullocks for cash from him. Like Albert after him, in 1955 Inkamala had his name removed from the list of wards of the state, giving him the status equivalent to that of a white man. When he died in 1960 he left an estate worth £4,500.

Painting had become a career but clearly not the only one. Nor was it an uncomplicated pursuit: in 1952, once again, the question of fakes arose. This time it was more serious. Paintings turned up in Adelaide and Melbourne that were not just wrongly attributed, but appeared to be deliberate forgeries. Battarbee, in Adelaide, told the press that he was *certain someone was forging signatures...I have an idea who the guilty person might be but it is hard to prove anything definite... anyone who buys a painting by an Aranda artist...which does not bear the stamps on the back runs the risk of buying a forgery.* However, unless unsold works were pre-dated, which seems not to have happened, the stamp would appear only on works made since the licensing system was established in 1951; a forger could easily claim a date prior to that for his fakes; most of the works of the Hermannsburg School, like almost all of Namatjira's, are undated.

The issue went national, as did anything connected with Namatjira now, and many people began to doubt the authenticity of their acquisitions. One man, a foreign diplomat, on an official visit to Alice Springs before returning to his home country, brought two paintings with him to be authenticated. In Adelaide *The News* reported that Battarbee, *Australian artist and leader of the Aranda Arts Council took one look at the paintings and said: 'They are both fakes. Albert Namatjira did not paint them. In fact, one is a copy of a fake.'* The forged paintings were skilfully executed but the signatures were often wrong: since 1938 Namatjira had signed his work with the surname in printed capitals in the bottom right hand corner; with the Christian name always present and only very occasionally in cursive script. Some of the forged works had the whole signature in running writing, others had it printed diagonally and some erred by using only the surname.

The story played out in the press for years until a resolution of a kind was reached. After the death of the caretaker of the local swimming pool in Alice Springs, police found among his belongings a suitcase containing what purported to be Namatjira paintings. They bore no stamps and were signed diagonally across the bottom. Albert, called in to inspect five of these works, said: *I have never seen these paintings before.* Gordon Simpson, who had for some years acted as sub-agent for sales in Alice Springs and was a member of the Aranda Arts Council, concurred: *the paintings I inspected at the Police Station appeared to be clever copies of Albert's style and only an expert would recognise these were copies.*

It was not established that the swimming-pool caretaker, a

middle-aged man, was in fact the forger; he might have been an agent. In January 1954 *The News* reported: *Last year the police investigated three fakes sold for 40 and 50 guineas in South Australia. After that, the police...seemed to wipe their hands of the matter. The Council believes the faker is still at large, carrying on a lucrative business.* The one person who did not seem unduly upset by the controversy was Albert himself, who remarked that forgeries didn't concern him because he could always paint more paintings: an attitude perhaps understandable for one who, in his camp at Morris Soak, *was living in a wurly of tree boughs, old bags and rusty galvanized iron.*

Albert might have been a fringe dweller in Alice Springs but he was also peripatetic, a confirmed wanderer who sometimes seems to have been, in his oeuvre, assembling a kind of composite map of his ancestral country. He also went further afield, painting pictures of the lands of the eastern Arrernte, for instance at Love's Creek, and on at least one occasion going far south, where he painted flat-topped inselberg Mt Conner; and west to Uluru, where Pitjantjatjara men told him he was not entitled to paint the rock. After his trip to Darwin, Albert expressed a desire to go to Perth next and asked Native Affairs for permission to do so. The plan was reported by Eric Charles in the *West Australian*, which announced the visit was to take place in January 1953.

Namatjira's decision, the paper said, *is the result of a long emotional battle which reached a crisis with the refusal of the authorities to let him build a house and studio in the Alice Springs 'white area'.* Said Albert: 'I'm sick of not being able to do what I like and go where I like. I earn my money like a white man and pay my taxes. Why can't I spend like a white man?' In the event, Native Affairs refused Albert permission to go to Perth and, adding insult to injury, declined to give any explanation why; it would not be surprising if the report in the *West Australian*, and in particular Albert's own quoted remarks, were part of the reason. There was undoubtedly animus towards Namatjira amongst a minority of the white population in Alice Springs and this was shared by others who lived in Darwin: he was an uppity black who had to be kept in his place.

The adoption of the cause of Albert's freedom by journalists and writers of various descriptions, while well-intentioned, was not necessarily of any advantage to him personally and may in fact have made things worse. It's significant that Battarbee, on the evidence of his diaries, tried never to feed a sense of grievance but attempted always to accentuate the positive. Of all of those who adopted Albert as a cause, the most vociferous and indefatigable was Frank Clune: in some respects, as Brackenreg replaced Battarbee as Albert's agent, so too did Clune replace Bob Croll (who died in 1947) as the chief proselytiser on his behalf. In both cases a gentlemanly old-fashioned approach to business gave way to something more in accord with the entrepreneurial spirit of the age: Clune's accountancy firm, like the businesses Brackenreg founded, is still extant and still in the family.

Francis Patrick Clune was a Sydney-sider, born the Catholic son of an Irish navvy in Darlinghurst in 1893, who grew up in nearby Redfern. He left school at fourteen and became a newsboy; when the war broke out he was working as a seaman and had already, in Kansas, joined up and then deserted from the United States Army. In May 1915 he enlisted with the Australian Imperial Force and at Gallipoli in early August that year, after just five days ashore, was wounded in both legs and evacuated to Cairo; he was discharged in 1916. Clune worked as a commercial traveller and studied accountancy at night; he founded his tax consultancy business in 1924, a year after he married his second wife, a twenty-one year-old saleswoman called Thelma Cecily Smith, who would later make regular appearances in his newspaper columns as *Brown Eyes*.

Clune's first book, *Try Anything Once*, came out in 1933 and was a bestseller; it is based upon *his adventures at sea, as a trooper in the American cavalry, at Gallipoli, bootlegging in Canada, touring Queensland in the chorus of an opera company, and as a mouse-trap salesman* and established the template for sixty odd other books published over the next four decades. Many of these were written in collaboration with former communist, writer, editor and publisher PR (Inky) Stephenson; an early champion of Aboriginal rights, Inky helped organise the Day of Mourning and Protest to mark the sesquicentenary on 26 January 1938. He and Clune were masculinists, nationalists, propagandists, rapscallions who on occasion played fast and loose with the truth. Clune wrote in the first issue of his eponymous *Adventure Magazine* in 1948: *We don't want stories of snoopy sex, written by anaemic lounge lizards and pub-crawlers. Action is the password to these pages. This is reading for men with red blood in their arteries.*

Clune, who also wrote for the newspapers and for magazines like *Smith's Weekly*, from 1945 until 1957 had a regular show on ABC radio called *Roaming Round Australia* with an audience estimated at about a million people. And in the 1940s, with his wife Thelma, he started an art gallery in Kings Cross. Russell Drysdale, John Passmore and the Clunes' lifelong friend, William Dobell, were among those whose work could be seen there. Subsequently the Terry Clune Art Galleries (Terry was Frank and Thelma's youngest son), opened, first on the corner of Challis Avenue and Macleay Street, later at 59 Macleay Street, where it became an exhibition space for younger artists like John Olsen, Stan Rapotec, Robert Klippel and Robert Hughes; and was in the late 1960s the home of Martin Sharp, who re-named it The Yellow House and re-invented the gallery as a kind of continuous art installation-cum-happening.

In June 1953 Clune was camping with Albert at Dashwood Creek, out towards Haasts Bluff, when he heard on the car radio that Namatjira had been awarded the Queen's Coronation Medal.

11,500 of these were distributed in Australia alone and Pastors Albrecht and Gross were among the recipients – though not Clune himself. According to Joyce Batty, Albert *showed little enthusiasm...had little to say; he was more interested in planning some landscapes.* She says that Clune took four paintings back to Sydney, all with the same subject but each painted by a different artist: Albert, Enos, Oscar and Ewald Namatjira. Reg Harris recorded an alternate version: Clune *arrived in town, took Albert for a trip out bush and, according to Rex Battarbee, arrived back in Alice with an original Namatjira; and Albert with a bottle of scotch.*

The Namatjira painting that was traded for a bottle of whisky is most likely the one of Haasts Bluff now in the National Gallery in Canberra. It has, below the signature, looking slightly cramped and written, unusually, in Albert's ornate copperplate script, the words *to Frank*. Dedications are as rare as dates on Namatjira paintings; one of the few others is inscribed *to Thelma* – clearly Thelma Clune. The Haasts Bluff painting that Clune commissioned, then gave to lawyer, politician and judge Robert 'Bob' Ellicott, who in turn gave it to the National Gallery, is both a reprise of the one the Adelaide gallery bought in 1939 and a magnificent work in its own right: a line of yellow-green shrubs gives way to a white plain covered with blue-grey trees that lead the eye on to the red and purple, eloquently shadowed mountain reposing beneath the eternity of a high blue sky.

Subsequently the *Telegraph* reported: *Swooner Crooner Frank Sinatra will sing one song to Mrs Frank Clune, wife of the Australian author explorer, at his home this afternoon. In return he will receive a boomerang carved by aboriginal Albert Namatjira. Offering the boomerang to Sinatra last night Clune said 'Namatjira carved it for me. I value it very much but if you sing one song for my wife, it's yours.' Accepting the offer Frankie said: 'It's a deal, you name it, I'll sing it.' Clune visited Sinatra at Glen Ascham* [a private hotel in Darling Point]...*to let him* view the latest painting by Albert Namatjira. Clune brought the painting to Sydney last month after meeting Namatjira near Dashwood Creek in the Centre of Australia. Clune also presented Sinatra with a volume of prints of Namatjira paintings – and six volumes of books written by himself with Australian themes.

It is a massive but not inappropriate irony that Namatjira's opportunity to travel for the first time beyond the Northern Territory came only because the Queen commanded it. Albert received an impromptu shoe shine at the Alice Springs home of his friends, the Tuncks, before going out to the airport for his first-ever flight in an aeroplane; he was farewelled by the Battarbees, who by now, with the birth of their son Robin Gilbert in 1953, were three, and by writer Alan Wauchope. When they landed in Darwin, he was met by Ngarla Kunoth (Rosalie Kunoth-Monk), the young Arrernte girl cast as the female lead in the feature film *Jedda*, and taken to the set where Charles Chauvel was shooting the scene in which Robert Tudawali (Bob Wilson), the male lead, dances with an eleven-foot snake. *Good tucker that feller,* Albert said. *I'll have to keep an eye on that snake,* Chauvel replied. *One man's meat is another man's python.*

Ted Egan recalled: *When it was announced that the Queen would visit Australia in 1954, I was told to organise a group of 21 Aboriginals who would...dance for the Queen and included in the group was Albert Namatjira, the painter, who was to be formally presented. He stayed with Rae and me for a couple of weeks while the group rehearsed. Among other things I had to take Albert to George Lim, tailor and publican, to get two suits made to measure. The government paid, so George charged plenty, but did a great job...in searching for a single adjective to describe Albert Namatjira only one comes to mind: dignified. In fact he was the most dignified person I ever met, dignified almost to the point of aloofness. A 'more quiet man altogether' is how the Aboriginals would describe him.*

From Darwin Namatjira flew, by Constellation airliner, to

Sydney, where he looked at the mean terrace houses in the industrial suburb of Mascot and asked, incredulously, if people really lived in them? In the capital he stayed at the Canberra Hotel and, on the morning of 15 February, rose early to practise his bow. As he stepped forward, in his brand new white linen suit, he was watched by, among others, a group of the Royal Papuan and New Guinea Constabulary, a Manus Island naval detachment and the brass and pipe bands of the Pacific Islands Regiment. *Among the many distinguished Australians presented to the Royal visitors*, one observer wrote, *the tall, handsome, dark Aboriginal artist was without a doubt the most outstanding personality.* Afterwards Namatjira said the Duke asked if he painted as a hobby? *No sir,* he replied, *it is a full time job.* Of the Queen he remarked: *She was a nice little kwara kwaka* (young girl).

After three days in Canberra, during which he attended the State Ball in Kings Hall, Parliament House – *the most glittering social occasion in Australia's history* – Albert returned to Sydney where he stayed for a week as a guest of the Clunes in their Vaucluse mansion. There he told the special correspondent at the *Sun Herald*: *I wanted to see the important men in Canberra who work on our affairs, but there was the Queen to see and I could not. There was no time. I am getting old but I can remember when there were no reserves. We are tired of walking around reserves like animals, and of living in tents like new people...I have painted for twenty years and always I have had to guard my paintings when the wet comes, so the rain does not soak them as it soaks me. This is no good, I am old now and I'm tired of moving with my tent. I would like to settle before it's too late.*

In Sydney, for the first time, Albert attended one of his own metropolitan openings. The exhibition was at Anthony Hordern's Fine Arts Gallery; there were twelve Namatjiras among the sixty-eight works by ten Arrernte artists. A crowd of 500 people came. Albert spoke after the Lord Mayor, Alderman PD Hills, had declared the exhibition open: *Well ladies and gentlemen I haven't been in a city before in my life. I think I have three times now had pictures coming on exhibition in this place here and I am pleased to thank you for being here.* Subsequently, while he was autographing catalogues, a mêlée developed: *As the crowd closed around the dais, several women knelt down on all fours and thrust their catalogues between legs towards Mr Namatjira. One elderly woman in a bright yellow dress crawled across the dais, her handbag in one hand and a catalogue in the other. The microphone began to sway and at length it fell into the crowd.*

People followed him wherever he went: to the opening of an exhibition of newspaper art at David Jones' Gallery; at a party in his honour at the Clunes; at the Art Gallery of New South Wales, where the assistant director received him on the steps and many of those in the queue to enter an exhibition of royal regalia left it and followed him through the portrait and landscape sections of the gallery. His responses to the work he saw went unrecorded but he would have known already that he was not represented in the collection. The *Bulletin* commented that it was *really shocking that the NSW gallery does not own a panel of these most interesting watercolours and hasn't bothered to buy a Namatjira painting*.

Meanwhile Brackenreg, who had just published another edition of Namatjira prints, saw an opportunity: *Because of great public interest in the work of our leading aboriginal artist and because the State collection so far does not contain a single specimen of his unique talents, Mr John Brackenreg of Sydney is offering to lend the trustees two of Namatjira's most important paintings.* It does not appear that the offer was taken up. The gallery director, Hal Missingham, had already, in 1951, stated his position and saw no reason to change it now. *When Namatjira comes up to standard,* he said, *we will hang his pictures.*

Namatjira took a train to Melbourne, where he was hosted by Lutheran Pastor Philipp Scherer, who prepared an itinerary that attempted to avoid the kinds of public occasions, and the public hysteria, that occurred in Sydney. However police had to be called when Albert was mobbed while walking down Collins Street; and there was another mêlée of autograph hunters when he attended a show of Australian art at the Town Hall. There was a dinner with JK Moir, of the Bread and Cheese club, to whom he had dedicated Mountford's book; boating on the Yarra; a drive through the Dandenongs and an excursion into orchard country at Doncaster; a visit to the Shrine of Remembrance. He also attended a meeting of the Aborigines Welfare Board and went to the Wycliffe Summer School of Linguistics, where he swapped phrases in Arrernte and Pitjantjatjara with the Superintendent of the United Australian Mission Languages Department, Wilfrid Douglas of Kalgoorlie.

It was an exhausting schedule: after Melbourne, Adelaide, to which he also travelled by train and where, again, he was hosted by Mission folk: Pastor Lohe and his old friend and patron, Charles Duguid. There were two official receptions: one by the Aboriginal Advancement League, of which Duguid was president; the other by the Royal South Australian Society of Arts which, out of respect for Albert's compulsory teetotalism, was a dry function. At the National Art Gallery of South Australia the director, Robert Campbell, showed him the painting of Haasts Bluff McCubbin had bought in 1939; but Campbell, like Daryl Lindsay in Melbourne, later on that year declined Battarbee's suggestion that they purchase more works by Namatjira.

Bernard Smith, at the time working at the Art Gallery of NSW, wrote that *Hal Missingham, Robert Campbell and Daryl Lindsay believed that Namatjira was painting the wrong kind of art. It was not for them 'primitive' enough. If Australia's most famous painter, Sidney Nolan, could paint primitive paintings then surely a real primitive man ought be able to do so.* Alan Wauchope later asked Namatjira what he thought of the remarks, made by gallery people in Melbourne, that his latest works were *frightful...absolute pot-boilers.* Albert replied: *If I want to boil a pot, I light a fire – and use some of the paper those blokes write on... can't waste good painting paper.* And of the paintings by the great masters he had seen in the cities: *When they painted them, they had to work hard for their money like me. So they did their best.*

It is one thing to live at home and know you are famous; another to go abroad into the larger world and experience it personally. It might exacerbate your sense of grievance, especially when you return to reduced circumstances, to a kind of enforced exile, at home. While in Adelaide Albert went up to the Barossa Valley, met with Albrecht's superior, Pastor Reuther, and walked in his beautiful gardens; and, at his own request, visited Mr and Mrs Heinrich at Gawler, recalling the time, thirty years before, when he had met them off the train at Oodnadatta and driven them by wagon up to Hermannsburg. He seemed disconsolate and told the Heinrichs that, for all his material wealth, money could not buy him the one thing he wanted most: a home of his own in Alice Springs. He returned there by train, accompanied by two Hermannsburg staff, and went straight out to his camp at Morris Soak to see his wife, his children and his friends and relations.

It was at Morris Soak, late in the year, that Namatjira was arrested and jailed for the first time for an alcohol-related offence. It was on the face of it a minor transgression: taking a sip of wine from a bottle he had been offered. He spent a night in the cells and appeared in the Police Court at Alice Springs on Christmas Eve 1954. Two men in the camp, a half-caste and a full-blood, had offered him the wine and he said that he had, to be friendly, taken a drink. *I am not a drinking man. I am an aboriginal and I know it is wrong.* Battarbee, who was a non-drinker, appeared as a character witness. *With all due respect,* he told the court, referring to a law that allowed people of so-called mixed blood to drink, *I believe the Full Citizenship Rights Bill for half-castes will be the downfall of the full-blood aborigines.* He also said that in all the years he had known Namatjira he had never seen him drink alcohol.

The arresting officer confirmed that Namatjira was not drunk and that he readily admitted the offence. The magistrate found the facts of the case proven but declined to impose any penalty; however the man who supplied the wine, whose second offence it was, got nine months. Albert himself was shaken by his night in the cells. As soon as he was free to go, he left Alice Springs and went bush; and spent most of the next year, 1955, out in the tribal lands west of Hermannsburg, coming into Alice Springs infrequently and then only to deliver paintings or to get more supplies of paint and paper. On those occasions when he did come into town he seemed changed. He was, his first biographer wrote, *embittered, disillusioned, his quiet pleasant manner replaced by an attitude of resentment towards everyone and everything*.

9. Painting from Memory

In 1954 the Commonwealth Literary Fund gave Irish-born Australian poet Roland Robinson a grant that enabled him to spend a year in the Northern Territory recording Aboriginal mythology for a book he would call *The Feathered Serpent.* Robinson was one of the Jindyworobaks, a group of nationalistic writers enamoured of Aboriginality, which they thought could be a source of renewal for the culture as a whole. He was also a trained ballet dancer and, in the 1950s and 60s, wrote as dance critic for the *Sydney Morning Herald.* He and his wife lighted out for the Territory by motor cycle, carrying all the gear they needed in their saddle bags: *silk tent, silk sleeping bags, light aluminium cooking gear and immediate food and water...we travelled many thousands of miles lightly and economically.*

At Areyonga they became *good friends with a certain native and his wife. This man was, unknown to me, a son* [it was Keith] *of Albert Namatjira, the painter...when we eventually reached Haasts Bluff we found we had been preceded by a most helpful introduction to a large section of the north-western Aranda tribe camped there.* Not long after they arrived *a big heavily built man walked up to our camp and introduced himself. He was Albert Namatjira.* Namatjira, whom Robinson calls by his tribal name Tonanga, took him down into a sandy creek-bed to meet several old men sitting beside a shelter made of branches leaning against a gum tree.

We sat down in the sand and one man pulled a corn-sack out from under the shade. This corn-sack was placed in Tonanga's lap as he sat cross-legged. Out of the sack Tonanga drew a large, flat, black oval stone inscribed on both sides with totemic designs. This stone was the Talkara, the body and spirit of Tonanga's mythical ancestor. Each man...placed the ball of his thumb in turn on the central design of the stone while Tonanga explained the significance and the meaning of the object to me. Then the stone was put back in the sack and hidden under the shade again. Robinson subsequently spent days in the creek-bed taking down the men's stories. Some of these accounts were performative: *I can still see Tonanga on his hands and knees in the sand enacting for me the myth of Erintja the Devil-dog.*

The story of the devil dog is one of three myths Tonanga told, and Robinson published, in *The Feathered Serpent*; the others are *The Eagle-men of Alkutnama* and *The Old-man and his Six Sons, the Namatuna*. Each is a substantial, complex, detailed and mysterious tale, carried in the memory and handed down in oral form from tribal sources: perhaps Albert's father Jonathon; perhaps other initiated men of his generation. There was more: *Tonanga's parting gift to me*, Robinson wrote, *was a painting of his three main ceremonial objects done while we sat in the creek-bed under the ghost gums with the purple and violet and ochre-red mountain of Haasts Bluff rising out of the spinifex.*

This painting, though not its explanation, survives in the State Library of NSW: an oblong sheet of brown paper with what look like a *tjurunga*, a bull-roarer and ceremonial pole design in watercolour upon it. Its existence, the glimpse into an alternate creation given by Robinson's account of his researches, and Tonanga's myths themselves, emphasise something often overlooked: that Namatjira was an initiated man, a custodian of traditional stories as much as he was of ancestral places and, by the 1950s, one of the elders of his tribe.

That his knowledge was rarely communicated to anyone not of the Arrernte is hardly surprising; that it is not readily seen in his paintings is more intriguing. Aspects of traditional knowledge, traditional stories, may be apparent in Namatjira landscapes to those who already know them, but without that special knowledge they retain an inscrutability that is as much a part of their appeal as their apparent verisimilitude.

A further question is raised by Roland Robinson's research: the place of memory in Namatjira's art. From at least as early as 1950 a critique had arisen among white commentators of what they called *painting from memory*. Apropos of Albert's plan to build a house in Alice Springs, McCoy of Native Affairs said that if Namatjira were to live in town he might become inactive and lose interest in his work, *perhaps adopting the technique of...painting from memory and selling whatever he could obtain for his pictures*. Why a civil servant should think it appropriate to advise an artist on his method of composition is unclear; but the conviction that works painted in situ were authentic whereas those made out of memory were not, is perfectly plain.

And absurd: for, as Tim Rowse has written, *one of the traditional functions of Aboriginal graphic symbols is to be mnemonic...painting from memory cannot be said...to threaten a tradition which has long been an art of memory*. Not only that: Lee Robinson observed at least ten years earlier that Namatjira possessed a prodigious visual memory and could reproduce with preternatural accuracy a landscape that was not before his eyes. Moreover, later practitioners of the Hermannsburg School, like Wenten Rubuntja, made it clear that there were usually two stages to the process of making a work:

getting the sketch, which might involve *plein air* drawing, and the actual painting, which could be, and often was, completed away from the landscape that was the subject of the work.

Yet McCoy persisted in his condemnation of the practice, essentially because he believed it was connected with the so-called 'black market' in art. He wrote to his superiors in Darwin that, if the illicit trade could be curbed *the lamentable practice, now adopted by even Albert Namatjira, of painting from memory will be abolished*. It never was, and never could be: memory, as Jean Paul Richter said, is the only paradise we cannot be evicted from; and one way of looking at Namatjira's late paintings is as works that use memory to evoke country that, like the fenced-off bluff at Illara Creek, is no longer accessible to the artist, perhaps no longer accessible to anyone any more, except through the agency of memory itself. Tragic is a word too often used to describe the artist's fate; and perhaps better employed with reference to his work.

Whether painted from memory or not, the illicit trade – that is, the bypassing of the Aranda Council with its official pricing system and its stamps of authentication – continued and led in the end to exasperation amongst those attempting to regulate sales and protect the artists' incomes. Early in 1956 Battarbee had had enough. He issued a public statement announcing that he was resigning from the Council and that he would no longer be acting as Namatjira's agent or as the agent of any of the other Hermannsburg painters either: *I have been associated with the Aranda*

painters since their artistic childhood, he said. *Now, like any parent who has guided his children's footsteps I feel the time has come for them to strike out for themselves.*

In a letter to Harry Giese, the Director of the Welfare Branch at Native Affairs, he was more explicit about his reasons: *I would be pleased to continue if these aboriginal artists were really honest to the Aranda Arts Council, as unofficial paintings by these artists are for sale in several shops…this position makes my job intolerable.* Battarbee was persuaded to stay on as Chairman of, and advisor to, the Council, which was reconfigured as an agency of the Welfare Branch with the power to disburse money and to appoint official sales agents both in Alice Springs and the wider world beyond; but in reality the Council, although it continued on with a nominal existence for a time, was defunct.

Legislation amending the Police Offences Act so as to make it a crime to buy a painting by an Aboriginal artist without the permission of the Native Affairs Branch (six months imprisonment or a £100 fine or both) proved ineffective, indeed unenforceable and anyway looked draconian; and the illegal trade continued. As if to make this crystal clear, a survey of so-called official agencies – a florist, a café and a general store – showed that ninety per cent of works on sale did not have the official stamp. It isn't clear if this survey included the premises of John Cummings, a pharmacist who moved to Alice Springs in the 1940s after seeing Albert's work in a sell-out show at Anthony Hordern's. Cummings was a trusted dealer to whom Namatjira gave about four paintings a week throughout the 1950s; he offered them for sale in the gallery next door to his chemist shop.

Elsewhere, mark-ups, especially for Namatjira works, were considerable and paintings bought for £20 might be resold for a hundred; or else sent to Sydney where demand remained high and prices even higher. Meanwhile Namatjira himself owed money all over town, as much as £1300, mostly for repairs on his various vehicles – a three-ton four-wheel-drive truck, a half-ton utility and a second-hand saloon car, none of which he drove much himself, but all of which were used regularly by friends and relations.

Battarbee at this time gave some insight into the nature of his business, telling *The News* in Adelaide: *In the last year of my sole agency in Alice Springs* [1955], *for all native artist's work including Namatjira, I sold 1034 paintings by 18 artists for about 7,600 pounds. I got 10% for my trouble and was happy to help them. But now unauthorised dealers want only Namatjiras and Albert's contemporaries in Alice Springs are having a lot of trouble finding markets.* Rumours of a rift between the two old friends remain unsubstantiated but there is no doubt that, as Battarbee himself recognised, *taking a broad view it looks as if the artists want to sell their own pictures*; and he cannot be blamed for deciding to leave them to it.

The recent birth of his and Bernice's second child, a daughter, Gayle Florinda, might have been an influence here, since the need to care for small children usually has the effect of focussing the mind upon time available for other pursuits; and it was certainly the case that Battarbee felt that he had for years neglected his own work in favour of the promotion and sale of that of others; and now wanted more time to paint. Battarbee's paintings are difficult to see these days, there are very few in public collections and, since he has not yet been given a retrospective, those held in private hands remain obscure. Some can be tracked through the records of auction houses but they are not many and rarely illustrated. Nevertheless, it's clear that his decision to step down from his role as agent and dealer bore immediate fruit in his work.

Two works from 1956 show him at his best; both are paintings of gaps in the Western MacDonnell Ranges; both feature red rocky walls that have been compared to slabs of dripping meat. They were each made into prints, which Rex signed in the same year, and had framed together to make a diptych. The left-hand image, of Standley Chasm, shows the two cliffs plunging down to meet at the base of the picture in a V shape; past the intricate exchange between them we see a coil of greyish stones like viscera topped by a blue corner of sky. The gap in the right-hand image, perhaps Ellery Creek Big Hole, is wider and more generously disposed. Here the two rock faces regard each other equally and in profile; in the water below, their reflections look like two old men talking. The wide belt of sand that separates image from reflection resembles a pair of lips and the tree that can be seen beyond the gap seems in certain lights to be an eye, beneficently gazing down upon this ancient conversation.

It may be fanciful to see here an acknowledgement and a celebration of the twenty-year professional relationship between Battarbee and Namatjira; and, given its timing, a kind of elegy for it too. Anthropomorphism is much more unusual in Rex's work than it is in Albert's and its successful appearance here may be seen as a kind of homage from the former to the latter. If the analogy can be sustained, then we may begin to hear fragments of the words the two painters are saying to each other: they are talking about red, they are talking about blue, about trees and rocks and water; most of all about the mysterious process by which the addition of water to pigment allows the representation of a world that can include rocks and stones and trees as well as conversations like these.

1956 was also the year in which Brackenreg's Legend Press published the book on Battarbee roughed out some years before. While it does include the promised sixteen colour plates and is more or less the size of an *Art and Australia* magazine – and like other books from the same publisher is well-made – it does not serve Rex particularly well. The major text is a long, rambling, sometimes incoherent essay on art by Ted Strehlow; and among the colour plates are six reproductions of paintings by artists other than Rex himself – including two of Albert's. This is presumably because of the need to continue promoting the Hermannsburg School but their appearance in the book, especially since it came out just as Battarbee had decided to step back, is not only confusing, it also takes something away from Rex as an artist: as if he were an adjunct, rather than an inspiration, to those he has mentored.

Apart from Strehlow's essay (and, oddly, one of his own colour photographs showing *totemic markings*), the book includes a brief anonymous biographical introduction, presumably written by Brackenreg, and an afterword, *Why I Paint In Central Australia* by Rex himself. The primary reason he gives is its natural beauty: *My love for this land has become so much a part of my life, that I have built my home in Alice Springs…the ever glorious thing about The Alice is Mount Gillen…especially at sunrise, when the play of light on this rugged mountain bluff bathes its rocky face with such a rosy red glow, that one could believe it to be a huge red-hot ember lying across the plain.*

On the front dust jacket is a portrait, in profile, of *Nabi, a Pintupi Tribesman*, from 1940; and on the back, white on grey, a *tjurunga* design. Beneath the dust jacket, white on black, are six more *tjurunga* running top to bottom on the right-hand side of the hardback; but there is no explanation as to what they mean or whose permission might have been sought for their reproduction.

The question of reproduction rights, and of Legend Press's ownership of them, was about to flare up: a Melbourne printer and publisher, FR Barlow, in July 1956 wrote to the proprietor of the Rendezvous Cafe in Alice Springs, a Mrs Woods, asking for the right to reproduce paintings by Albert Namatjira, Otto Pareroultja and Herbert Raberaba which he had bought from her; he enclosed permission forms for each artist to sign. In the next month, August, he wrote to Battarbee in his capacity as Chairman of the Aranda

Arts Council: *We feel we are justified in asking that you approve of these Rights as in our opinion we do not consider any one company – such as Legend Press – should have any priority, especially when these paintings are controlled by a public body such as your Committee.* The Secretary of the Council replied: *There is no question of any particular company having the sole right to reproduce the works of Aranda artists.* That was, however, about to change.

Brackenreg entered the fray, alleging that Barlow, who went ahead and published his prints, obtained his permissions fraudulently – by asking the artist for an autograph and then later adding words to make it appear a genuine assignment. He wrote to Battarbee suggesting *you could have a stay of proceedings issued against the firm on the strength that Albert Namatjira, being a ward of the government, was not in a position to grant authority...it is not in the least bit of good allowing it to go further, because this is only the beginning of a flood of work that could be brought out by others who have similar authority from the artists.*

Legend Press, up until this challenge from Barlow, had had a free run. Since 1949 Brackenreg from time to time reproduced works of Namatjira's, paying for each pro rata; there does not seem to have been any arrangement with respect to royalties nor any formal agreement on copyright. A subsequent legal investigation by an officer appointed by the Northern Territory government found that Barlow had committed no offence and also that his reproduction authority, signed by Namatjira, appeared genuine; although rumours persisted that this was not so. Now Brackenreg mobilised his resources in an attempt to protect his (de facto) assets by redressing his oversight in not drawing up a proper legal agreement. He moved swiftly and, with the support of Battarbee, within a year or so of Barlow's letter, effectively owned Namatjira's copyright. The first document towards this assignment of rights was tendered in Sydney during Namatjira's second visit there towards the end of 1956; and the process was complete by early June in the following year.

Meanwhile Albert was more concerned with familial than with commercial matters. In March, 1956 his father Jonathon died, aged about eighty, at Hermannsburg. He had seen in those years the eclipse of one way of life and its transformation into another, hitherto unprecedented, indeed unimaginable. Although he was born and raised in the bush, over the half century since conversion his Christianity never wavered; neither had his commitment to the old ways and his custodianship of tradition. He was proud of his son's achievements as an artist and remained a presence in his life, often appearing in photographs and also in Mountford's film, where he is among those who crowd into an exhibition of paintings and examine the work on the wall.

In family photographs he usually sits in profile, cross-legged, looking out of the frame as if across the landscape: an hieratic figure like a guardian of the mysteries. In a portrait by Axel Poignant, taken in 1946, his mane of white hair and his knotted white beard contrast with his dark skin and enigmatic, hooded eyes; in an earlier uncredited photograph from the 1920s he has his head

thrown back and his eyes closed in a pose reminiscent of some of the asylum photographs taken by Georges Pastier of Antonin Artaud. Another shot shows him in the dusty compound of Hermannsburg with hat and cane, at once terminally dishevelled and sartorially elegant. In almost every photograph he appears in profile; in every one without exception you sense the presence of a silent witness who insists that his perspective, however oblique, is an integral part of the meaning of the image. Now he was gone.

His death, according to Joyce Batty, affected Albert deeply: *even though for some years he had not seen much of him.* She quotes a fragment of speech which may or may not be verbatim: *'Albert, him very rich, him Big Boss now',* he would say; but adding that he was sad *Albert had left the Mission;* and goes on to remark that Jonathon died in ignorance of the financial difficulties his son was in. The reach of that ignorance might be widened to include a great deal more than just monies owing: Albert's predicaments were manifold and increasing but they all stemmed from a common source, which can be understood as an ultimate lack of control over the direction his own life was taking. In that sense the loss of Jonathon's vigilant, if silent, presence as an over-seer probably increased Albert's vulnerability to outside, perhaps inimical, forces. Chief among these was Frank Clune.

Clune's latest scheme was to bring Namatjira to Sydney once more: this time to receive the gift of a new Dodge utility truck from the petrol company, Ampol. He had to obtain permission from Canberra for Albert and his son Keith to leave the Northern Territory; Canberra in turn had to ask Native Affairs in Darwin. The Administrator, Giese, expressed some misgivings about the purpose of the trip but Clune told him it was all for the sake of Albert's art. Giese telexed the Department in the capital: *Have received firm assurances that purpose of visit is purely social. The only function arranged being a morning tea at David Jones.* This was untrue. The week was made up of a relentless schedule of civic functions and public appearances. Nevertheless permission was granted, albeit only hours before Albert, Keith and their chaperone, taxi-driver Bert Gardiner, were due to board the plane. Gardiner had been hired by Clune: *I was told to get the bushman look off them – clean them up, shave them, suitcase them and put them on the plane.*

Namatjira was introduced to the Governor of NSW, the Police Commissioner, the Lord Mayor and Cardinal Gilroy. He went to the zoo, he went boating on the harbour, he met Father Christmas at a city emporium. On Monday night he went to see Gilbert and Sullivan's *The Gondoliers* at the Empire; and on Thursday night enjoyed the Tivoli's *Good Old Days*, a vaudeville show featuring singers, dancers, comediennes, contortionists, impressionists and jugglers. He was a guest at a cocktail party held for athletes who had competed at the recent Olympic Games in Melbourne and he met the American Davis Cup tennis team. He was persuaded to set up an easel in Martin Place but could find there nothing to paint: *I can't feel anything about these buildings,* he said. *Perhaps a greater artist could paint them. I'm only good enough for the rough bush.*

A dinner was held in his honour at Princes where Doc Evatt and Dame Mary Gilmore, then ninety-one years old, were among the guests. Crowds gathered outside to watch the celebrities arrive; Albert, sitting between the statesman and the poet, spent much of the time in conversation with Dame Gilmore and afterwards helped her down the stairs; but the meal itself was an ordeal. *He sat in puzzled silence listening to one speaker after another eulogising him and his work in terms he could not understand. He just bowed solemnly every time he heard his name spoken.* There was a visit to a dentist, where he was given a set of false teeth. And there were four sessions sitting for artist William Dargie to paint his portrait.

Namatjira always woke early and so, given his busy schedule, that was when the sittings took place: between 5–8am at an improvised studio – probably the Clune's gallery, later the Yellow House – in Macleay Street, Potts Point. Dargie, whose painting won the Archibald prize in 1957, said: *Albert has tremendous inner dignity. It reminds me of the tranquillity one finds in antique statues, Roman*

portraits and in the Arabs in the desert. *He has the most wonderful face for a portrait I have ever seen.* Albert appreciated the company of a fellow painter: *I went with him to several parties and receptions. I very soon saw that he was most unhappy in this strange environment. On one occasion he came up to me, pushed me in the back and…whispered, 'We go now – we go back to your studio and talk about pictures.'*

From Dargie we get a rare glimpse of Albert as critic. Of a well-known, though unidentified, Australian painter he remarked: *He does not know how to make the side of a tree which is in the light look the same colour as the side of the tree in shadow. If you turn that picture upside down the mountain in the distance would look closer to you than the tree. That is not right. I know how to do it better.* He met other painters in Sydney, including Charles Blackman, who said he had the saddest eyes he had ever seen in a man.

When Elizabeth Riddell interviewed Namatjira at the Clunes' Vaucluse house he reiterated points he had been making for years: *I am a man of Central Australia but in my own land I have no freedom...I like a quiet place. Morris Soak is alright except it has no water so we have to cart it all the time. I would like to build a hut there, not live under a tent flap... a hut at the Soak and a truck, that's all I want. I feel these Native Affairs people want to keep me down all the time. For a long time I was like a blind man – he pressed a handkerchief over his eyes – but now I can see and I see they want to keep me down.*

The Dodge truck, the ostensible purpose of the visit, was presented to Namatjira by radio personality Jack Davey, the compere of the Ampol Show, live on air and with a studio audience watching; in the photos Albert is wearing a Santa Claus suit like a robe open at the front. And it was on Davey's luxury Halverson Cruiser, *Sea Mist*, that he spent his day on the harbour – his most enjoyable experience of the visit, he would later say. There are photographs of this, as of all the other events: Namatjira sits on the deck of the *Sea Mist*, wearing a checked shirt, looking uneasy, between two fashionably dressed young women, both in sunglasses; while in the background we see the waters of Sydney Harbour and the rocky shores of South Head. Davey, as an act of courtesy, locked the *Sea Mist*'s lavishly appointed liquor cabinet for the duration of the voyage.

And then, on 18 December, John Brackenreg provided Albert Namatjira with a document to sign; which he duly did, with Frank Clune as the witness: *I confirm that your company has been and at this date remains sole publisher of prints of my work. I now authorise you to take for my name, or otherwise as you may consider best, such legal or other action as may be appropriate to stop the publication and sale of my prints by Barlow & Sons.*

Brackenreg followed up this coup by flying on Christmas Eve to Alice Springs, where he visited the Woods, who owned the Rendezvous Cafe and were selling Barlow's prints; presumably this was to assert the authority Namatjira had given him. He also had meetings with the Secretary at Native Affairs and with

Rex Battarbee; the outcome was a draft of a proposed contract which Brackenreg sent to the Administrator for his approval on 31 January 1957. He had to do this: Namatjira's legal status as a ward of the state precluded him signing any such agreement without the state's consent; but there were already rumours abroad that this legal status was about to change.

Albert had preceded his agent, driving back to Alice Springs, with Keith and Bert Gardiner alternating at the wheel. They were farewelled outside Romano's restaurant by WG Walkley, the journalist after whom the awards are named, and must have been relieved to leave all the hoopla behind. On the back of the truck, amongst much else, were a dining table and chairs and a refrigerator donated by a white goods manufacturer – even though there was no electricity at Morris Soak. There, in Ted Strehlow's words, it *stood out...in the sand and mulga rotting...it was a cheap gimmick.* Somewhere on the road, according to one his biographers, they

surprised some geese: both Albert and Keith leapt from the truck and chased the birds into the scrub, catching one and bringing it back to cook and eat on the spot. Along the way they also acquired one of the illuminated merino ram signs used as a logo by Golden Fleece petrol stations. It was a present for Biddy.

Albert's first stop in Alice Springs was the hospital where Rubina was recovering after an operation; he gave her the frocks, scarves and blankets he had bought in Sydney; and, a few days later, brought in a watercolour as a gift for the nurse, Sister Schneider, who looked after her. Alan Wauchope saw him not long afterwards *in the picture theatre here on Saturday night and said 'Good Evening'… Albert had just decanted about 20 young and old relations from the new utility…I asked Albert how he had enjoyed his trip and the unshaven artist grinned and said, 'Everybody talked too much'. He then moved out into the theatre's closely adjoining lolly-pastry-fish-and-chip-soft-drink shop to buy half a dozen bottles of lolly water to share among the multitude he had shouted into the cowboy picture.*

The gift of a painting to Sister Schneider was not an isolated act; Namatjira, while fully aware of the value of his art, was at the same time prepared to give pieces away if the circumstances were right. He would also dedicate himself to causes if he felt they were just. Hence, in April 1957, he made his long-delayed visit to Perth, principally to attend Namatjira Button Day on Friday 26 April. He flew west on 22 April to stay with Mr and Mrs Claude Hotchin at their property, Mandalay. Hotchin was a long-time admirer of Namatjira's work who arranged his first Perth show in 1946. He recalled Albert in his bedroom reading religious verses from a birthday book: *I like the verses in this book,* he said. *I read them whenever I can.*

He was there for a week. There was a reception by the Trustees of the Perth Museum and Art Gallery and lunch with the Rotarians; visits to the railway workshops, Fremantle Wharf,

Kwinana Oil Refinery; a scenic drive. Despite attempts to insulate him *thronging crowds fought and pushed frantically to get a glimpse of him. Many tried to touch him. Hundreds besieged him for autographs.* His purpose in coming was to support an appeal organised by the Native Welfare Council to raise money to establish a Native Hostel and Community Centre *which all natives could call home and from which they would not be turned away.*

The *Westralian Aborigine* reported: *He said he would never forget the Coolbaroo Dance on the last night of his visit. In a packed hall he was welcomed with joyous enthusiasm. He looked relaxed, more so than when attending previous functions in Perth – he was with his own people and what a friendly lot they were. The President of the Coolbaroo League thanked him…Namatjira was glad to meet W.A.'s aborigines and talked and joked and enjoyed his supper…people…sang 'For He's a Jolly Good Fellow', 'Why Was He Born So Beautiful?' and 'Auld Lang Syne'. As he left the hall he waved. Outside the hall he was still smiling but it was noticeable that there were some little glistening drops in his deep thoughtful eyes. 'In Sydney they called me the cowboy from Central Australia,' he said with a laugh.*

Not long after Namatjira's return to Alice Springs the Register of the 15,711 wards of the state in the Northern Territory was published – without Albert's or Rubina's names on the list; their children and grand-children, along with most of their close relatives, remained upon it. This exclusion is the basis of the often-repeated claim that Namatjira was the first Aboriginal to be granted Australian Citizenship; he wasn't, there were others before him who, for one reason or another, also had their names removed from the Register: his nephew Adolf Inkamala, for example.

Nor was it, properly speaking, a grant of citizenship. All it meant was that he was no longer subject to the rules and regulations that so-called full-bloods had to observe and thus, from one point of view, was less an invitation to join white Australia than an excision from his own people; he would now be legally obliged to apply for a permit to visit the reserves that were his own tribal lands. There's no evidence that Namatjira wanted to be granted this privilege and some suggestion that he actively opposed it; Battarbee records that he inquired into the possibility of legal action to prevent it happening. There was no celebration.

He was not even told officially; he only heard the news after the Register was published. Alan Wauchope went out to Morris Soak to see Namatjira and gauge his reaction: *Was greeted courteously, as usual, by the burly artist, but although we have been friends for a long time, I felt an air of constraint… 'Now that you've citizenship rights are you going to apply for land for a house in town?'…he got up and walked to the open side of the bough shed and looked around at the encampments of his friends and relations for a long time before he answered. 'What's the use? We're better off out here. I don't think they'll try and kick us out of here…anyway, I don't feel any different now than I did before – let's talk about these things some other time – when I've had more time to think.'*

There were, however, two immediate consequences, both of which proved ambiguous, to say the least: those not on the Register were, like so-called half-castes, permitted to buy and consume alcohol whenever they wished; and they could also enter freely into legal agreements with other entities. The history of Albert's drinking is murky, the chronology of his indulgence in alcohol unclear: there is the bottle of whisky that Clune allegedly gave him back in 1954, there is the court appearance for the sip of wine at Christmas that same year; it's quite possible that there were other episodes between then and mid-1957, when it became legal for him to drink.

It is also alleged that, after publication of the Register, officials of the Native Affairs Branch collected him from Morris Soak and took him to a pub in town and bought him celebratory drinks.

Certainly, the press had paid inordinate attention to the matter of Albert's drinking, or not, since his visit to Darwin early in the decade and it came up frequently in reports of functions he had attended during his visits to the cities. It's possible that the excision of his name from the Register merely transformed an intermittent illegal indulgence into one that was, catastrophically, legal.

Rex Battarbee seems to have thought so. In June, 1957 he addressed his last meeting as Chairman of the Aranda Arts Council at which, according to McCoy, he delivered *an involved dissertation on the evils of strong drink, which was strongly resented by the artist members present.* Subsequently he resigned as Chair but was persuaded to stay on to continue pricing paintings. McCoy concluded his report of that meeting by observing that the majority, (which included some non-wards though it isn't clear if Albert was among them), *were firmly of the opinion they could now manage without the assistance of the Aranda Arts Council and were no longer interested in maintaining it as a means of disposing of their paintings.*

Battarbee was a teetotaller who would, in the next decade, ask his children to sign the Pledge. He had always been abstemious where alcohol was concerned and, although there are suggestions in his diaries that he might now and again have taken a drink on social occasions (he mentions champagne during an outing to the north of Alice Springs in the 1930s), by the 1950s, and perhaps under the influence of his wife, he was a confirmed non-drinker who, like Albrecht, had begun to deplore, publically, the effect that excessive use of alcohol was having upon some of the artists. Unfortunately, as on this occasion, preaching against the evils of strong drink does not seem to have had any other effect apart from sparking a feeling of resentment in those so admonished.

The other consequence of Albert's new status was that he could now sign away his copyright without the consent of the Northern Territory government or anyone else; and on 8 June 1957 he did so. The agreement was substantially the same as the draft Brackenreg had prepared back in January: *In consideration of Ten Pounds paid by The Legend Press Proprietary Limited, I, Albert Namatjira, artist of the Northern Territory do hereby grant to The Legend Press Proprietary Limited the sole and exclusive right, privilege and authority to print or otherwise use, reproduce by any means any or all of my original paintings or other works of which I am the author upon the following terms and conditions*; the main one being *a royalty fee of twelve and a half percent on all sales at retail prices.*

Brackenreg had consulted widely before this agreement came into force and was, naturally, a strong advocate for it. He wrote to the Administrator: *It may be an advantage to him to retain the right to sell his original paintings wheresoever he pleases. The matter of his copyrights would be best safe-guarded in the hands of an experienced publisher, and Albert was willing to appoint us sole agent in this respect. I had drawn up an agreement for Albert to sign, with the consent and approval of the Aranda Arts Council, which Mr Battarbee thought was the best and fairest proposition, as far as Albert was concerned, he had seen.*

Legend Press has indeed safe-guarded Namatjira's copyright,

tenaciously so; following his death in 1959, the administration of his estate passed to the Public Trustee for the Northern Territory Government which received a yearly royalty cheque from Legend Press's accountants, Price Waterhouse, then disbursed the monies among the Namatjira family. But this task was, it seems, increasingly onerous; and so, in 1983, for the sum of $8,500, the NT government sold Namatjira's copyright outright to Legend Press, thereby extinguishing the right of his descendents to benefit from income from the reproduction of his works.

It was a mysterious decision that, while barely noticed at the time, has since become controversial. Some among the Brackenreg descendents believe it was motivated by a weariness in the Public Trustee's office at the exigencies of dealing with the demands, not to say the importunities, of the Namatjira family. They wanted to hand the problem over to someone else. There were two options: one was to return the copyright to the family; the other, to sell it to Legend Press. It does not appear that there was much enthusiasm for, or consideration of, the first course of action; instead, in 1982, the Public Trustee wrote to John Brackenreg offering the copyright for sale; the deal was done the following year. With the extension of the term of copyright after death from fifty to seventy years as part of the free trade agreement between Australia and the United States that came into force in 2005, Namatjira's copyright remains the property of Legend Press until it expires in 2029. Unless, of course, it is given back.

There is a Namatjira painting of a West Australian scene, distant blue rocky hills with yellow rocks and pale green scrub in the foreground: a place called Kariltynja or Kariltjnja (the word is written in Albert's hand on the back) that is otherwise unidentified. It joins other rare out of the Centre works like the Darwin seascapes and another, which is probably of a Sydney beach, now in the National Gallery. There were almost more: in 1956, in Sydney, Albert was offered a commission by Blake Pelley, the Chairman of mining company Rio Tinto, to paint six views of the company's new Mary Kathleen uranium mine in north-west Queensland; here, between 1958 and 1963, 4,500 tons of yellowcake uranium oxide were extracted.

The terms of the commission were negotiated over the first part of 1957 between Rio Tinto and the Northern Territory government; and agreed before Albert's trip to Perth in April. He was to be flown up to Queensland at Rio Tinto's expense and paid a hundred guineas for each of the six landscapes. The flight was booked for 2 May and the Managing Director, a Mr Poole, flew to Mary Kathleen to meet Namatjira; who, however, failed to arrive. He had been ill with a bronchial infection and had not yet got around to signing the agreement. Mr Poole flew back to Melbourne and contacted the Administrator's negotiator, a Mr Archer, who in turn, upon investigation, found that Albert wasn't even in Alice Springs: he had gone with Frank Clune on a painting trip to Glen Helen.

Rio Tinto was advised that Albert was too sick to do the work at present; when they made another attempt to finalise the agreement, they were told that an accident prevented him from painting. The company gave up on him and employed another artist to make the works, which had already been scheduled to be exhibited overseas. By this time Namatjira was off the Register and so could accept or refuse commissions for himself. Why he did not bother to pursue the Queensland paintings, and the 600 guineas they would have earned him, is unclear: simple disinterest, a presumed lack of empathy for landscapes not his own, or something more intrinsic, some malaise? Maybe it had to do with the 'secret' British atom bomb tests at Emu Fields and at Maralinga, that poisoned the tribal lands of the Maralinga Tjarutja, a southern branch of the

Pitjantjatjara? As so often, Albert did not say and we do not know.

It's not necessarily the case that he was averse to corporate sponsorship. When, later in the year, a second film about him was made by Sydney-sider Norman Wallis, Ampol bought the picture off the film-maker; in return, the last shot of *My Father's Country* shows Albert at an Ampol bowser filling the tank of the truck the company had given him with the company's product. Wallis recounts his first meeting with Namatjira: *we travelled on to the Gorge, arriving at nightfall, and found Albert and his wife and three sons Ewald, Enos and Oscar, sitting around a campfire with a number of tribal relatives, shy little piccaninnies and their pet dogs. This was just as I had hoped.*

It was on this occasion that Namatjira told the much-quoted story of his father, the flying ant. Less often repeated is the coda: *Albert then went on to say sadly that many of the sacred 'mysteries' must die with him, as his sons were not tribally worthy of the 'big magic' and he did not care to pass it on to those who could not be relied upon to preserve it.* Some stories however, like that of the dancing girls who came up from a thousand miles south to live with the hitherto companionless Arrernte men, could still be told: *When these women died, their spirits returned to the crests of the hills over which they danced and took the shapes of trees that can be seen there to this day.* Mt Sonder, one of Namatjira's favourite subjects, is sometimes seen as the reclining figure of a woman; and the dancing girls are also able to be glimpsed in the cliffs at the mouth of Glen Helen gorge, another favourite.

The accident that may have prevented him taking up the Rio Tinto commission was not an excuse – he'd spilled boiling water over his foot and the burn had become infected; he'd gone to Hermannsburg for treatment and they had sent him on to Alice Springs hospital where, by choice, he checked into the Aboriginal ward even though, as a citizen, he could have gone to the white ward. He was looked after by the same Sister Schneider who had cared for Rubina. She said later that, after he left hospital, there was a deterioration in his health, which she attributed to poor diet and the amount of alcohol he was drinking: *He mostly rode around in a taxi as his new Dodge utility was often out of order...some of his sons were selling...very shoddy efforts by Albert for as little as £10.* Some of these were probably collaborative works; but there was nothing in Arrernte custom that proscribed collaboration.

Early in 1958 he was back in hospital again, this time because the bonnet of his truck had fallen on his hand and lacerated the index finger so badly it had to be amputated. Fortunately it was not his painting hand. When Alan Wauchope visited him in hospital he described him as resigned and listless: *A long well-shaped finger of the right hand traces a little square in the dust. 'They want me to paint little pictures now...they tell me there's not much money in the cities where I sell my pictures. I got to make them smaller and take less money'.* These days he had to paint even if he didn't want to; he was under contract to Brackenreg to supply a certain number of pictures annually.

Nevertheless, Albert refuted allegations that he was drinking heavily and painting badly or not at all: *I went out to Glen Helen Gorge with my agent some little time ago,* the *Northern Territory News* reported, *and I painted solidly for five weeks. I painted nine big canvasses which I value at about a hundred guineas each. I also painted a number of smaller pictures of lesser value at the insistence of my agent. After this I got a bit tired of the work – I am not a machine even if those who market my work would like to have me that way. I decided to have a couple of days off. I got a friend of mine to bring me out a little bit of beer – two cartons – in company with some of my friends I drank them. I enjoyed them and I enjoyed the relaxation from painting.*

As these comments imply, all was not well between Namatjira and Brackenreg. The *Northern Territory News* continues: *the next thing I knew was that my agent said to me: 'We are finished, you and me.'*

He seemed annoyed that I had taken some time off after hard work. After all, he wasn't the one doing the painting that was to bring in the money. I was hurt and bitter at his attitude, but I will wait until I hear from him again before I finally sever my connection with him. I haven't been able to sleep worrying about this business. I wish people would leave me alone for a while and let me work as I want to work – like any other painter – when I see something lovely enough to make me want to paint my best.

Brackenreg disputed this. He told the *News* the Glen Helen trip was primarily to seek a place for Albert to build a house; which he, Brackenreg, would finance, on land that had been offered by the station owner Bryan Bowman; but that Bowman's offer was withdrawn after the drinking party. Brackenreg reiterated that, as far as he was concerned, it was Albert's drinking that was the problem and, if it stopped, he was happy to keep on representing him: *Only two days ago I spoke to our common friend, Rex Battarbee, and I authorised him to select Albert's work. I told him to tell Albert that I wanted to help him. However, I will not pay him money that he is going to squander.* There was at this time mention of an application to have Albert's citizenship rescinded; that is, for his name to go back on the Register. This did not happen; nor did Namatjira sever his business connection with Brackenreg.

There was, for many Aboriginals, a relationship between alcohol and citizenship. Ted Strehlow, in a talk given soon after Namatjira's death and later published under the title *Nomads in No-Man's-Land*, described the association in these terms: *If this pioneer-honoured method of extracting the maximum amount of alcoholic fun out of hard-won earnings is borne in mind it will be easier…to understand why alcohol acquired such a superlative importance in the thought of the aboriginals and part-aboriginals who had been watching their white employers 'having a good time' at the inland hotels…many of the applications for exemption* [from the Aboriginal's Ordinance in the 1930s] *that came before me officially mentioned as the main ground (and sometimes the only ground) for exemption that the applicant wanted to live as a white man and 'go for a drink to a pub same as any white man'.*

Drinking, he says, became a way to flaunt emancipation from former inferior social status; but, he goes on, Namatjira's mistake was to forget *that his skin colour automatically precluded him from safe indulgence in this aping of traditional white bush behaviour. In the Territory the sight of a drunken white man had never been an uncommon phenomenon...but no white man could stomach 'a drunken nigger'.* As late as 1975 Basil Sansom recorded drinkers in Darwin's Wallaby Cross camp tapping their beer cans with their finger nails whenever the word *citizen* was mentioned: *it is a word to be said with an obligatory nod to grog.* This association was compounded by a belief among some Hermannsburg painters in an historical connection between art and alcohol: as artists they were supposed, like van Gogh or Gauguin or any number of others, to drink.

Namatjira, Strehlow continues, *generally contented himself with having liquor brought out by taxi to his camp at Morris Soak, a secluded place in the hills a few miles west of Alice Springs. Here not only his sons and some other male relatives gathered around him but also a considerable number of natives who had police records for drunkenness and other petty offences. At Morris Soak wine was consumed by the flagon, and spirits by the bottle...although Namatjira himself took no part in them, drunken brawls became common among his hangers-on...Namatjira paid for all the alcohol consumed in his camp but possessed no powers of restraint, tribal or otherwise, over the motley crew of wasters.* This lack of powers of restraint was to have fatal consequences.

A decline in the quality of Namatjira paintings had been anticipated, discussed, forecast, hoped for and proclaimed for a decade or more. Many people feel such a decline did in fact occur in the mid to late 1950s but, given that most works are undated, it is difficult to be sure if this really is the case. It is more likely that, as with many painters, Namatjira produced high quality along with lesser works throughout his career; it appears that the proportion of weaker works did increase later on. There is however a change of a different kind detectable in the later 1950s, one that may be due to the fact that, as he aged, he travelled less into remote areas; his subject matter became more restricted and so too the character of his painting altered. But this had also to do with the fact that he had a new dealer, a new agent and that, while well-intentioned, John Brackenreg, living in Sydney, was perforce more remote from the situation than Rex Battarbee had been.

On the evidence of two illustrated books that came out in the 1980s – Brackenreg's own *Central Australian Artist Albert Namatjira* (1984); and Nadine Amadio's *Albert Namatjira: The Life and Work of an Australian Painter* (1986), the catalogue for the retrospective that opened the Araluen Centre in Alice Springs – neither Legend Press nor the Araluen Centre had access to a wide range of Namatjira's work. It appears that, with one or two exceptions, the selection of works was made from later and less distinguished work. Namatjira's painting appears in these publications, and in the parallel reproduction, from the 1950s on, of cards and prints, drink coasters, tea towels, place mats and other ephemera, as most people still think of it: the gum tree on the left (or the right) with rocky hills and mountains beyond; a generic and representative landscape of unknown provenance; a fading blue sky over a dry stony valley.

Whether this was because the best was past or because most of what was really exceptional was sold before it could be photographed is not clear; it was probably a bit of both. As a heavy seller who exhibited almost exclusively in commercial galleries, which did not keep detailed sales records, Namatjira's strongest work tended to disappear into private collections; where it stayed until

about the turn of the twenty-first century, when remarkable paintings began to appear at auction and to command prices in the tens of thousands. This tendency was exacerbated by the fact that the metropolitan state galleries were only faintly interested, if at all, in making purchases of their own. The Art Gallery of New South Wales, for instance, still owns just two Albert Namatjira paintings.

There is a further point: some late Namatjiras are apparently what might be called synoptic works, indeed painted from memory, that do not represent any known or actual place so much as a generic landscape, a placeless place, a feeling as much as a real location. Not all of these are mediocre paintings; some are masterpieces. In these works it is as if the painter has called up from memory country he will not see again, not because it is no longer there but because it is no longer accessible to him in the form it once was; these glowing, jewel-like, late works can be understood as paintings of exile, imprisonment and loss. They show, to quote AE Houseman, *those blue remembered hills...the land of lost content*.

One lingers in the mind. It is called *The Valley, MacDonnell Ranges, NT*, is undated, and was recently (2010) sold by Christies of London for £22,500. A picture of chromatic harmony in predominant shades of white, olive green and brown, it has the ubiquitous gum tree on the left before a landscape that recedes past spiky outcrops and mounded hills to a distant, mountainous skyline. The dark aperture in the base of the tree has a lighter purple slit at its centre, intensifying the feeling of an opening through to another, thoroughly sexualised, world; there are eyes in the trunk of the tree, more eyes in the mid-ground rocky outcrops, a face in profile looking out of the picture to the left; but what makes the painting memorable is not to be found among the details but in the whole: consummate beauty, a composition perfectly realised, a place beyond places.

Namatjira was, amongst much else, a superlative painter of water, with the ability to make it seem to lie clear, transparent, water-coloured, upon the ground which we see revealed through it; anyone who has seen a freshet arrive down a hitherto dry central Australian watercourse will recognise that peculiar transparency, that preternatural clarity, as if there were no dust in suspension, no pigment within, that which is also possible, with pigment, to capture. One of the ironies of Namatjira's residence at Morris Soak was that, despite its name, there was no ready source of water in the camp. It had to be brought in by container via taxi from the town supply. In the morning, when Namatjira was ready to paint, he would send a child down with a tin cup to get him the water he needed to mix his paints.

Some of these children, like Kevin Wirri, used to stay on to watch him paint, picking up both techniques and materials; so too did some adults, such as Wenten Rubuntja, then in his thirties: *When that old man chucked his paint tubes away – after he had finished with them – I used to pick them up and take them back home. I asked the old man for a brush and he gave me a brush and said to me, 'Eh, what for, you going to learn, eh?'...I went and hid behind a rock to paint. I was remembering how that old man was painting – his handwork, his mixing and his ideas. After that I brought the painting up and showed it to old Namatjira and he said, 'Eh, who taught you? You've got good ideas.' Then he showed the painting to Mrs Battarbee. She said she'd start me off with five pounds, just for a start only.*

Wenten Rubuntja became a maker of both watercolour landscapes and acrylic dot paintings; the first, he said, were about country, the second about law. Others, better known as dot painters, also watched Namatjira at work or painted early works in the Hermannsburg style: Clifford Possum Tjapaltjarri, who as a young man in the mid-1950s met and painted with Albert in the Glen Helen area; and Turkey Tolson Tjupurrula, who moved to Papunya in 1959 while Albert was living there. This handing on of the knowledge and methodology of the school was in accord with the transmission of traditional culture but was also, and in a profound sense, an act without precedent: neither Turkey Tolson nor Clifford Possum was a blood relative of Namatjira's, nor even a tribal brother; Possum was an Anmatyerre and Tolson a Pintupi man. From now on the art movement, while its subject matter may still have derived from tribal lore, would be in outlook ecumenical.

10. Papunya and After

On the morning of 21 July 1958, at Morris Soak, Enos Namatjira found the battered and mutilated body of Fay Iowa, a sixteen year-old Pitjantjatjara woman, lying dead on the ground. She was pregnant; had been killed by an unknown person during the night; and her murder was, though Enos could not have known it, the beginning of the end for his father. Fay Iowa's husband, twenty-four year-old Sandy Nitjenburra, was alleged to have been the culprit but was eventually acquitted (and then imprisoned for alcohol related offences) so the case remains officially unsolved.

There was no doubt as to whom the powers that be thought was to blame for the events of 20–21 July and for other acts of drink-induced violence that occurred at Morris Soak around this time. It was Albert Namatjira, who some say was the father of Fay Iowa's unborn child and thus, even though he did not commit it, was ultimately responsible for the crime. So they decided to act – swiftly, vengefully, fatally – against him. It was as if all of his achievements as an artist and a man counted for nothing; or rather, as if those very achievements were now to be weighed against something both irredeemable and unforgiveable: his Aboriginality.

The inquest into the death of Fay Iowa took five days to complete and more than twenty witnesses, many of whom did not speak good English nor understand the court procedures, appeared before it. Namatjira, though he had little that was material to say about the matter, was the star witness; his arrival at the court was reported nationwide in the most sensational terms. *Albert walked into the court slowly, shakily, grief in every line of his face*, Douglas Lockwood in the *Sydney Morning Herald* wrote. *He looked old and haggard, thin and ill, distressed and shaking. His left hand, from which he had lost a finger, was bandaged. So was his left leg, which he had burnt long ago in a camp fire. The tragedy of all Australian aborigines was written in his face.*

There was, coincidentally, a painting by Walter Ebatarinja hanging on the courtroom wall. Albert identified himself, took the oath, said he understood he would be punished if he didn't tell the truth, then gave his evidence. He had bought beer, wine and rum (reputedly *Treasure Island*) on the night of the murder; had drunk two bottles of beer and some rum before locking the rest of the alcohol in his tin trunk. *I went to sleep because my head wasn't right. I was full and could not put my head right. I didn't know anything until I woke up next morning and my son, Enos, tell me about the murder.* He also testified that the liquor he'd locked in his trunk the night before was still there, untouched, the next day.

The coroner, Mr Lemaire SM, did not believe this. After committing Sandy Nitjenburra to trial in the Northern Territory Supreme Court on a charge of murder, he called Namatjira – *dressed in a shabby grey suit coat and old trousers and still with grey beard stubble on his face* – back to the bar table and gave him a lecture: *There is evidence before me that you brought alcohol to the camp…and that Sandy Nitjenburra and the dead lubra drank some of it. As a result they got mad with drink…I want your undertaking that you will keep liquor away from your camp.* Albert replied: *I will keep liquor away from my camp.*

Lemaire made him repeat the promise and then said that, if he didn't keep it, he would be sentenced to six months in jail.

After leaving the court Albert, accompanied by four of his sons, retreated to Hermannsburg; but he would have needed to go a lot further away than that to escape the controversy raging around him and his drinking habits. The Territory press was unremitting in its attacks upon him and in their calls for something to be done about *natives mad with drink*; while the metropolitan papers were more inclined to defend him against what they saw as an outrageous persecution.

Unfortunately, although Albert was no longer there, drinking parties, and occasional violent acts, continued at Morris Soak; late in August eighteen men were charged with drinking while wards of the state and there were reports of a young woman lying partly paralysed in Alice Springs Hospital after an iron spike had been driven through her throat; of an elderly woman with severe head injuries from having, the *Advocate* said, *her head split open*. Morris Soak had become a dangerous place for women to be: Rubina had left already and returned to Hermannsburg, after allegedly being threatened by Albert with a gun while he was drunk one day; he is said to have claimed that his citizenship entitled him to shoot people if he wanted to.

Meanwhile both Albrecht and Battarbee had spoken up; Albrecht, to suggest that Namatjira be reclassified as a ward of the state and hence forego the privileges of citizenship, including the right to buy alcohol; while Battarbee, even before the murder inquiry, said that *citizenship had been forced upon Albert, he had foreseen the problems it would bring and…engaged a lawyer to appeal against it. It only meant the right to purchase liquor.* Pastor Doug Nicholls did not agree: *Albert's drinking is being used as an argument for taking away his rights*, he said, *and people are using his case as a weapon against full citizenship for all aborigines.*

Rex responded to the coming crisis in another way; he asked Albert to sit for him and painted his portrait: head and shoulders, in three-quarter profile. Namatjira is wearing an orange windcheater, open at the neck, over a blue shirt. He is bearded and has his long hair swept back from his forehead in the style of a 1950s rocker. His lips are slightly parted, as if in speech, and his eyes, heavy-lidded, intense, look out of the picture to the left; the lines on his face, particularly his forehead, suggest both suffering and resolution. Oddly enough – though typically of Rex's portraits – it is not, on the evidence of the photographs, a very good likeness; but it is a strong painting and an image of a resilient, a durable man; which might have been the point.

While public controversy continued, behind the scenes the authorities were preparing to act. Within days of the Fay Iowa inquest, a Namatjira File had been opened and there were rumours, encouraged by press coverage, that he was going to be charged with supplying liquor to a ward of the state. Olive Pink responded by telegramming Paul Hasluck, then Minister for Territories, saying that a private letter was on the way containing a list of names of white Territorians, including high government officials, *who do the same things but are not imprisoned*. Included on the list was *Frank Clune, who got Albert to paint pictures in the Todd River and filled him up with beer*. McCoy of Native Affairs responded by saying that Namatjira was neither arrested nor in jail; however, he also said that inquiries had been made and the relevant papers sent to Darwin. The die was cast.

A Constable Harvey served a summons on Albert on 15 September 1958; he screwed it up and put it in his pocket, saying his solicitor would fix it. He was charged with four counts of supplying liquor to members of his tribe who were wards of the state and ordered to appear in court on 22 September; the offences were said to have occurred on the 26th and 27th of August. In the event, because of his earlier comments, Lemaire excused himself from presiding and the case was heard on 6 and 7 October by Mr S Dodds SM, of Darwin. Albert, neatly clad in blue jeans and a grey windcheater, stood silent and motionless throughout the proceedings. He appears to have thought, initially at least, that with the help of his solicitor, Mr E Carter, the whole matter would be resolved quickly and without any penalty being imposed. He was wrong.

Five witnesses were called: two police officers; a taxi-driver, George Bray; the acting manager of Hermannsburg Mission, Ralph Kernich; and Henoch Raberaba, the artist. Albrecht, even though his wife Minna was ill, was in the courtroom every day. What happened is this: Albert had been out at Glen Helen painting before returning to Hermannsburg. Bray picked him up there on the 26th and took him in to Alice Springs to do some shopping. Then they'd gone out to Morris Soak and collected Raberaba before setting out for Hermannsburg again; as they left Constable Browning, in what must have been a prearranged move, stopped the cab, searched it, found beer, wine and rum aboard and warned Namatjira against taking liquor back to his camp.

Bray said he stopped the cab at Namatjira's request twice on the eighty mile return trip to the Mission; both times Albert went into the bushes, presumably to go to the toilet. Namatjira had a bottle of rum with him in the front seat, which he opened and drank from; according to Albert's testimony Henoch, who was sitting in the back, asked him for a drink, he refused but the other man persisted: *We are artists*, Raberaba said, *we are supposed to drink*. The first time they stopped, near Jay Creek, Albert left the bottle on the front seat and the second time placed it upright on the roadside. It was on these occasions that Raberaba drank the rum.

About seven miles from Hermannsburg they stopped for a third time, both men got out and there was a tribal argument

– about a place west of Haasts Bluff – which culminated in a physical fight. Albert got back into the taxi and continued on alone, leaving Raberaba *barely able to stand* beside the road. Before entering Hermannsburg itself the taxi made one more stop so that Namatjira could cache the flagon of wine and a dozen bottles of beer, which he buried beside the road.

Raberaba was picked up soon after by Manasse driving the Mission truck and arrived at Hermannsburg, Kernich said, only a little while after Namatjira; he got a big stick and went to Albert's camp to continue the fight. The next day Albert sent his son Enos and two other men to retrieve the cached beer; he didn't mention the wine, so they drank it on the spot before bringing the bottles of beer back. Kernich – with, it must be assumed, the advice and consent of Albrecht – informed the police and, the following day, the 28th, Constable Browning arrived to take statements. Albert was sick – hungover. He signed the statement Browning typed up for him but said later he did not fully understand it. He was, however, certain that he had not given the bottle to Henoch to drink from; but he had, just as certainly, left it in a place where he was free to help himself; and that is what led to his downfall.

Three of the charges were dismissed but the fourth, that of supplying Henoch Raberaba, was not. *I think*, Dodds SM said, *to make this Ordinance operate, that if a man puts a bottle down knowing that a ward would have a drink, it must constitute supply.* He sentenced Namatjira to six months imprisonment with hard labour. Joyce Batty wrote that *Albert seemed stunned by the sentence and the conviction. He stood for a moment quite motionless, his face expressionless, his eyes half closed.* He spoke briefly to his solicitor before being escorted from the courtroom by a uniformed constable and taken by truck to police headquarters. Half an hour later he stepped from a police van in front of the Alice Springs jail and, *stooped and haggard*, went inside.

The recently formed Federal Council of the Aboriginal Advancement League (FCAA) hired a prominent Melbourne-based barrister and Queen's Counsel, Maurice Ashkanasy, to take Namatjira's case and he began work towards an appeal against both conviction and sentence. Ashkanasy was a Jewish lawyer with a strong interest in civil rights issues and, during his preparations for the appeal consulted, among others, the then Dean of the Faculty of Law at the University of Melbourne, Zelman Cowen. Cowen was on the way to becoming one of the leading constitutional lawyers in the English-speaking world; he would also, in 1977, succeed John Kerr as Australia's Governor-General.

Once the appeal had been lodged, on 10 October, Albert was released from prison and went back to Morris Soak, where he remained until the case was heard in mid-December. He was too despondent to paint; he spent a lot of time sitting staring into the distance. He made one trip out to Hermannsburg in an attempt to persuade Rubina, who was living there with their married daughter Maisie, to return with him to his Alice Springs camp; she refused. He packed up the few paintings he had left there during his previous sojourn and went back to town. Some people who had been his friends now avoided him; others, like Olive Pink and pharmacist Peter Ryan, remained loyal. Ryan recalled that when Albert found him sunbathing in the garden behind his shop, he insisted on putting a shirt round his shoulders to protect his fair white skin from being burned.

Meanwhile the Victorian branch of the FCAA decided to mount a legal challenge to the Welfare Ordinance itself. Two activists, Stan Davey and Pastor Doug Nicholls, travelled to Alice Springs and there organised a petition. When Namatjira's appeal began in Darwin on 15 December, the Supreme Court was informed that a writ against the Commonwealth had been issued by Enos and Keith Namatjira, Otto Pareroultja and Claude Emitja, on the grounds that the Welfare Ordinance and the Register of Wards were unconstitutional because they subjected those listed or unlisted to a change of status and loss of liberty and proprietary rights while denying them any recourse to law. These were also grounds for Albert's appeal against conviction and sentence. Further grounds lay in the contention that Namatjira was required, by tribal law, to share whatever he had with his tribal brother Henoch Raberaba. Finally, even if the conviction was upheld, the sentence was too harsh; there was provision in the legislation for a fine of not less than £30.

None of this had any effect on the conviction. Nor did nationwide protests, the petitions, the newspaper articles, the impassioned pleas for a more humane solution. In a written judgment that ran for thirty-six foolscap pages Mr Justice Kriewaldt, who himself owned two pictures by Albert's sons, upheld the validity of the Welfare Ordinance and declared that Namatjira's obligation to share liquor with his tribal brother Raberaba was unsubstantiated. A fine, he said, was inappropriate. He did however halve the sentence to three months. The decision was stayed until the fifteenth day after the first sitting of the High Court in Melbourne early in 1959; there was one more avenue of appeal.

The Left rallied. The crews of SS *Iron Wyndham*, *Iron Baron* and the *Iranda* demanded Namatjira's immediate acquittal. Trades Hall in Sydney issued a statement proclaiming the need for a comprehensive overhaul of all legislation pertaining to Aboriginals as citizens. The Builders Workers Industrial Union of Australia said that, faced with the alternative of breaking a stupid law, or departing from the very fine way of life of the Aboriginal to share everything with his people, Namatjira chose the latter. The Universal Declaration of Human rights was invoked, along with Convention 107 (1957) of the International Labour Organisation, promoting the protection of indigenous rights and identity worldwide. Even the antediluvian Premier of Victoria, Henry Bolte, wrote to Prime Minister Menzies asking for Namatjira's release on humanitarian grounds.

Namatjira's art, too, remained contentious and there were calls for galleries, as a gesture of solidarity, to hang his work. Hal Missingham in Sydney did not resile from his earlier statement: *When Namatjira comes up to standard we will hang his work.* English-born Eric Westbrook, in Melbourne, agreed: *Namatjira's work is just not up to standard...there are twenty or thirty white Australian watercolourists who depict Australian landscape with greater skill.* Robert Campbell in Adelaide concurred, saying *it was only because he was a full-blooded Aborigine that his work received attention. Curiosity, not aesthetic value has made him so popular.*

Dr Duguid, a prime mover in the establishment of the FCAA, pointed out that other artists had led less than exemplary lives without compromising their work; so did William Dargie, who predicted that gallery directors would soon be falling over each other in an attempt to buy Namatjira paintings. Noel Counihan, artist and writer, said it was disgraceful that he was not represented in the national galleries. *He has done a remarkable thing. He has bridged a gap of several hundred years between the primitive artist and the modern European painter.* Counihan had earlier organised a letter of protest against Namatjira's trial and imprisonment. It was signed by fourteen artists, including Arthur Boyd, John Brack, Ernest Buckmaster, Charles Bush, John Percival, Clifton Pugh as well as Counihan himself.

Ashkanasy, on 12 March, in Melbourne, applied to the High Court for leave to appeal the prison sentence imposed by the Supreme Court on three grounds: that the judge was wrong in law to dismiss the appeal against the conviction; that the judge should have allowed the appeal and set aside the judgement; that in the exercise of his discretion the judge should have imposed a fine not a prison sentence. Five learned men heard the application: Sir Owen Dixon, Sir Edward McTiernan, Sir Wilfrid Fullagar, Sir Frank Kitto and Sir Victor Windeyer. On the day of their decision Albert came in from his tribal country to see his solicitor, Carter; then, seeming a little less despondent than he had been, went to spend the night at Morris Soak.

He heard the determination, which was unanimous, next day: he had supplied liquor to Henoch Raberaba; there were no grounds for doubting that the trial judge had exercised his discretion appropriately in ordering a term of imprisonment; he could not appeal again. Namatjira, according to *The News* in Adelaide, said: *I cannot go on like this. I cannot stand it any longer. I would rather put my rifle to my head now and end it all than go on. Why don't they kill us all? That is what they want.*

He did indeed take up his gun but it was wrestled away from him by his son Enos. It was only when he was told that he would be allowed to serve his sentence in open country rather than in a prison that he calmed down a little. He continued: *Why can't they leave me alone? I have nothing. They have taken everything. They told me I would not have to go to gaol. They told me it would be fixed in Melbourne. What is left for me? I am an old man. I have worked hard. They have taken a lot of my money in taxes, but now I must go and do hard labour.*

The arrest papers, which had already been prepared, were mailed south from Darwin to Alice Springs where Inspector Mackinnon collected them and then drove out to Morris Soak to bring Albert in. This was the same man who, as Mounted Constable William McKinnon of the Northern Territory Police, had in the early 1930s commissioned Namatjira to decorate a dozen plaques with pokerwork images of his camel patrol; they had known each other for three decades. Mackinnon said that, over his long period of service, it was one of the unhappiest duties he had to fulfil; but Albert himself did not appear to mind. He was delivered secretly to the town jail – the authorities did not want a crowd of any kind forming – and, next morning, the official announcement of Namatjira's imprisonment was made.

He was supposed to stay only briefly in the jail but there was a complication. Areyonga Native Reserve, which had been selected as the place where he would serve his term, was populated mainly by Pitjantjatjara people and Fay Iowa was a Pitjantjatjara; threats had been made that not only Namatjira, but any Arrernte man, would be speared if he entered Pitjantjatjara territory. Albert asked if he could go elsewhere, the Administrator was informed of the problem and the order was altered. He would be sent instead to Papunya Native Reserve, north of Haasts Bluff in Arrernte-friendly country.

Papunya, famous now, was then a relatively new settlement. Like Yuendumu it was a government settlement, established in the mid-1950s essentially as a replacement for the old Lutheran out-station at Haasts Bluff, now Ikuntji, which was running out of water. Near the old Popanji Bore, about twenty miles north and west, some houses were built; those residing permanently at Haasts Bluff were encouraged to move to the new settlement; as were the wild people to the west who still lived unsequestered on their desert lands.

In 1959 the Superintendent of the Reserve at Papunya was Ern Fietz, a Lutheran who'd lived twenty years at Hermannsburg and there married Hilda Wurst, the teacher who served on one the art committees set up to regulate the trade in pictures in the 1940s. Both Mr and Mrs Fietz, then, knew Albert well. Paul Hasluck, Minister for Territories, who had to endure some high-level criticism for allegedly overruling the judiciary by allowing Namatjira to serve his sentence in the open, arranged for Fietz to be appointed an officer within the Prison Ordinance; and he became Albert's keeper.

Namatjira was given a medical examination at Alice Springs jail and found to have high blood pressure and an enlarged heart; the doctor said hard labour was inappropriate and recommended light duties only: sweeping paths, gardening, preparing vegetables for meals. He seemed apathetic, resigned, probably depressed; nevertheless, special precautions were taken. Staff weren't allowed to speak to him and he was to be segregated from the 600 or so other Aborigines, many of them Pintupi or Kukatja, who lived at Papunya. There were no cameras allowed and only two visitors a fortnight; he was under constant surveillance. The Fietzes, however, upon his arrival invited him in for tea and offered to let him take his meals with them and their four children; he refused, preferring to sit outside in the shade by himself to eat.

But when Fietz asked if he'd like to come out with him on his regular inspections of the Reserve, Albert agreed and trips through country he had known since he was a child began to revive him: *He recalled the tribal legends associated with each landmark...the mighty totem heroes who had created the mountains, ravines and rock pools... the prowess of his tribe in the great battles and feasts which followed and the corroborees of victory his father had participated in.* Soon the Fietz children were sitting outside with him when he had his meals under the tree; he began reading his Bible and his hymn book (both in Arrernte) again.

He wasn't painting however and he was missing Rubina; so a visit was arranged that was also a reconciliation. Rubina could have stayed at Papunya – there was no law against it – but she would still have been able to visit Albert only when regulations permitted; that is, once or maybe twice a fortnight. When she was told this she broke down and cried and, despite reassurances that her husband would soon be released, left Papunya in tears to return alone to Hermannsburg. There she told family and friends that Albert *waters the garden and looks after the chooks.*

The sentence was reduced from three months to two. The release date was 18 May but he had to be transported back to Alice Springs jail in order to receive his formal discharge. He went by truck and, as they passed through Hermannsburg, Rubina recognised the vehicle and, seeing Albert sitting within, ran to greet him; but she wasn't allowed to go to him. She was there next morning, outside the jail, along with their sons and other relatives, when he walked out. Curiously, before returning with his family to Hermannsburg, Albert made two visits in town: one to his tax advisor, a Mr Owen, and another to Reg Verran, who on occasion shipped his paintings to John Brackenreg in Sydney. Both of these visits seem to have been attempts to straighten out, if not finalise, his business affairs.

The hut he lived in at Papunya was his if he wanted it and Mission staff at Hermannsburg, concerned at his lack of activity and his propensity to sit for hours gazing into the distance, urged him to take up the offer. He and Rubina did move to Papunya and there he did resume painting. Fietz mentioned seeing some works with *harsh, almost aggressive colours* and one of these, at least, seems to have survived: it shows the north-facing cliffs of the Belt Range, part of the Haasts Bluff complex, in sombre purples behind sandy ridges and red rocks and altogether lacks the extension of space typical of most of Namatjira's work: it is landscape figured as prison walls. Albert himself said that he might give some paintings to Enos to take to Battarbee and perhaps he did. Certainly, Battarbee later published a reproduction of one of Namatjira's last paintings, made at Papunya; but there is nothing untoward about the colours nor is it in any way uncharacteristic of the late work.

Rubina went back to Hermannsburg in late July to be with

their daughter Maisie, who was having a baby. She asked the Fietzes to look after Albert and they said they would. However, he still refused to take his meals with them and, soon after, Ern Fietz found him crouched in a corner of his hut complaining of chest pains. He would not be admitted to the hospital at Papunya so the Sisters contacted the Flying Doctor Service, which offered to send a plane; but on consideration Papunya decided his condition was not

that serious and arranged to take him to Alice Springs by truck instead. He sat on a mattress on the back and waved as he was driven away. The truck was met along the way by an ambulance and, at the hospital in Alice, his condition was said to be satisfactory. Two days later he had a heart attack and deteriorated rapidly, there was a sudden onset of pneumonia and his condition was soon critical.

Rubina came in from Hermannsburg and so did Pastor Albrecht. They kneeled at the bedside and said the Lord's Prayer. Albert, according to Albrecht, tried to join in but was too weak to speak out loud: *halfway through the prayer I realised he was whispering the words...just before the end his voice faded out. I had a very strong feeling he was seeing God's forgiveness.* He did, said Joyce Batty, whose main informant was Rubina, manage to say the *Amen* before lapsing into a coma. He died two hours later, towards evening on Saturday 8 August 1959, one year to the day since his appearance at the inquest into the death of Fay Iowa. He was fifty-seven years old.

The funeral was at four o'clock the following Sunday afternoon, with Albrecht officiating; about 200 attended: *his own people were all present, most of them had come in from Hermannsburg.* The *Sydney Morning Herald* reported *a moving ceremony, half in the Arunta language and half in English, with an aboriginal choir singing in the background. The text used at the graveside…was from Corinthians 15:10* – *'By the grace of God I am what I am'. Wreaths were laid on behalf of the Northern Territory Administrator and the Native Affairs Department as well as many leading citizens of Alice Springs. Pastor Albrecht said…'I have never seen so many white people at a native funeral.'*

He was buried in the Lutheran section of the Alice Springs cemetery, to the south of Heavitree Gap. As the service ended and the sun began to go down in the west Rubina, her whole head veiled, came forward carrying a small bunch of flowers and threw the first handfuls of earth onto the coffin. The Alice Springs Gliding Club had taken to the air as a mark of respect and one of the gliders, circling overhead, passed its shadow like a great bird over the open grave and over the mourners gathered around about it.

After the tumultuous events of the previous year, Rex and Bernice Battarbee made a commitment: *The sadness of Albert's death to my husband,* Bernice said, *brought us to analyse the situation…and we decided that there had been so much sensationalism…that we would not under any circumstances add to it…we would not write for ten years… until we had time to contemplate all that had happened.* They did, however, as reported in the *Australian Women's Weekly* on 17

February 1960, turn their *sunroom into a small gallery housing nine Namatjira watercolours covering the entire 23 years of his work*. Rex also described what he thought would be an appropriate memorial to his friend and colleague: *An amenities centre, a theatre, with showers, toilet block, a laundry and canteen, a large assembly hall where meetings could be held and entertainment provided…with baby care facilities to help young mothers.*

Towards the end of 1960, in November, Rex did consent to an interview which, although it began as an attempt by Ted Strehlow *to record some details of your personal story*, inevitably moved on to a consideration of Albert's achievements as well: *I am certain that his fame will grow,* Rex said, *because his work…will stand up…they have got much more luminosity; a good watercolour has much more luminosity than an oil painting, and a good watercolour will improve. I've got some of Albert's pictures painted up to 24 years ago and some are still improving in quality.*

Rex also ventured upon a rare assessment of his own painting: *I have spent the last 25 years helping these men…naturally I haven't had the time to paint as many pictures as I would like to paint but that doesn't say that I still can't paint some of my best pictures…I'm not stale yet…I feel that as time goes by, when I have say been dead 25 years, my work will become much more important than it is now because I feel I have painted this country sincerely and my colour sense I feel is very sound. Some of my best pictures I feel will live and posterity will judge my work.*

Rex did speak out again, in January 1962, to contradict reports that forgeries were once more flooding the market, in part because Namatjira paintings were so easy to fake. The *Bulletin* reported: *Battarbee, who concentrates quietly on his own paintings, disagreed emphatically. At his best Namatjira would be no easier to forge than Rembrandt…Battarbee for years fostered the Aranda Art group*, the magazine continued, *but today he says they are capable of looking after themselves and should be allowed to paint and sell at will. 'They should find their own level...the policy of protection...isolates them from the struggle that is part of the making of every great artist'.*

Among the visitors to Tmara Mara, now more usually called the Battarbee Gallery, were the Queen and the Duke of Edinburgh. Their 1963 visit to Australia, during which they toured all states and territories, was to preside over the jubilee celebrations commemorating the fiftieth anniversary of the naming of the capital, Canberra; in Alice Springs, as well as Tmara Mara, they visited the Royal Flying Doctor base. Security was tight. Sir Roy Dowling, the Queen's Australian Secretary for the duration of the visit, was warned about mosquitoes: *You could be placed in an extremely embarrassing situation,* he was told, *if the Queen's skin was marked and if the press published pictures and stories about those marks.*

It was 15 March, Gayle's birthday, and she had been given a Box Brownie as a present; Scotland Yard thought it might have been a bomb. At 10.45am Her Majesty's personal flag attendant, the gate keeper, the gallery barriers, the press, radio and TV personnel, umbrellas, six Aboriginal artists with original paintings and Mr and Mrs Battarbee were all *in position*. At 11.14 the Royal car arrived, the Battarbees approached, the Royal couple alighted, her Majesty's personal flag was broken out on the masthead. The Battarbees greeted the Royals and conducted them into the gallery, where Enos, Oscar and Ewald Namatjira, two of the Pareroultja brothers and Richard Moketarinja were introduced and a specially autographed and bound copy of *Modern Australian Aboriginal Art* presented.

By 11.45 it was all over. The car had gone, the flag was struck, lowered and given into the custody of a police officer. The Duke bought two of Battarbee's pictures and, so Rex later told the Minister, mentioned several times that he thought the artists should paint in oils. The context for this communication was Battarbee's distress at what was happening in Alice Springs; the artists did not need the Duke's advice, he felt; they had difficulties enough: *they need a place to paint and sell their work…at the moment the artists hawk their paintings up and down the streets of Alice Springs. They should have a chance to keep their work on a higher plane. The art movement has been important to the Aboriginal people.*

Rex did keep on painting. His daughter Gayle recalled: *We had a caravan. Mother drove – she was capable. He couldn't or wouldn't drive because of his injuries. Mum and brother would sit in the front – Dad and I in the back. I was six, I would sit on his knee. 'Alright Gayle,' he would say, 'separate these colours by their temperature. Which are the complementaries?'* It remained a Christian household: *Sunday was family time, the gallery was closed – but the tourists still showed – look out the window and there they would be.* When Rubina came to town *she got the full treatment…the dining room, the ironed linen table cloths, the china cups, everything.*

In the heat of summer the family would put the car on the Ghan, rail it down to Port Augusta then drive to one of the southern or eastern cities for a holiday, staying in hotels or motels. On one of these visits, in Sydney, Battarbee discovered that Brackenreg had marked *Copyright Legend Press* over some prints he had made of Battarbee paintings; no such agreement had been signed and Rex asked that the claim be withdrawn. It was. Rumours of copyright problems reached as far as London. One day the phone rang at Tmara Mara; it was Buckingham Palace, inquiring as to just who did hold reproduction rights to the Battarbees the Duke of Edinburgh had purchased? The Palace was re-assured to learn that those rights were still held in the family; where, indeed, they remain.

Brackenreg was, however, generous in other ways. He continued to remit regular amounts of money to the family, via the Public Trustee, in the years after Albert's death; and Rubina, at his expense, had a house built for her at Hermannsburg. Albrecht, who resigned as a trustee of Albert's will because of lack of experience and the difficulty of dealing with *those Namatjira boys*, reported: *Last Thursday, Rubina and most of her family moved in, after the manager had unlocked the door and handed her the keys. It has a cement floor, wide eaves, a fireplace and shower recess. She was very happy and I don't remember how often she would come and squeeze my hands. Rex Battarbee was there.*

It is melancholy to record that, with the exception of Oscar (1991), who lived to the age of seventy, none of *those Namatjira boys* exceeded their father's fifty-seven years. Enos was the first to go, in September, 1966: *The afternoon before he died he called in at the Battarbee Galleries in Alice Springs, and being somewhat the worse for liquor he was warned of its possible dangers. All he said was, 'I have citizenship rights, I am supposed to drink.' Next morning he was found dead in his camp.* They were all big strong men, recalled a woman who knew them; yet they all died suddenly, usually after sleeping out on cold nights. Keith went in 1977, aged forty; Maurice, who was also forty, in 1979; Ewald in 1984 at the age of fifty-four. Rubina herself died in 1974, following the death of her one remaining daughter Maisie; in some accounts she sang herself to death, in others, simply turned her face to the wall. There were and are grand- and great-grand-children, many of whom are also painters.

Rex remained capable of changing his mind. In a rare public appearance in the mid-1960s, before a Parliamentary Committee Inquiry into Assimilation in Alice Springs, he was asked if he had anything to add to his written submission and replied: *in my opinion every Aboriginal who wants to vote should be able to apply in writing to get the right. These people are ambitious but are kept down by the mission and the government. The missions have done more than anybody for the natives but they will not give them freedom or the opportunity to express themselves.*

Ten years ago I would not have said this, **Rex** continued, *but I have had 29 years experience with the Hermannsburg mission and my own opinion is that the missionaries wanted to be there, simply because they wanted to be missionaries – if the natives were not there they would be out of a job. Pastor Albrecht said that the cattle experiment there was a failure – I was there when it grew, I remember travelling over those rough roads for hours and hours. Pastor Albrecht wanted it to be done in his own lifetime.*

I've great respect for Pastor Albrecht but I think that people living in missions take the one view, that the native is subservient and that he is sub-normal unless he can get out of the rut straight away – he is useless. There was no cleverer man in the world than Albert Namatjira, and his sons have proved he was not a freak. The policies of the governments and missions have been wrong – they go a certain distance then clamp down on the natives.

By the late 1960s Rex was not a well man. Duodenal ulcers, probably related to the wear and tear of a long and active life on a body severely damaged by war injuries, meant that he had to go to Adelaide for prolonged medical treatment. Bernice and the children went too; the gallery in Alice Springs was given over into the care of the son of church-going friends of the family and a shop front opened in Adelaide itself, where the trade in art continued. However, the man left in charge of Tmara Mara abused the trust he had been given, buying and selling works without putting them through the books and pocketing the proceeds. When the Battarbees returned in 1968 the business was much reduced and Bernice had to work hard to restore its profitability.

A second book was prepared, co-authored by Rex and Bernice, and published by Rigby of Adelaide: *Modern Aboriginal Paintings*

(1971). There is a short introduction by Bernice, followed by a number of brief biographies of artists, sixteen in all, accompanying reproductions of their works; then an afterword by Rex. All the paintings illustrated were part of the permanent collection of the gallery. It is a judicious selection, the reproductions are of high quality and among them are some powerful works by Henoch Raberaba.

There are four Namatjiras. The very early *Amphitheatre, Palm Valley* (1936), which Rex had bought after the first painting trip he and Albert took together, is illustrated next to *Late Afternoon in the MacDonnell Ranges* (1959), painted at Papunya during the last two months of Albert's life. Rex quotes in the caption something Albert said at the time: *With such emotional upheavals and disappointments behind him, he expressed his thoughts as 'All that is in the past is in the past and there is a new beginning.'* Insofar as Rex was concerned, then, his friend *was at peace with himself and prepared for what was soon to come.*

The painting shows an outcrop of rust orange rock at the left of a gum tree which stands before a wide plain covered in small trees, with purple then blue hills in the distance; the two triangular-shaped apertures in the trunk of the tree are painted in the same purples and blues as the distant hills, suggesting a kind of continuity between interior and exterior, subjective and objective views; as if dark blue were the ground of being.

Halfway up the trunk, where a branch has fallen and left a bole behind, is a single eye, staring and somehow glaucous, looking directly out at us; but that is the extent of the picture's anthropomorphism. The handling of the paint in the rendition of the rocky outcrop is unusually tentative and thus reminiscent of the naïve treatment of similar formations on the verso of the 1936 picture: for the poignancy of this juxtaposition we must thank Rex Battarbee, that unobtrusive man who nevertheless remains remarkably influential.

There's a photograph, taken by Rennie Ellis, of Rex in his gallery in 1970. He is wearing a checked tweed jacket, a dark tie with a red pattern upon it, a white shirt and stands, slightly to the right of frame, looking directly at the camera. His greyish-white hair is combed neatly across his head; perhaps it is brylcreemed. His eyes look somehow weary, even sad: as if he has seen too much. The left eye in particular looks rheumy and as if it might have begun to wander. Behind, there is a wall of paintings, hung two or three deep or propped up on ledges. Some of them are probably his own but, since they are out of focus, it is difficult to say for sure what they are and who has painted them.

As with all good photographs, a description of the image does not entirely account for the feeling it carries. Although he looks old and tired, there is still something of Rex that has escaped the rigours of age. Some quality of optimism, of humour, something that might be described as mischievous; as if he might be about to crack a wry joke or point out some hitherto unnoticed marvel or beauty in the world. As if he was still moving forward, still leaving the past behind. Here, you cannot help but think, is an honest man; someone whose conscience is clear, who has lived his life according to certain principles, still honours those principles, and always will.

In 1970 Bernice herself fell ill. She had cancer and, after two extremely difficult years, died in 1972. Rex was inconsolable. He began to wander in the night, looking for her. Their son Robin, who had been expected to train as an accountant and take over the business side of the gallery operations, left to join the navy the day after his mother died. Their daughter Gayle had been taken out of school when Bernice became sick, to look after the artists and the exhibitions; she had been taught to draw and paint by her father in anticipation of this role. Extensions to the house, to provide more

exhibition space, had been made but not yet paid for: the expected flowering of the business, which included lecture tours and sales overseas, could not now occur.

Rex Battarbee was himself pursued by the Tax Office towards the end. He wrote in explanation of his financial, physical and psychological state: *I now feel tired after painting for short periods of half an hour. In the last two months I have painted one painting. I have earned 511 dollars in the past six months, mainly from works painted 30 years ago.* His last painting, of a corkwood tree before a western landscape, took two years to complete; according to his daughter Gayle, there is a self portrait concealed in the trunk of the tree; the painting is hanging on the wall behind Rex in the last photographs taken of him at Tmara Mara.

He needed care, and went in to the Old Timers' Home in Alice Springs. He was still wandering and in an attempt to bring him back his daughter bought him a new sky-blue jacket, which he wore constantly. On 2 September 1973, Father's Day, Gayle arrived with gifts of lemonade and marshmallows. He was outside, in a wheelchair; and *the sky was back in his eyes*. He told her he was going home. She said that was impossible; alluding to a stressful visit they had made to Warrnambool the previous year. *No*, he said, *I'm going home*. She intended returning to Tmara Mara to fetch Bernice's wedding ring, the one made from an opal got at Coober Pedy, and the portrait of her Rex had made; but she had to go to the office first. She covered him with a blanket and went; and then heard the ambulance coming.

Rex was buried with Methodist forms in the town cemetery; his passing was noticed with severe economy. Under the headline *Namatjira Teacher Dies at 80*, one newspaper account said only: *the man who taught aboriginal artist Albert Namatjira has died*.

The Papunya Art Movement, initiated by teacher Geoffrey Bardon, had begun at Albert Namatjira's last home, north of Haasts Bluff, in 1971, and continues to this day. It was a refuge for people from the west, who brought their Dreamings in with them and learned how to make them over into paintings. Bardon had in 1972 come in to Alice Springs to see if Battarbee would like to become the agent of the new movement but Rex was not at home that day.

Papunya has become the model for many similar art centres across the desert lands of Central Australia, providing a unique means of returning country to its original owners. The Haasts Bluff Reserve, of which Papunya is a part, was itself transferred back into Indigenous ownership in the 1970s; in 1982, so too was Hermannsburg. Some of the town camps at Alice Springs are still extant and now accepted as permanent settlements; but Morris Soak was razed in 2012.

A significant act, and a vindication of Battarbee's vision of a community centre as a memorial to Albert Namatjira, was the construction of the Araluen Art Centre, designed and built around a 300 year-old corkwood tree considered sacred by the Arrernte. The art gallery opened in 1984 with a retrospective of Namatjira's painting and now holds a substantial collection, with some examples of his work always on display. It is the one place where you might be able to see a Battarbee and a Namatjira hanging side by side.

The Art Centre is part of a larger cultural precinct, which includes a theatre, a craft centre, several other galleries, a museum and, since 1991, the Strehlow Research Centre where much of that controversial man's collection of Indigenous artefacts is held in the basement: as if returned to a simulacrum of one of the caves they were taken from so many years before. The precinct was built on land that once belonged to Eddy Connellan, the pioneer aviator; Connellan Air's original hangar, associated heritage buildings and the Araluen homestead are still there. The site is also culturally significant to the Arrernte people. There are seven registered sacred sites and trees of significance, all part of the Two Women dreaming track which runs through it.

Closer still to Battarbee's vision of a place to paint and sell their work is Ngurratjuta Iltja Ntjarra, the Many Hands Arts Centre, an Aboriginal-owned and operated institution set up precisely for this purpose. There painters may go to sit and paint; and prospective buyers go to look and, perhaps, purchase. Ngurratjuta currently supports over 300 artists and has *a special focus on encouraging the Hermannsburg School style watercolour artists, who continue to paint in the tradition of their grandfather, Albert Namatjira.* Many Hands has recently relocated to the Desert Park to the west of Alice, in the shadow of Mt Gillen.

Meanwhile, on the other side of town, on the east bank of the Todd River, the house that was Tmara Mara, and thus the first art gallery in what is now a town of galleries, still stands. Somewhat dilapidated, much altered, with a green roof and dusty pale ochre walls, and a jacaranda tree Rex planted shading the iron gate, it is now a private residence that might deserve restoration as another kind of museum: to the farm boy from Warrnambool who went away to war and nearly lost his life; and came home to make a unique contribution to the cultural and artistic life of his times and ours. Or perhaps not; perhaps its modesty and unobtrusiveness are a more characteristic memorial than anything official might be.

In the 1960 interview Battarbee told Strehlow: *They say that you can't judge an artist until he has been dead a hundred years, whether he is really a great artist. Even then he may have had so much publicity in his lifetime that he may still be famous; but there are so many petty jealousies, and when you come to look at the art only in the last, say, 50 or 60 years – take men like van Gogh who could sell only one picture in his lifetime and he has only been dead 70 years and his pictures now bring up to £100,000; the pictures are still the same but the public had to be educated.*

It would be wrong to suggest that Battarbee was a van Gogh; he had his period of fame and fortune as an artist in the 1930s and was then, through his own efforts, eclipsed by those he set himself to help. It is certainly time another look was taken at what he accomplished: the distant purple ranges knotted like muscles along the skyline or standing as ramparts against the blue; the sand hills and gorges, the rocky faces like slabs of meat; his trees with their tracery of light and dark along the trunks; his tribal portraits and portraits of his fellow artists, some of which are awkward and strange and others replete with insights nobody else has had; most of all, at the quality in his work that Helene Burns, Pastor Albrecht's daughter, identified when she said: *with Rex's painting, it's almost as if you are looking at a delicate curtain.* That curtain has now fallen; but it may still be raised again.

When men of the western tribes first saw the watercolours of Rex Battarbee they thought they were magic: the essence of the land they knew came before them in another form. Not abstracted, translated, or reinvented; not even reproduced: recreated in a way only the Dreaming was supposed to be able to do. It was the same perception, differently expressed, that led the old men to instruct Namatjira to paint no more portraits; and made Rubina insist he abandon the picture of her he had begun. Portraits were not versions, they were the real thing; somehow doubled into eternity. So too were landscapes.

The European tradition is inclined to dismiss such speculations as childish superstition; but there are still some who subscribe to the view that paint is a magical substance and painted images an actual creation. Rex Battarbee had his life taken away and given back and paint was the way he witnessed the world he saw after rebirth. He once said his only teacher was nature; in his writings the word that reccurs as the touchstone of what he was attempting to paint is *luminosity*, the paradoxical quality that material things like paper and pigment can have to manifest the ineffables of light.

When we look today at the works of Battarbee, Namatjira and the school they founded, it is their clarity, their luminosity, that seem at first most remarkable; with time the forms disclosed in that clear white light begin to come forward in their familiarity and their strangeness: presences which, especially in the case of Namatjira, ask to be evoked using the antiquated currency of romantic description: ancient, immemorial, primordial.

The ability to construct an image out of pigment and some kind of support is indeed older than Lascaux, older than Chauvet, and has always appeared to partake of the miraculous; but you don't need to invoke the supernatural to explain it: the mere fact that such humble materials can create a world is enough to make most people wonder. And this wonder will outlast explanation, whether mystical or not. Paint as an artefact has been used throughout human time as a form of transport: towards awe and revelation; and equally towards abnegation and oblivion, especially when used on the body and associated with dance.

Battarbee in his art was showing the world as he saw it; whether he thought of it as God's creation was something he never said but it may have been so. Namatjira took the methodology offered by his teacher and used it in a similar, if not identical way: to paint the world created in the Dreaming and, in his belief, constantly recreated through human action. His paintings are recreations as much as testaments; real as opposed to invented things. They are not simulacra of landscapes but the landscapes themselves, re-dreamed.

Namatjira shared with, and perhaps learned from, Battarbee, the ability to deliver a world in close up; the intricacies of bluffs and cliff faces, the living complexities of rocky outcrops, the transparency of water pooling in the bed of a stream; most of all, the paintings of trees as entities that possess the emotional characteristics of human beings, expressed in a mythic form. Namatjira went further than Battarbee: his landscapes are comprehensively anthropomorphised; they are all, in a subtle yet pervasive manner, portraits; often group portraits.

He was also an incomparable painter of space. Lloyd Rees said: *I find in his work a marvellous sense of distance and of space. His eyes can look so far away and seem to know what's there.* But what was there? What did he see with those far-seeing eyes? Sometimes it seems that those immense vistas transform, in the way such things do out among the galaxies, from space into time; so that, when we look into the far reaches of a Namatjira landscape we are looking back in time towards the beginning; and perhaps we are.

NOTE ON SOURCES

Introduction

The account of Arrernte ways is adapted from a culture summary prepared by Martin Malone for the *Ethnographic Atlas* published by the Centre for Social Anthropology and Computing at the University of Kent at Canterbury (nd). This was checked against Malone's principal sources, Baldwin Spencer and Frank Gillen's *The Arunta: a study of a stone age people* (1927) and TGH Strehlow's *Aranda Traditions* (1947). The work of WEH Stanner, who in his *The Dreaming and other essays* (2009) coined the word 'Everywhen' as an alternative to Gillen's 'Dreamtime', also informs this account.

The early European history of the Lutherans is derived from *Persecution of the Lutheran Church in Prussia from the year 1831 to the Present Time* (1840) by JD Lowenberg. The early history of the Lutherans in Australia and the progress of their mission among the Dieri is recounted in Christine Stevens' *White Man's Dreaming: Killalpaninna Mission 1866–1915* (1994).

Peter Vallee's *God, Guns and Government on the Central Australian Frontier* (2007) has material on the early days of the Lutheran Mission at Hermannsburg. CD Rowley's *The Destruction of Aboriginal Society* (1970), apart from its general introduction to the trilogy of which it is the first volume, includes a useful chapter titled 'The South Australian Frontier 1860–1911'.

Pastor Philipp Scherer edited *The Hermannsburg Chronicle 1877–1933* (1995) which includes summaries of annual reports by the Superintendent to his superiors in Adelaide for most, if not all, of those years. Information about Harry Hillier, Namatjira's first teacher at Hermannsburg, comes from Philip Jones and Peter Sutton's illuminating *Art and Land – Aboriginal Sculptures of the Lake Eyre Region* (1986).

A further source of information about the Carl Strehlow years at Hermannsburg is *The Heritage of Namatjira* (1992) by Jane Hardy, Ruth Megaw and Vincent Megaw. Much of the material gathered during the writing and editing of this book is in the Megaw Archive at the Flinders University Art Museum library. Ted Strehlow's *Journey to Horseshoe Bend* (1969) includes valuable insights into the Hermannsburg of the early twentieth century.

Barbara Henson's biography of FW Albrecht, *A Straight-out Man* (1992), is effectively a history of Hermannsburg from 1926 until 1984. I read a selection of Albrecht's own writings, mainly pamphlets, letters and addresses, in the Lutheran Archives in Adelaide.

Some of this material, along with much else besides, is also in an archive Nigel Roberts assembled during research in the 1990s for a documentary film that was never made. His 70-page unpublished ms, *A sequential narrative – an assembly of contemporary reportage & official documents that attempts to account for A.N. in his time*, was an indispensible guide.

Albert Namatijira

The first book about Albert Namatjira, *The Art of Albert Namatjira* by Charles Mountford, was published with an introduction by Bob Croll and some excellent illustrations by the Bread and Cheese Club in Melbourne in 1944. Subsequent to Namatjira's death in 1959, two biographies appeared. The first, *Namatjira of the Aranda* (1962) by Vic Hall is, at best, anecdotal. The second, *Namatjira: Wanderer between two worlds* (1963) by Joyce Batty, is more comprehensive. Her main informant was Rubina Namatjira, and other key figures, such as

Pastor Albrecht, Inspector McKinnon and Ted Strehlow, contributed to her research.

A third biography, *Albert Namatjira 1902–1959* (1989) by Andrew MacKenzie is, as the author notes in his subtitle, a sketch rather than a fully researched life. It is well illustrated and, though brief, is an accurate and informative account of the main events of Namatjira's life. MacKenzie went on to construct a website called *In The Artists Footsteps*, a large section of which is devoted to Namatjira.

Shorter accounts of Namatjira's life have appeared in exhibition catalogues and monographs, beginning with the first retrospective held at the Araluen Centre in 1984; the accompanying catalogue was written by Mona Byrnes, who was the daughter of Gerhardt Johannsen, one of the Hermannsburg missionaries.

That same year John Brackenreg's Legend Press published *Central Australian artist Albert Namatjira* (1984); it is essentially a collection of images with a brief reminiscence by Brackenreg at the head. Two years later Nadine Amadio published her *Albert Namatjira: the life and work of an Australian painter* (1986), which includes a biographical outline.

Hardy, Megaw and Megaw's *The Heritage of Namatjira*, was in one sense a culmination of this flurry of publications in the 1980s. It remains, twenty odd years later, the standard reference on the Hermannsburg School. There is a detailed chronology, by Ruth Megaw, at the front of the book, and the ten essays it contains are scholarly, well-researched and written in an accessible style; the book is generously illustrated in both colour and black and white.

A major retrospective of Namatjira's work, *Seeing the Centre*, was curated by Alison French at the National Gallery of Australia in Canberra in 2002 and accompanied by a handsome publication of the same name. This includes a biographical introduction by French, followed by a number of themed chapters concentrating upon aspects of the Namatjira oeuvre. It remains by far the best published collection of images of Namatjira's art, and the biography that introduces the plates is well supported by black and white photographs. There are also excellent notes to the text and a full catalogue of works.

In the Roberts Archive are hand-written transcriptions of a manuscript written by Bernice Battarbee in the 1960s. These are drafts of passages from a biography of Namatjira she intended to write and from them I derived my account of Namatjira's courtship of Rubina and also the story of the Namatjira family's dramatic journey through the flooding land to reach the Battarbee wedding in time.

Rex Battarbee

Legend Press's *Rex Battarbee, artist and founder of the aboriginal art movement in Central Australia* (1956), written by Ted Strehlow and illustrated with a selection of the artist's works, includes a brief biographical sketch that provided the basis for my subsequent research into his early life. The family background was filled out by Gayle Quarmby, in correspondence and in person when I visited her at her home in Reedy Creek in South Australia. I found online a memoir of Warrnambool written by a cousin of Battarbee's called Robert Cust, and used that in my reconstruction of the early twentieth-century town.

A short biography of Walter Withers appears in *Golden Summers – Heidelberg and Beyond* (1985), the catalogue for an exhibition mounted in Melbourne. This was augmented by Withers' entry in the *Australian Dictionary of Biography* and from other sources. There is a chapter on Wilmot Abraham in Jan Critchett's *Untold Stories: Memories and lives of Victorian Kooris* (1998).

As part of my research into Battarbee's military service I read Les Carlyon's majestic *The Great War* (2006), in which there is a detailed account, and analysis of, both the first and the second battles at Bullecourt. Gayle Quarmby showed me her father's war memorabilia, including the newspaper article about Rupert 'Mick' Moon, the penny that turned a bullet away, and the bullet that came out of Rex's chest years later.

She also gave me copies of the message with which his father farewelled Rex on his way to war, and of Rex's battlefield drawings. Much of the information about his activities immediately post-war comes from the store of her father's memorabilia that Gayle has; including the notebook in which his first sketches were made.

Battarbee taped an interview with Ted Strehlow in 1960; both the tape and a transcript are in the National Library in Canberra. On this occasion Battarbee talked about his teacher, Cyril Leyshon White, and his time spent studying commercial art in Melbourne in the early 1920s. He also recounts meeting Jack Gardner and describes their decision to buy the Model T Ford and go out on the road in 1928.

From that point on, Battarbee's *Diaries* are a major source of information about him and also, after 1934, about Namatjira too. The *Diaries* themselves belong to Gayle Quarmby; copies of all of those up until 1944 are in the Megaw Archive at Flinders University and most of these are also, in transcription, in the Roberts Archive; which includes excerpts from diaries written after 1944 as well.

Gayle Quarmby also has an extensive archive of photographic material. One of the diaries, from 1932, has a photograph album accompanying it but it is not clear if any, or all, of the others do too. Philip Jones, in his *Images of the Interior: Seven Central Australian Photographers* (2011), includes a chapter on Battarbee and reproduces a number of fine images in both black and white and colour.

Rex Battarbee published two books himself, *Modern Australian Aboriginal Art* (1951), and, co-authored with his wife, *Modern Aboriginal Paintings* (1971). They are essentially art books but both include short biographical statements by Battarbee and the first, a series of chapters he wrote about painters of the Hermannsburg School, includes one on Albert Namatjira.

Battarbee gave a number of newspaper interviews over the course of his life; the Roberts Archive in Sydney includes most of these, as well as miscellaneous correspondence to and from Battarbee.

Artistic Traditions

The initial discussion of the nature and characteristics of pre-contact Arrernte art is from Ted Strehlow's *Aranda Traditions*. I also consulted Josephine Flood's *The Riches of Ancient Australia* (1990) and her *Archaeology of the Dreamtime* (1995). *The Heritage of Namatjira* includes, in the introductory chapters, some speculation on what things might have been like for Arrernte artists before there were European observers on the scene.

The Commercial Art School, where Battarbee studied, has left a paper trail of advertisements through the classified sections of

Melbourne newspapers of the 1920s. I have a 1940s publication by the school, which includes reproductions of several works by Leyshon White. Examples of Battarbee's early work as a commercial artist are with the rest of the Battarbee Collection in the Araluen Centre.

John Gardner was at the Commercial Art School with Battarbee and he also studied at the National Gallery School; I researched his teachers, and other art world figures of the 1920s, including Harold Herbert, in the pages of the *Australian Dictionary of Biography*. The Koshare Indian Museum has a website devoted to the Taos Society of Artists; and I also own a copy of the Hans Heysen number of *Art in Australia* from March 1926.

Leyshon White published fragmentary accounts of Battarbee's and Gardner's travels in Melbourne in the early 1930s, and Gardner much later contributed a series of interviews to *A Vagabond and his Easel : a biography of John Gardner* (1984) by Kaye Dowdy. A journal he kept in 1930 at Wilpena Pound is a contemporary account of how he and Battarbee lived and painted while on the road. It is in the Fisher Library at the University of Sydney.

My research on Walter Withers led me back to the English watercolour tradition and particularly to painters like Peter De Wint and David Cox. *The Great Age of British Watercolours, 1750–1880* (1993) by Andrew Wilton and Anne Lyles, an exhibition catalogue, was a good source here. John Ruskin, in 1857, published his *Elements of Drawing*, which Battarbee may have known; it includes advice on the techniques of watercolour painting.

Just when the word 'luminosity' entered the Battarbee lexicon is unclear but it was probably in the early 1930s. Gayle Quarmby pointed me to the breakthrough painting of Bitter Springs Gorge, with its emphasis upon a heavy layering of pigment as a means of attaining the desired luminosity.

Bruce MacEvoy (www.handprint.com) writes at length on the debates in the nineteenth century about the transparency or otherwise of watercolour pigment, and the philosophic, moral and religious positions that may derive from differing positions taken in that debate.

In Chapter 6 of *The Heritage of Namatjira*, titled 'The Hermannsburg watercolourists: The view from the art museum', and written by Daniel

Thomas, I found confirmation that an anthropomorphic element may be found in Namatjira's painting. Thomas visited Hermannsburg as a child and, as a young art historian, rejected the Hermannsburg School as uninteresting painters of realist landscapes; but he changed his mind about Namatjira's work when he saw a particular painting of a ghost gum in Alice Springs in 1979.

The seventh and eighth chapters of *The Heritage of Namatjira*, by Sylvia Kleinert ('The critical reaction to the Hermannsburg school') and Ian Burn and Ann Stephen ('Namatjira's white mask: A partial interpretation') elaborate upon the manner in which art historians have interpreted Namatjira's work over time. Sylvia Kleinert's master's thesis, which she kindly sent me as an electronic copy, surveys the locations in Central Australia that Namatjira painted and attempts to reconcile the frequency of his depictions with the sites' significance, or not, as dreaming places among the Arrernte. Meanwhile Burn's and Stephen's essay is a re-interpretation of Namatjira's strategy as a painter suggesting he was, in certain crucial respects, very un-European in his use of composition.

I have mentioned Battarbee's career as a photographer; he introduced Namatjira to cameras and their uses in the 1930s and both men habitually framed their compositions using the model of the viewfinder of a camera. Their participation in the making of Charles Mountford's 1946 film adds another layer of complexity to this engagement. The Roberts Archive includes a scrapbook which contains a detailed account of the shooting of this film and its aftermath, and also an hour-long video interview with film-maker Lee Robinson, recorded towards the end of his life. Quotes from Robinson in the text are taken verbatim from this unpublished video interview. The correspondence between John Reed and the Department of Information is also in the Roberts Archive; it has not to my knowledge previously entered the record.

The Town Grew Up Dancing (2002) by Wenten Rubuntja, with Jenny Green, largely an oral history, is important for its insight into a practitioner's view of what the painting is about. Rubuntja, who painted in both styles, says that dot painting is about law whereas watercolour painting is about country; his son Mervyn, a watercolour artist, at a seminar in Sydney in 2013, gave a moving account of how he has to feel the country singing through his mind and body before he can set its lineaments down on paper.

In Conclusion

There is nothing resembling a catalogue raisonné of the works of either Namatjira or Batterbee. I spent many hours online tracking their paintings (and in Namatjira's case, the *objets d'art* he made). There are extensive online databases of both men's works, which chart their movements through auction houses and other points of sale, both here and overseas; but these databases are chaotic, with items appearing multiple times under different titles or with different items listed under the same, or similar titles. Unless a work is illustrated it is usually impossible to identify it securely; and even then its provenance may remain obscure.

Because there have been two Namatjira retrospectives, it is possible to locate a core of examples of his work, either in public institutions or else with well-known private collectors. Nevertheless, the oeuvre, in scholarly terms, remains in disarray. The situation is exacerbated by the refusal of Namatjira's copyrighter-owners, Legend Press, to allow material from the Araluen Centre in Alice Springs or from the National Gallery of Australia in Canberra, to be reproduced. These repositories hold the two largest and most significant collections of Namatjira's work and without access to their holdings it is not possible to represent his oeuvre in any coherent manner. Our decision not to include colour plates of paintings in this book is a consequence of Legend Press's intransigence.

Battarbee's achievement is even more occluded; his personal collection is in the Araluen Centre in Alice Springs, but the holdings in other public galleries are meagre and it is clear that the bulk of what he made, if it is not altogether lost, is held in private collections.

ACKNOWLEDGEMENTS

I would like to thank Gayle Quarmby, Rex Battarbee's daughter, for her enthusiasm and commitment during the research and writing of this book; and Nigel Roberts for his unstinting help and support at all times. Stephen Williamson at the Araluen Centre in Alice Springs showed me through the Battarbee and Namatjira collections held by the Museum and Art Gallery of the Northern Territory. Iris Bender, at Ngurratajuta Iltja Ntarra – Many Hands Arts Centre, facilitated conversations with inheritors of the Hermannsburg tradition of watercolour painting, including Albert's grandson, Kevin Namatjira and his fellow painters Mervyn Rubuntja, Kevin Wirri and Ivy Pareroultja. Also in Alice Springs, Penny McDonald of the Northern Territory Film, Television and New Media Office, made it possible for me to see inside the house, still extant, that Rex Battarbee built. Nic Brown at the Flinders University Art Museum helped navigate me through the collection and the Megaw Archive there; Rachel Kuchel at the Lutheran Archives in Adelaide provided indispensible research aid. Staff at the National Gallery of Australia and at the National Library in Canberra provided access to their collections.

Particular gratitude is due to Melinda Jewell and Suzanne Gapps at the Writing and Society Research Centre at the University of Western

ACKNOWLEDGEMENTS

Sydney, where this project was developed as a doctoral thesis between 2010 and 2012. I would also like to thank Tom Carment, Hart Cohen and Nick Jose for the conversations; and Ivor Indyk, for his wise and generous guidance throughout.

Details of photographs featured in *Battarbee and Namatjira* are as follows:

p.41: Rex Battarbee, c.1914, Courtesy Gayle Quarmby.

p.59: Axel Poignant, Jonathon Namatjira, 1946, National Archives of Australia.

p.85: Rex Battarbee, c.1920, courtesy Gayle Quarmby.

p.116: Rex Battarbee and Albert Namatjira, c.1938, courtesy Gayle Quarmby.

p.139: Axel Poignant, Albert and the camels, 1946, National Library of Australia.

p.140: Rex Battarbee painting, 1930s, National Library of Australia.

p.171: Albert Namatjira painting, 1946, National Library of Australia.

p.177: Axel Poignant, Albert Namatjira and his wife Rubina at a camp, 1946, National Archives of Australia.

p.193: Albert Namatjira and his paintings, c.1940s, courtesy Gayle Quarmby.

p.204: Namatjira house at Hermannsburg, 1946, National Library of Australia.

p.209: Axel Poignant, Albert Namatjira, Axel Poignant and Rex Battarbee, 1946, National Library of Australia.

p.215: Albert Namatjira and Lee Robinson, Production still from *The Phantom Stockman*, 1952 © National Film and Sound Archive.

p.231: Axel Poignant (England; Australia; England, b.1906, d.1986) Albert Namatjira and his family 1946, printed 1981, gelatin silver photograph, 35.3 x 45.4 cm, Art Gallery of New South Wales, Photo AGNSW © courtesy Roslyn Poignant.

p.258: Rex Battarbee and Albert Namatjira, c.1950s, courtesy Gayle Quarmby.

p.266: Albert Namatjira outside Government House, Sydney, 1956, National Library of Australia.

p.274: Neil Murray, Rex Battarbee, 1954, National Library of Australia.

p.280: Axel Poignant (England; Australia; England, b.1906, d.1986), Albert Namatjira's father Jonathan Namatjira 1946, printed 1981, gelatin silver photograph, 45.4 x 34.7 cm, Art Gallery of NSW, Purchased 1984, Photo: AGNSW © courtesy Roslyn Poignant.

p.283: Keith and Albert Namatjira with Sir Edward Hallstrom, 1956, National Library of Australia.

p.285: Albert Namatjira on Jack Davey's boat, 1956, National Library of Australia.

p.289: Albert Namatjira, 24 September 1958 © *Sydney Morning Herald*.

p.298: John Tanner, Albert Namatjira 1958, National Archives of Australia.

p.314: Rubina at Albert Namatjira's funeral. All efforts have been made to contact the copyright holder.

p.319: Rex Battarbee and Oscar Namatjira, c.1960s, courtesy Gayle Quarmby.

p.323: Rex Battarbee c.1970, by Rennie Ellis, type C photograph, Collection National Portrait Gallery Canberra, Purchased 2006.

This project has been assisted by the Commonwealth Government through the Australia Council, its arts funding and advisory body.

For a list of links to paintings by Rex Battarbee and Albert Namatjira, please visit our website:
www.giramondopublishing.com/non-fiction/battarbee-and-namatjira